D0082861

The Stone and the Scorpion

Recent Titles in
Contributions in Women's Studies

The Stone and the Scorpion

THE FEMALE SUBJECT OF DESIRE
IN THE NOVELS OF
CHARLOTTE BRONTË, GEORGE ELIOT,
AND THOMAS HARDY

Judith Mitchell

Contributions in Women's Studies,
Number 142

Greenwood Press
Westport, Connecticut • London

Library of Congress Cataloging-in-Publication Data

Mitchell, Judith (Judith I.)
   The stone and the scorpion : the female subject of desire in the
novels of Charlotte Brontë, George Eliot, and Thomas Hardy / Judith
Mitchell.
       p. cm.—(Contributions in women's studies, ISSN 0147–104X ;
no. 142)
   Includes bibliographical references and index.
   ISBN 0–313–29043–1 (alk. paper)
   1. English fiction—19th century—History and criticism.
2. Feminism and literature—England—History—19th century.
3. Women and literature—England—History—19th century. 4. Brontë,
Charlotte, 1816–1855—Characters—Women. 5. Eliot, George,
1819–1880—Characters—Women. 6. Hardy, Thomas, 1840–1928—
Characters—Women. 7. Desire in literature. 8. Sex in literature.
I. Title. II. Series.
PR878.F45M57 1994
823'.8099287—dc20   93–43751

British Library Cataloguing in Publication Data is available.

Copyright © 1994 by Judith Mitchell

All rights reserved. No portion of this book may be
reproduced, by any process or technique, without the
express written consent of the publisher.

Library of Congress Catalog Card Number: 93–43751
ISBN: 0–313–29043–1
ISSN: 0147–104X

First published in 1994

Greenwood Press, 88 Post Road West, Westport, CT 06881
An imprint of Greenwood Publishing Group, Inc.

Printed in the United States of America

The paper used in this book complies with the
Permanent Paper Standard issued by the National
Information Standards Organization (Z39.48–1984).
10 9 8 7 6 5 4 3 2 1

Copyright Acknowledgments

The author and publisher wish to thank the following for permission to use their material in this volume:

Extracts from Thomas Hardy: *Far from the Madding Crowd*, ed. Suzanne Falck-Yi and Simon Gatrell, Oxford World's Classics edition, 1993; *The Return of the Native*, ed. Simon Gatrell, 1990; *Tess of the d'Urbervilles*, ed. Juliet Grindle and Simon Gatrell, 1988; *Jude the Obscure*, ed. Patricia Ingham, 1985—by permission of Oxford University Press.

Extracts from Charlotte Brontë: *The Professor*, ed. Margaret Smith and Herbert Rosengarten, 1987; *Jane Eyre*, ed. Margaret Smith, 1980; *Shirley*, ed. Herbert Rosengarten and Margaret Smith, 1981; *Villette*, ed. Margaret Smith and Herbert Rosengarten, 1990—by permission of Oxford University Press.

Extracts from George Eliot: *The Mill on the Floss*, ed. Gordon S. Haight, 1980; *Middlemarch*, ed. David Carroll, 1986; *Daniel Deronda*, ed. Graham Handley, 1984—by permission of Oxford University Press.

Extracts from Judith Mitchell, "George Eliot and the Problematic of Female Beauty," *Modern Language Studies*, vol. 20, no. 3 (1990): 14–28.

Extracts from Judith Mitchell, "Hardy's Female Reader," in *The Sense of Sex: Feminist Perspectives on Hardy*, ed. Margaret Higonnet, 1993, 172–87.

The author gratefully acknowledges the generous support of the University of Victoria in providing research grants and study leave in the production of this book, as well as the invaluable assistance of Penny Sippel, Senior Production Editor, Greenwood Press.

To Leonard and Betty;

To Bob;

And to some of the strong female subjects I am lucky enough to know: Audrey, Carla, Connie, Claire, Donna, Jean, Jenni, Joan, Kathleen, Kathy, Liz, Lynne, Pam, Sharon, Sheila and Tracey

Mutual desire is not at issue. Feminine desire itself, woman as the subject of the discourse of desire, seems unthinkable. At best, it is in excess of what is required. The feminine part is to consent or refuse (to be taken) rather than to desire or will (to take). (Ellen Rooney, "Criticism and the Subject of Sexual Violence" 1273)

The desiring woman and her excessive sexuality may be theoretically unrepresentable. (Mary Ann Doane, *The Desire to Desire* 122)

When asked about their sexuality women cannot answer. (Andrea Nye, *Feminist Theory and the Philosophies of Man* 172)

She felt the jolt of desire: not her desire, but the man's. As, since girlhood, . . . [she] had always felt, not her own, but the other's, the male's desire. (Joyce Carol Oates, *Black Water* 115)

CONTENTS

1

✧ ✧ ✧

INTRODUCTION:
THE EROTIC SUBJECT

There is something wrong with erotic relations in our culture. Exactly what that something might be has been the subject of massive and ongoing speculation by theorists in widely disparate fields, the gist of which I shall try to summarize in the following chapter. The succeeding chapters constitute a re-reading of the erotic in twelve well-read canonical novels, a reading that seeks to define and locate a somewhat elusive entity, a female subject of desire.

The objectification of women in Western culture has become a critical commonplace in several fields of inquiry, and my search for a female subject in literature parallels a similar search that is currently taking place in film criticism and visual arts criticism.[1] The realist novel is a particularly intriguing genre to approach in this way (as are mainstream cinema and representational art), first because its ideological assumptions are so persuasively embedded in the structure of the work itself, and also because such an examination inevitably addresses the wider issue of whether realism itself is in fact complicit with patriarchy, as some theorists have suggested. This project can be seen as a small part of the larger, immensely important intellectual enterprise which has been taking place over the past few decades, namely the disruption of dualistic modes of perception. The disruption of male-female dualities, in particular, is essential in the re-creation of erotic relationships in our culture. The urgent search for a new wholeness is not only (or should not only be) a feminist undertaking; that my project is subsumed under a feminist label is in fact part of the problem.

At the moment, however, such an inquiry is ineluctably feminist, and as such needs to be justified in two ways, namely in my choice of both male and female writers and in my choice of canonical writers. I have chosen to examine the work of both male and female novelists simply because I do not believe feminism to be a gendered attribute;[2] and I have chosen canonical writers, even though there are already many existing readings of their novels, to illustrate that reading in order to discover a female subject of desire is in fact a new (âlbeit largely ahistorical) reading.

My project, then, is to re-read several novels by Charlotte Brontë, George Eliot and Thomas Hardy in order to analyze, in Elaine Showalter's terms, their "symbolic construction of gender and sexuality" (*New Feminist Criticism* 10) and thus to discover the erotic ideologies embedded in them. This will not always be easy, first because of the transparent nature of the "truths" of realism (as Lennard Davis remarks, "Novels parallel ideology, which attempts to destroy the veil of its own artifice and to appear as natural common sense," 25) and second because of the balancing act that is always required of the female critic in confronting the texts she cut her critical teeth on. Jonathan Culler describes this balancing act in *On Deconstruction* (43–64), and Patrocinio Schweickart elaborates on his description: "A feminist reading . . . is a kind of therapeutic analysis. The reader recalls and examines how she would 'naturally' read a male [or canonical, male-interpreted] text in order to understand and therefore undermine the subjective predispositions that had rendered her vulnerable to its designs" (50–51).

I have chosen these novelists in particular for several reasons. They nicely span the period; they have all been loosely categorized as feminist; and their novels all embody some form of erotic desire. As a group, these novels seem to stand a chance of portraying varying degrees of female subjectivity as well as varying degrees of eroticism. Their heroines, who include such distinctive personalities as Jane Eyre, Maggie Tulliver, Gwendolen Harleth, Tess Durbeyfield and Sue Bridehead, comprise a formidable array of fictional females. If such a construct as a female subject (as opposed to object) of desire is possible, she should surely be found among them. Whether such a construct is possible, or even imaginable, within the constraints of the Victorian novel is one of the questions I shall attempt to answer. Other questions arise in the course of such an inquiry: To what extent does each novelist "dare" to invest his or her female characters with erotic subjectivity? How is this achieved? Is there any progression in degrees of such subjectivity within the career of each novelist? Is there any progression in female subjectivity in novels written over the latter half of the nineteenth century? Such speculations, of course, inevitably point to a larger question: does our ideology even now admit of such a construct as the female subject of desire? Even now, do we have a language, in our literature or in our culture, in which female desire can be authentically expressed?

The Victorian novel is a particularly rich source of material germane to such an inquiry, embodying as it does a sexual ideology that is at once so overt (in its severe polarization and coding of acceptable sexuality) and yet so covert (in its rigid taboo against explicit eroticism), so easy and yet so difficult to "read," and above all so formative in relation to our own literary and cultural mores. The sexual reticence of the Victorian novel does not preclude preoccupation with the erotic (in fact, as Michel Foucault points out, such reticence more likely betrays a ruling obsession); conversely, the sexual garrulity of the twentieth century does not indicate its greater erotic wisdom (as George Steiner remarks, "Reticence is one kind of stylization; total explicitness is another," 122). Although Foucault, especially, fails to acknowledge his own implicitly gendered stance, largely taking for granted the primacy of the male subject, his work contributes some useful insights for feminism, and I shall allude to it again in the course of the following discussion.

EROTIC DESIRE

Erotic relationships as they are constituted in our culture are characterized by the troubled and destructive nature of an interaction between an active, desiring subject (usually male) and a passive, desired object (usually female). It is interesting to note that most traditional commentators on erotic desire have tended to take this hierarchical dichotomy for granted, speaking exclusively in terms of the complications that can arise for the male subject. Such commentators include writers like Denis de Rougemont, various other philosophers and theorists, and assorted literary and cultural critics. René Girard, one of the latter, in *Deceit, Desire and the Novel*, advanced a theory of desire that seemed especially masculine, in that it was triangular, competitive and de-emphasized the position of the object or third term of the triangle. In fact, Girard's work provided one of the formal models for Eve Kosofsky Sedgwick's theory of homosocial desire, in which the important relation is ultimately formed between the competing (male) subjects rather than between the male subject and the desired female ("The impulse toward the object is ultimately an impulse toward the mediator," Girard 10). In addition to reinforcing the concept of sex as a power struggle, such theorists also tend to underwrite the split between sex and love, and to promulgate the Platonic need for the transcendence of the latter over the former. ("Eventually desire is replaced by a love which is no longer erotic. . . . The trouble of desire is then at an end. The problem is, how to shut out the third party who will begin it again," Scruton 244.)

By and large, the addition of feminist commentary to this discourse of the erotic has effectively burst it wide open, speaking the anger of the elided object and questioning the bases of "normal" erotic structures. The relation that is uniformly troubling to feminists, the opposition that needs to be disrupted, is of course the male subject/female object configuration, with its power-based hierarchy, encompassing as it does so many other hierarchical values: active/passive, strong/weak, rational/irrational, dominant/submissive, culture/nature, mind/body. Such values and such a dualistic way of thinking are at the very heart of Western society, making the task of feminism seem gargantuan but also underlining its importance.

Undoubtedly the most dangerous opposition that is subsumed in the male/female relation, and the one which will inform my critical approach in this book, is that of subject/object. This split characterizes the way Western man perceives and acts upon his world, which is tragic since it is a dysfunctional (some would say immoral) mode. Its confrontational and controlling mentality fails to satisfy either member of the dyad. The detriment to the "inferior" term—the slave, the victim, the loser of the competition or war—is easy to see, but the detriment to the "superior" partner has become increasingly obvious. Feminist psychoanalytic gender-relations theory provides a relevant context for any discussion of the formation of erotic desire, and I would now like to investigate some recent speculations in this area in the belief that these theories have the potential to shed light on, and possibly even to alter, our readings of male/female relationships both inside and outside novels.

SUBJECT AND OBJECT

What exactly is wrong with a subject/object interaction, not only between sexual partners, but between any two entities? First of all, and most obviously, it is a lonely interaction in which neither the subject nor the object can experience recognition as a human Self. Jessica Benjamin, referring to Hegel's master-slave dialectic and to the work of Georges Bataille, characterizes this interaction as one of "erotic domination." Benjamin, one of the most articulate of modern feminist gender-relations theorists, traces the tendency to objectify other people to what she terms "false differentiation" from the mother in early childhood, by which she means differentiation occurring with no appreciation of the mother's subjectivity. A falsely differentiated individual is able to act as if other people are subjects, but is unable to experience them as such in any meaningful way. Such false differentiation, according to Benjamin, represents the stance of "normal" masculine maturity in our culture:

Both in theory and in practice our culture knows only one form of individuality: the male stance of overdifferentiation, of splitting off and denying the tendencies toward sameness, merging, and reciprocal responsiveness. . . . This way of establishing and protecting individuality dovetails with the dualistic, objective posture of Western rationality. To be a woman is to be excluded from this rational individualism, to be either an object of it or a threat to it. To be a man is not merely to assert one's side of the duality, the supremacy of the rational subject. It is also to insist that the dualism, splitting, and boundaries between the male and female postures are upheld. ("Bonds" 46–47)

The split, then, is usually along gender lines, with the male in the position of the (over)differentiated subject and the female in the position of the desired/feared object. This relationship—and herein lies the real difficulty of the subject/object configuration—is always necessarily one of control rather than reciprocity. Inherent in the subject/object opposition is the more invidious opposition of domination/submission ("When the two poles of the unity become split, the relationship of domination emerges. . . . Nonreciprocity is a constant undertow in any dyad," "Bonds" 49, 59).

In a patriarchy such as ours in the Western world, the male fears outlined by psychoanalytic theorists give rise to the wholesale objectification of women and the valorization of control and complete autonomy as ruling virtues. Plato's (male) subject, centuries before Freud's or Lacan's, was split, into a lower self which had to be controlled by a higher. As feminists have noted, this mind/body opposition has been reinscribed in Western culture in the male/female opposition, with women embodying corporeal "nature" as opposed to androcentric "culture." The need of the latter to control the former makes somatophobia and misogyny virtually synonymous, as Marilyn French points out in *Beyond Power*. The Platonic ideal of transcendence reflects this body-hatred:

Male morals are designed to permit male transcendence. Life—that mass of breathing flesh, sweating pores, darting sensation, uncontrollable being—is rooted in nature, in the fetid swamp, the foul murk. . . . Above these, stark, pure, beyond the pull of heart or genitals, soar a rigid set of principles, rules, taboos. To prove his full manhood, . . . a man must cleave to these and abandon the other, which is the realm of woman. (523)

The classical privileging of mind over body described by French, our epistemological inheritance, is reflected in modern psychoanalysis: both Freud and Lacan postulate a linear progression from merging (with the mother's body) to differentiation, from the pre-oedipal to the oedipal stage, from the imaginary to the symbolic. The subject is male, and the tasks are control and transcendence. Only recently have feminists begun to challenge this hierarchical paradigm and to re-evaluate the pre-oedipal and imaginary realms, envisioning not a progression from one state to the other, but a balanced interaction between them. Nancy Chodorow has described this interaction as one in which, after a "confident separateness" is established, "one's relational self can become more central to one's life. *Differentiation is not distinctness and separateness, but a particular way of being connected to others.* This connection to others . . . in turn enables us to feel that empathy and confidence that are basic to the recognition of the other as a self" (11). Other theorists, too, envision a similar dynamic autonomy which maintains a balance or tension between separateness and relatedness, seeing traditional male models of "healthy" autonomy as pathologically rigid and defensive

("The more secure the central self, or ego core, the less one has to define one's self through separateness from others," notes Chodorow 10).

We can see, then, that any discourse of subjectivity is inextricably bound to discourses of gender. We can also see that the dualistic, oppositional thought patterns of traditional Western epistemology (reinforced at various points by such thinkers as Descartes, Kant and Hegel) are reflected in the splitting or breakdown of wholeness in the Western psyche, in which subject is opposed to object, love is opposed to sex, mind is opposed to body, action to passivity, male to female.

SOLUTIONS AND POSSIBILITIES

What, then, could heal the split in our cultural psyche and disrupt the hierarchical oppositions that contaminate male-female relationships in our world? An early solution to male dominance was for women to become more male-identified, appropriating power in order to become more autonomous. While this solution, which is still operative, did much to improve material conditions for women in society, it did little to solve the psychic difficulties inherent in erotic relationships. It merely reinforced male values, assuming that the isolated stance of overdifferentiated male autonomy amounts to true subjectivity. Clearly, it is the configuration itself that requires disruption. Neither the subject nor the object position represents authentic desire, and righting the balance is not simply a matter of adding an already-defined female sexuality (which currently lacks expression) to an already-defined and expressed male sexuality.

And yet, somewhat astonishingly, some degree of domination and submission appears to be essential in any erotic relationship. Ethel Spector Person, writing about "Sexuality as the Mainstay of Identity," points out that "because sensuality develops in the relatively dependent, helpless child, with the earliest gratification attached to powerful adults, it is unlikely that sexuality will ever be completely free of submission-dominance connotations" (58). In the formation of erotic drives (as opposed to gender roles), it seems, it really does not matter whether the early caregiver is male or female. Inequality is still the earliest turn-on, and desire remains bound up with power and control. What does matter is the unequal allocation of this power between the sexes. Person notes that even though it may be impossible to rid sexuality entirely of its power-based overtones, progress will be made when dominance and submission are no longer automatically linked to male and female sexuality respectively (61). Other theorists, too, somewhat grudgingly acknowledge the "kernel of psychic domination or surrender" at the heart of all sexual relationships (R. Rich 547).

Such seemingly simplistic materialist accounts nevertheless accord with traditional accounts of the formation of erotic desire put forward by psychoanalytic theorists since Freud. In *Civilization and Its Discontents* Freud spoke of the aggression associated with erotic relationships, and in *Three Essays on the Theory of Sexuality* he stressed the sadomasochism of infant sexuality as well as the paradoxical nature of sexual desire, in that its pleasure is akin to a kind of pain (the pain of unfulfilled need). Lacan, too, sees desire as unassuageable, a result of the alienation of the subject from its own being as well as from other beings and directed toward ideal objects which remain forever out of reach. The sexism of both Freud's and Lacan's accounts is obvious, in that they both posit a male subject (film critic Mary Ann Doane wryly remarks of Lacan's scenario, "Desire may be insatiable, it may entail the constantly renewed pursuit for a perpetually lost object, but at least the male has desire," 12).

Basic to any such theories of desire formation are two tenets: the erotic is aggressive (it cannot be tamed) and it is paradoxical (it cannot be fulfilled). Also, it appears to be elusive and somewhat fragile: it is destroyed in the privileging of either the physical—pornography annihilates it, as Susan Griffin points out—or the spiritual. Feminists have described the erotic in lyrical terms; Ann Snitow calls it "that general . . . rapture which stokes life's energies" (169), and Audre Lorde refers to it as "that power which rises from our deepest and non-rational knowledge," "an assertion of the life-force of women," "the nurturer or nursemaid of all our deepest knowledge." The Wordsworthian echoes of the latter phrase coincide perfectly with the traditional psychoanalytic recognition that the erotic has its origins in the pleasures of infancy; Freud tells us that a child nursing at its mother's breast constitutes the original paradigm of all other love relationships.

What, then, could constitute a healthy expression of this powerful yet fragile force, in literature and in life? How is it possible to feel both regressed (submissive, merged) and yet comfortably autonomous (dominant, differentiated)? The only satisfactory answers are in themselves paradoxical. Benjamin maintains that these impulses need to be held in tension, in balance, both within and between both subjects, all of the time. Only in this way, she says, can we aspire to the goal that beckons on the horizon of all discourses of the erotic, namely that of mutual subjectivity. Benjamin foresees a utopian synthesis consisting of "a wholeness in which the opposing impulses for recognition and differentiation are combined" ("Bonds" 65), an "intersubjective mode, where two subjects meet, where both man and woman can be subject, [which] may point to a locus for woman's independent desire, a relationship to desire that is not represented by the phallus. . . . Here the desire to lose the self in the other and really be known for oneself can coalesce. . . . Otherwise one falls into the trap of choosing between [these modes], grasping one side of a contradiction that must remain suspended to be clarifying" ("Desire" 93–94).

The trouble, as we have seen, is that in "normal" erotic relations in our culture, the two tendencies are polarized and complementary: the male's desire is to dominate and the female's desire is to submit to his desire. What both really long for, according to Benjamin, is "ritual transcendence," the experience of losing the self, which yet remains intact. But such an experience is frightening, giving rise to fears of the boundless, of infinite ego loss, so that each partner wants the other to define the limits of the interaction. The submissive female object longs to be "released into abandon by another who remains in control" ("Desire" 97), and the dominant male subject needs his chosen object to be somewhat resistant. Edwin Mullins, in his account of this necessary feminine reluctance as it is revealed in the visual arts, attributes it to religious strictures against sexuality (which really amount to the somatophobia I noted earlier): "She has to say No. It is he who insists on it, while pretending it is she. . . . His God, who says he should deny women, is placated, while his own strongest passions are freed from guilt to fly out to her across the abyss" (136). In literature, too, instances abound of the male's need for resistance. Milton's description of Adam and Eve's lovemaking in Book IV of *Paradise Lost* is completely characteristic: "by her yielded, by him best received, / Yielded with coy submission, modest pride, / And sweet reluctant amorous delay." Thus the symbiotic and unhealthy domination/submission configuration, consisting of a desiring male subject and a female object who embodies, reflects, accepts or rejects his desire, is formed in our culture over and over again.

FEMALE DESIRE

It is small wonder, then, that it is so difficult to theorize a female subject of desire. According to some feminists—those I quote in the epigraphs to this study constitute a small but representative sample—a positive formulation of female desire itself does not yet exist in our cultural psyche. Such commentators, characteristically responding to the deeply embedded cultural repression of the very concept of a feminine libido with a sense of pained resignation, verify that in this sense, Freud's characterization of the sex drive as exclusively masculine was appallingly accurate.

In fact, the notion of an active female sexuality has been and continues to be viewed as unnatural or even dangerous, as we can see in the examples of Victorian "hysterics"; Nina Auerbach's hags, witches and demons; and more modern heroines such as those in Louis Malle's *Damage* and Adrian Lyne's *Fatal Attraction*. The latter film, which is particularly adept in arousing a murderous fear of the seductive woman, makes it appallingly easy for a modern audience to understand the witch burnings of an earlier time. Sadly, as Elizabeth Janeway points out, "A tamed Eve pleases men, a wild one frightens them, but in neither aspect does she serve the needs of women. The message she conveys is, Keep your sexual needs and pleasure at modest levels. . . . Passionate or passionless, you are still an object. Become something more and mythic terrors will rise like smoke around you" (17). Even when the woman is grammatically in the subject-position of erotica (as she is in D. M. Thomas's *The White Hotel* and Pauline Réage's *The Story of O,* each of which has occasioned much analysis), her role has remained one of passivity, as feminists have pointed out.[3]

It is no wonder, then, that so much of the feminist discourse on erotic relationships is suffused with anger and sadness.[4] The situation as it exists is unavoidably crippling, not only to women but to men as well. Women lose their entire potential for active sexuality, a terrible loss—Dorothy Dinnerstein calls it "the female burden of genital deprivation" that "most reliably cripples . . . human pride" (75)—and men, too, lose a vital part of their erotic potential. Barbara Sichtermann asks, "What about men? By seldom being desired, . . . the price they had to pay was that their narcissism, and their ability to be passive wasted away, as did their sexual pride as far as this is nourished by providing pleasure" (120). It is significant that both Dinnerstein and Sichtermann use the term "pride" to describe what it is that is damaged in conventional polarized relationships; the damage is to self-respect, to the central core of being. The grinding and debilitating effects of enforced female passivity, arguably the more oppressive of the two hardships, are not a recent feminist invention. They are most eloquently expressed, for example, in the harrowing diatribe of the narrator in Charlotte Brontë's *Shirley,* a reversal of patriarchal Biblical solace :

A lover masculine . . . can speak and urge explanation; a lover feminine can say nothing. . . . Take the matter as you find it: ask no questions; utter no remonstrances: it is your best wisdom. You expected bread, and you have got a stone; break your teeth on it, and don't shriek because the nerves are martyrised: do not doubt that your mental stomach . . . is strong as an ostrich's: the stone will digest. You held out your hand for an egg, and fate put into it a scorpion. Show no consternation: close your fingers firmly upon the gift; let it sting through your palm. Never mind: in time, after your hand and arm have swelled and quivered long with torture, the squeezed scorpion will die, and you will have learned the great lesson how to endure without a sob. (105)

What, then, would consist of the requirements for a female subject (as opposed to object) of desire in the Victorian novel? What would constitute a female character as a Self rather than an Other in erotic relations? The answer to this obviously entails a complex combination of reader-author-character relationships, ideological agendas both overt and covert, and the expression of these elements in the representation of women. Perhaps the most outstanding characteristic of an authentic female erotic subject, posited by both grass-roots and intellectual feminists, is autonomous activity as opposed to dependent passivity. Subjectivity is measured in action, either toward the male in the case of popular culture or apart from the male in the case of radical feminist theory. By refusing to be a passive object, the female can disrupt the domination/submission hierarchy in important ways.

But could the Victorian heroine ever constitute such an active subject? The answer, I believe, is one of degree. Feminists throughout the ages have intuited the debilitating effects of the subject/object opposition and have sought to disrupt it in various ways, and the degrees to which they have succeeded, however small, have marked important progress. Accordingly, I wish to examine a number of portrayals of women by Charlotte Brontë, George Eliot and Thomas Hardy for traces of erotic subjectivity, bearing in mind the severely polarized sexual ethos of the time. I shall take as my criterion the concept of erotic activity, namely the extent to which these authors permit their heroines to look, speak, feel and act on their desire within the (heterosexual) erotic encounter.[5] Such information, I think, should constitute a reliable guide to the sexual ideologies embedded in these novels and to the extent of their authors' feminism. It should also result in new readings of the novels, and therefore in new evaluations of them.

Basically, I shall conduct my search for the female subject of desire under three categories, namely the look of desire, the language of desire and the enactment of desire. Much work has been done in each of these categories in such extra-literary areas as film criticism, visual arts criticism and semiotics, and I would like briefly to examine some of this theory before I proceed with my readings of individual novels.

THE LOOK OF DESIRE

Looking, in the feminist lexicon, is not a neutral activity. As John Berger pointed out in *Ways of Seeing*, looking is an activity of control, a power hierarchy of the viewer over the viewed object. And, as the entire Western visual arts tradition testifies, it is men who do the looking and women who are looked at. Rosalind Coward succinctly enunciates the feminist view of this relationship: "In our society men can and do stare—at women. It is a look which confers a mastery. It represents a right to assess, pass judgment and initiate or invite on the basis of that judgment. . . . Sexual and social meanings are imposed on *women's* bodies, not men's. Controlling the look, men have left themselves out of the picture because a body defined is a body controlled" (52, 229). The male surveying the female in this way is of course directly parallel to (and in fact participates in) the domination/submission hierarchy. In looking, the male is acting on his desire, while the female is the passive recipient of it. According to Coward, this arrangement fails to work not only for women but for men as well, since men's refusal to be desired, she believes, ultimately results in a "sort of failure of will at the heart of heterosexual desire" (230). Also, many theorists have noted that the activity of looking yields a specifically masculine pleasure, while women's pleasure is much more bound up with the other senses, particularly the sense of touch. Such commentators point out that looking, with its automatic distancing of subject and object, is eminently suited to the typically over-differentiated male psychic configuration in our culture, providing a position from which it is possible to "possess" a woman visually without having to deal with her "in the flesh." The obsessive looking of pornography is an obvious instance of this, but all representations can be said to partake of such "safe" distancing between viewer and object.

Looking and being looked at, then, constitute a complex phenomenon, and much literature has appeared which deals with the power relations inherent in any form of imaging (generally referred to as the "politics of representation"). Susanne Kappeler's *The Pornography of Representation* is a good example, in which she categorically states that the fundamental problem at the heart of heterosexuality, "the root problem behind the reality of men's relations with women, is the way men see women, is Seeing" (61). Female subjectivity itself, it seems, is inextricably bound up with questions of visual representation. Kaja Silverman points out that "the structuration of the female subject begins not with her entry into language, . . . but with the organization of her body. That body is charted, zoned and made to bear meaning, a meaning which proceeds entirely from external relationships, but which is always subsequently apprehended both by the female subject and her 'commentators' as an internal condition or essence" ("*Histoire d'O*" 325). In other words, women internalize their position as looked-at objects. Silverman, referring to Foucault, likens the position of women in the seeing/seen dyad to that of the prisoners in Jeremy Bentham's Panopticon, a prison in which the guards in the central tower are never seen but see everything, while the prisoners on the periphery are seen all the time but see nothing. Vision is equated with power, and women, having internalized the male gaze, carry their own Panopticon with them wherever they go.

The oppressive effects of this seeing subject/seen object dyad can easily be detected in such obvious manifestations of looking as advertising and pornography; but representation is also integral to many of the arts, where its operations are much more subtle. Susanne Kappeler holds that the arts participate in a dialectic that is essentially pornographic, in that the definition of the aesthetic in our culture invariably includes women as objects of aesthetic attention (a definition operative in the novels of George Eliot, as I shall show). Women clearly have difficulty in taking part in such a discourse. "The fact that women, as individual subjects, have inserted themselves into the cultural audience (not without a struggle), have apprenticed to the male viewpoint which surveys women as objects and as products of fine art, is itself one of the most fundamental sources of female alienation: women have integrated in themselves, have internalized, a permanent outpost of the other gender—the male surveyor" (Kappeler 58).

The difficulties inherent in the position of the female viewer have been explored in feminist analyses of both film and the visual arts, forms which are almost purely representational. Mary Ann Doane stresses the necessity of examining representational structures themselves in any such analyses, pointing out that a crucial development in recent feminist film theory has been a shift in its critical focus, from questions of whether given representations of women are positive or negative to the more fundamental issue of "the very organization of vision and its effects" (176). The main problem, of course, is that this organization of vision is deeply ingrained not only in men but in women themselves, so that they must question their own aesthetic pleasures. Mary Gentile stresses the need for a "critical subjectivity" on the part of the female viewer, a stance that parallels Judith Fetterley's notion of the "resisting reader" of literature.

The woman's position as audience of the arts (including literature), then, is fraught with difficulties. Before examining these in more detail, I would like to turn briefly to the "normal" viewing paradigm, that of the male viewer, as it is into this paradigm that the female spectator must somehow insert herself. Feminist film critics have examined the audience/film construct in great detail, and their observations can easily be extrapolated to include the reader as the audience of the novel. It is generally recognized that traditional realist cinema has inherited the narrative conventions of traditional realist fiction; Annette Kuhn's description of classic Hollywood cinema, for instance, sounds remarkably like earlier descriptions of realism in the novel: "All films are coded: it is simply that certain types of film are coded in such a way as actually to seem uncoded. . . . This of course is one of the pleasures of the classic realist cinema: an address which draws the spectator in to the representation by constructing a credible and coherent cinematic world, which at the same time situates her or him as a passive consumer of meanings which seem to be already there in the text" (268). The viewer of a Hollywood film and the reader of a Victorian novel in this respect are in much the same viewing position, that of a "passive consumer" of the "obvious" meanings inherent in an already created fictional world.

Laura Mulvey's well-known article "Visual Pleasure and Narrative Cinema" subjects this position to a searching analysis. Mulvey discerns three different looks associated with the cinema: that of the camera, that of the audience, and that of the characters on the screen. These three vantage points have obvious parallels in those of the narrator, the reader and the characters of a novel.[6] According to Mulvey, all of these entities are male subjects, who together watch the woman, the sexual object, whose presence "connotes something that the look continually circles around but disavows: her lack of a penis, implying a threat of castration and hence unpleasure." Mulvey suggests that the male viewer responds to the resulting unconscious anxiety in two ways, through the defense mechanisms of either voyeurism or fetishism. Voyeurism is a function of the narrative, producing pleasure by "ascertaining guilt . . . , asserting control, and subjecting the guilty person through punishment or forgiveness" (21–22), whereas fetishism or what Mulvey terms "fetishistic scopophilia" allays castration fears by investing the female body with an excess of perfection in interludes of "erotic contemplation" that temporarily halt the narrative (19). Such extra-diegetic interludes occur during close-ups or musical numbers in films, and in passages of description and portraiture in novels, some of which I shall investigate in the following chapters.

In short, there are two kinds of visual pleasure in which the cinema audience is invited to take part: the obvious narcissistic pleasure of identifying with the controlling male protagonist, and the scopophilic pleasure of erotic stimulation through sight. Clearly, there is no place in this scenario for the female spectator (or for the female reader). How, then, do women participate as members of a viewing or reading audience, and what sort of pleasure do they derive from the experience? Film critics have devoted much attention to such questions and have come up with some interesting and informative replies. Mary Ann Doane speculates that a female viewer of a classical Hollywood film "has basically two modes of entry: a narcissistic identification with the female figure as spectacle and a 'transvestite' identification with the active male hero in his mastery. The female spectator is thus imaged by its text as having a mixed sexual body—she is ultimately a hermaphrodite. It is precisely this oscillation which demonstrates the instability of the woman's position as spectator" (19). This unstable, oscillating, bisexual subject position is also characteristic of the female novel-reader; Doane's account is strikingly reminiscent of Jonathan Culler's well-known account of "Reading as a Woman" ("Reading as a woman is not necessarily what occurs when a woman reads: women can read, and have read, as men. . . . To ask a woman to read as a woman is in fact a double or divided request," 49).

We can see, then, that women's pleasure in viewing films (and in reading novels) is peculiarly problematic, a tortuous negotiation with and insertion into the seeing/seen configuration. We can also see that this configuration leaves the woman's desire out of the picture, so to speak, and that once again it is female subjectivity which is in doubt. And it is in this respect, according to Doane, that "representations of the cinema and the representations provided by psychoanalysis of female subjectivity coincide. For each system specifies that the woman's relation to desire is difficult if not impossible. Paradoxically, her only access is to the desire to desire" (9). Other film critics agree, arguing further that the act of representation itself ultimately involves the repression of female sexuality, since women in our culture as a whole are invariably constructed as fetishized images which function automatically to validate male rather than female desire.

It is certainly true that if, as Linda Williams puts it, "to see is to desire" (83) in classical cinema, then film (and novel) heroines (as well as female viewers and readers) do little of either except in a highly convoluted and problematic fashion. We have already seen how this is true of the female spectator or reader as she regards images of women in films or in novels. It is doubly true of the images themselves: the heroines of classical realism, in order to maintain credibility as heroines, do not look at male characters with desire, nor do they return the latter's look (they look away or drop their eyes). Exceptions to this rule are consistently punished or regarded with suspicion, by the spectator/reader, by the events of the film/novel or by the other characters in the narrative. The seductive heroine, one who looks at (or at least looks back at) the male characters, is a case in point. Williams remarks that "the bold, smoldering dark eyes of the silent screen vamp offer an obvious example of a powerful female look. But the dubious moral status of such heroines . . . undermine[s] the legitimacy and authentic subjectivity of this look, frequently turning it into a mere parody of the male look" (85).

The woman's look of desire in both realist film and the realist novel is frequently portrayed as shameful, in fact, so that a desiring woman appears to be not looking but spying. There is a marked contrast, for instance, between Caroline's secret looking at Robert Moore in *Shirley*, which seems pathological rather than erotic, and Gabriel Oak's secret looking at Bathsheba in *Far from the Madding Crowd* or the reddleman's spying in *The Return of the Native*. Both of the latter looks not only have erotic overtones but also constitute acts of power and control by male characters, in which the (male) reader is invited to participate by the (male) narrator.

Mary Ann Doane points out that the female's desire in the love story film is invariably constructed as "imaginary" or "excessive" and is therefore invariably punished, often by death. The project of such films, in fact, is "the tautological demonstration of the necessity of the failure of female desire" (104). Such a demonstration is necessary, Doane suggests, because the love story has the audacity to posit "the very possibility" of female desire (118). Such speculations have significant ramifications for the way in which we read the Victorian novel, in which the love story is of primary interest. In light of Doane's observations, we can ask some interesting questions about the perception of female desire in such novels. Is it too portrayed as imaginary or excessive, and is it punished by the events of the narrative? And what about the male characters? Do they ever desire inappropriately or excessively, and if so, do they suffer for it? Detailed answers to these questions will emerge in the following chapters, but for now we can make some preliminary speculations. The list of female characters who harbor "excessive" desire is impressive, including Hetty Sorrel, Maggie Tulliver, Bathsheba Everdene, Fanny Robin, Eustacia Vye, Thomasin Yeobright, Tess Durbeyfield and Lucy Snowe. Others, like Dorothea Brooke,

Sue Bridehead and Gwendolen Harleth, are subject to prolonged bouts of "imaginary" desire in which they are portrayed as having over-active imaginations in regard to the feelings of certain male characters. And of all of these, a disproportionate number die as a result of their folly (Hetty, Maggie, Fanny, Eustacia and Tess), while others (such as Sue and Gwendolen, and arguably Bathsheba) might as well be dead. In any case, they are all "cured" of their inappropriate desires by the end of the novels they inhabit.

Male desire, on the other hand, is presented as being on the whole much less problematic. Male characters who love excessively or inappropriately include Adam Bede, Farmer Boldwood, and Jude Fawley (to give Hardy credit, he can at least imagine such characters). Others, such as Arthur Donnithorne and Clym Yeobright, have transitory episodes of inappropriate desire, from which they speedily recover, while in many instances the desire of the male characters is simply unsuccessful rather than excessive or inappropriate (take the case of Seth Bede, for example, or Philip Wakem or Alec d'Urberville). And they hardly ever die for their errors; Boldwood, Jude and Alec are exceptions. In fact, in all of the novels I shall discuss, only Boldwood is portrayed as having the kind of excessive or pathological desire that is so frequently associated with female characters—and it is interesting to note that in him such desire manifests itself as genuine madness. In women, this pathology is the norm; or rather, any hint of active sexuality on the part of women characters is automatically portrayed (and read) as pathological.

The look of desire in classical realism in the visual arts is deployed in much the same way; that is, it is the shared property of the male artist and the male viewer and its object is the female nude, whose nudity thus becomes a function not of her sexuality but of theirs. As in the pornographic scenario, the model's gaze reflects (usually in an inviting way) the male's desire, not her own. And, as in realist cinema, exceptions to this rule are seen as dangerous; according to Edwin Mullins, it is the desiring look of Manet's "Olympia" that provoked such a sharp critical reaction to it: "She is steadily regarding us; it is not we who are doing the sexual appraisal— she is. So she is not the ideal supine mistress; she is active, and she is waiting for a good lover. [Her] steamy female sexuality . . . seems aggressive and disconcerting. To the nineteenth-century peacock the experience of encountering an image of such erotic self-confidence in a woman . . . induced a state of ungovernable panic" (96).

It seems we must conclude, then, that the look of desire—in the visual arts, in film and by extension in the novel—is the property of the male. When the woman appropriates the look, she seems to usurp it, and her subjectivity is undermined as a result. And the objectification of the male is no solution; what feminist theorists advocate is a "mutual gazing" such as that which can occur in the mother-child relationship. Before this can

take place between the sexes, however, female desire itself must be legiti-
mated in the cultural psyche. Visual arts critic Sarah Kent laments "the
absence of a body of knowledge or an art form which recognizes and
describes female sexuality as a potent initiating force, rather than merely
as a response to masculine desire. The sexual drive . . . must first be acknowledged before it can be harnessed without appearing deviant, ob-
scene, evil or insane" (62–63). Indeed it must, but this is unlikely to happen
so long as the present system of the representation of women remains in
place.

Before I end my discussion of the look of desire, I should mention an
element of the seeing/seen dyad that complicates that look enormously,
and that is the element of beauty. In our culture, as many commentators
have observed, beauty is an almost exclusively female attribute, so much
so that both women and men regard women as beautiful and therefore
sexually desirable. In fact, representations of beautiful women are always
eroticized in our culture; E. Ann Kaplan's comment that "screen images of
women are sexualized no matter what the women are doing literally or
what kind of plot may be involved" (30) applies to all images, not just screen
images. A beautiful woman automatically and simultaneously functions as
both an aesthetic object and a sexual object, an object for the male viewer's
appraisal (and for the appraisal of other women and even of herself insofar
as women have internalized the beauty standard, the male Panopticon).
This automatic aesthetic and sexual objectification of women has enormous
consequences for the power relations between the sexes, as many critics
have recognized. Basically, it is a system of control that functions in two
ways: to control women themselves, and to control male fears of female
sexuality. In Laura Mulvey's category of "fetishistic scopophilia," for example, castration threats are mastered by "build[ing] up the physical beauty
of the object [the woman's body], transforming it into something satisfying
in itself" (21).

In film, the most striking instances of such fetishistic over-valuation
occur in close-ups of the heroine, which "freeze" the action and focus the
spectator's attention on the heroine as desirable object; in the novel such
moments are paralleled in passages of heroine description. Helena Michie
points out that these descriptions, like close-ups, halt the narrative action
and stand out from the text as discrete excrescences (Michie calls them
"cysts" or "ornaments," forms of "sexual disease, . . . eruption[s] in the text
that [have] a life and erotic energy of [their] own," 85). As the Victorian era
progressed, passages of heroine description grew progressively more detailed, with the details denoting both disclosure and concealment. "The
bodily parts that comprise the litany which in turn constitutes the female
body as it appears in the Victorian novel," says Michie, "are carefully
selected not only for what they represent but for the absences they suggest. . . . The Victorian novel aligns itself with *Playboy* in its sexual construc-

tion of the absent" (97). The ruling trope in such fetishistic description is synecdoche, and feminists have long realized that the fragmentation of the female body (which occurs throughout our culture, in advertising and pornography as well as in film, art and literature) is an objectifying and dehumanizing mechanism. In perusing the parts, the viewer misses the whole, and when the viewer is a woman the result is extreme alienation from the whole body and the whole self.[7]

We can conclude that the seeing/seen dyad plays a key part in the domination/submission hierarchy. Women's bodies are irretrievably eroticized by the male look of desire, and this look is primarily a look of control. Kaplan's seemingly sweeping statement about women in film—"[They] . . . do not function as signifiers for a signified (a real woman), as sociological critics have assumed, but signifier and signified have been elided into a sign that represents something in the male unconscious" (30)—applies to all realistic representations of women, including those in the Victorian novel, and what the "something" in the male unconscious consists of is readily apparent. In my discussion of Brontë, Eliot and Hardy I shall examine not only the extent to which their female characters are constructed as objects of the look of desire, but also the extent to which these characters are allowed to possess the look without earning the reader's disapprobation. The latter should serve as an indication, at least, of the room for female desire (and female subjectivity) that each novelist is capable of envisioning within the confines of each novel.

THE LANGUAGE OF DESIRE

Women's relationship to language is regarded by feminists as both problematic and highly complex. Sandra Gilbert and Susan Gubar, in a 1985 article entitled "Sexual Linguistics: Gender, Language, Sexuality," refer to "the widely accepted contemporary assumption that 'the feminine' is what cannot be inscribed in common language" (516), and statements to this effect have indeed become critical touchstones. Take, for example, Laura Mulvey's categorization of woman as "bearer of meaning, not maker of meaning" (15) or Julia Kristeva's oft-quoted statement, "In 'woman' I see something that cannot be represented, something that is not said, something above and beyond nomenclatures and ideologies" (137). The power dynamics of the seeing/seen dyad are replicated in the speaking/spoken to dyad, in that women in male discourse are relegated to the position of silent listeners, or if they do speak, their speech, like the female look, is regarded as somehow illegitimate (as Alice Jardine puts it, "Women's discourse is always perceived as unclean, transitory, of no ultimate import, *impropre*," 98). Speech is more complicated than sight in relation to the female object, however, as the latter is not only spoken to but also (perhaps more frequently) spoken about; also, the glance itself cannot be captured, but words can. And words, of course, are the constituent element of the patriarchal symbolic order, the realm into which the (male) infant, in Lacan's terms, is propelled by the "third term," the phallus, as it shatters his pre-oedipal imaginary unity with his mother. It is through language that the male subject can master the threat of castration and express desire for the (m)other.

But what about the female subject? Christine Gledhill summarizes women's position in relation to Lacan's schematic in the following way: "Women anatomically play a key part in the production of the symbolic . . . , but by virtue of this role (castration) women can only have a negative relation to language; they cannot wield control over the symbolic; they do not carry in themselves the symbol of the signifier, the phallic authority for signification, only the absence which sets the signifier in place. Thus their entry into human discourse must be tentative, highly negotiated, and ambiguous." Women, then, can only speak in what Gledhill terms "a highly negotiated fashion" (31–32). This complex, convoluted female speech has been described in various ways, all of which stress the enormous difficulty of using male language to describe female experience.[8]

Basically, women have difficulty in constituting themselves as speaking subjects in a language in which the "I," the superior term, is male. And it is only through language that people exist as subjects, as Emile Benveniste has pointed out ("It is literally true that the basis of subjectivity is in the exercise of language. . . . There is no other objective testimony to the identity of the subject except that which he himself thus gives about himself," 226). The subject, the "I," according to feminist philosophers such as Andrea Nye, provides a center around which all language is ordered, including demonstratives and personal pronouns. This central "I" that speaks is especially formed in confrontation with the "you"; and women have traditionally been placed in the position of the "you," the "other," the "it." Thus speech itself reflects the woman's otherness: the woman in such a linguistic economy is not she who speaks, but that which is spoken to or about (186).

According to the Lacanian system, then, sexism resides in language itself, in that the syntactic structure of subject and predicate mirrors the hierarchical division between subject and object, male presence and female absence. The referent, that which language is constantly trying to signify, is always feminine, partaking of silence, absence and lack, while the signifier is present and masculine. Margaret Homans sees a parallel hierarchy in the structure of metaphor, which, like the structure of male desire, "permits one term . . . to claim the authority to define the other—whether the feminine object of romantic desire or the second term of a metaphor" ("Syllables of Velvet" 573). In these concealed ways, English is a covertly gendered language, as several linguists have pointed out.[9]

The patriarchal symbolic is thus a realm in which women are silenced in various ways. Women characters, particularly within the Victorian novel, are silent as part of their virtue; women writers throughout the ages have been effectively silenced by the prevailing patriarchal literary canon; and then there are the more insidious silences within texts themselves, the gaps and omissions which simply "write out" or "write off" women's experience and point of view. Edwin Mullins gives a good example of the latter tendency in his discussion of the "objective" language of art history: "It is what it does not say, does not question, that is the weakness of art history. . . . The museums of the world could be hung exclusively with pictures of women being tortured and raped, and the language of scholarship would remain the same" (77). This awareness that texts also operate through what is not said in them, through their absences as well as through their presences (an insight articulated in the work of Pierre Macherey), has been useful for feminist criticism, particularly in the re-reading of canonical texts. Elizabeth Ermarth, for example, speaking of Flaubert's Emma and Hardy's Tess, remarks that "theirs is an absent voice and, as with victims of violence generally, the absent voice has exquisite importance" ("Fictional Consensus" 15). Silence itself can be revealing, as Margaret Higonnet emphasizes in her article on women's suicide, entitled "Speaking Silences."

In fact, the power relations embedded in the speaking/spoken to relation are by no means straightforward. On one hand, to silence someone is to reduce that person to powerlessness, a fact that Christine Brooke-Rose sees as motivating the male fantasy of the ideal woman as dumb ("Woman as a Semiotic Object"). Men need women to be silent for fear of what they would say if they spoke—which would have something to do with desire, with "speaking from [the] body," as Christine Froula puts it (335)—and they also need women to be silent in order to constitute them as listeners of male speech. Susanne Kappeler contends that the masculine subject-position can be maintained only in relation to such listeners, and that therefore one of the constructions of the feminine in our culture is that of woman as a "speech-object," a "passive masochistic counterpart to men's aggressive and sadistic linguistic assault" (194). Kappeler sees a parallel between this sort of linguistic availability and sexual availability, a parallel which emphasizes the connection between silence and powerlessness.

This connection is not an equation, however. For, while silence can undoubtedly be a sign of submission (the "good" woman is silent as well as beautiful), it can also be an attribute of power. Susan Gubar's discussion of Isak Dinesen's story "The Blank Page" illustrates this beautifully: in the long gallery of framed blood-stained sheets, each bearing witness to a royal bride's "honor," the single blank sheet is utterly and powerfully enigmatic, a conundrum that is simply unavailable to patriarchal analysis. The absence of speech can admit of multiple meanings; as Margaret Homans points out in Bearing the Word, often "what seems from the point of view of symbolic language to be silence is in fact a rich, nonsymbolic language" (38). Certainly it is true that the one who speaks is not always the most powerful term of the speaking/spoken to dyad. In the case of confessions, for example, the listener acquires power over the speaker by virtue of the silent acquisition of knowledge. Unfortunately, however, as Rosalind Coward puts it, the literary confession has become "sexualized" in both senses of the term: it is about sex and it is by women. While Victorian heroines were characterized by silence, in the modern novel "the female protagonist has become the speaking sex," and what she speaks about—endlessly, garrulously, according to Coward—is sex itself, thus perpetuating the relegation of women to the private sphere of affective interpersonal relationships (178–79). Also, the confessional mode clearly carries with it the implication of guilt; women's sexual knowledge, as displayed in the confession, is by inference guilty knowledge.[10]

And this brings us back to the issue of female desire and the question of what would constitute its authentic expression. How can it be "spoken" within patriarchal discourse? The answer is that perhaps it can't. Anaïs Nin spoke of "woman's sensuality, so different from man's and for which man's language [is] inadequate" (100). More modern feminists speak of this same inadequacy, citing as its source the symbolic objective of patriarchal language, that is, the eradication of the lack that woman represents. In this view, it is hardly surprising that female desire cannot be expressed, since its very existence would logically entail a symbolic desire for self-annihilation.

French feminists have also determined that female desire is unspeakable within male discourse because it has been "submerged" by Western male logic. According to Luce Irigaray, "Within this logic, the predominance of the visual, and of the discrimination and individualization of form, is particularly foreign to female eroticism. Woman takes pleasure more from touching than from looking, and her entry into a dominant scopic economy signifies . . . her consignment to passivity: she is to be the beautiful object. . . . [But] her sexual organ represents *the horror of nothing to see*" (25–26). It is through language, Lacan's symbolic, that female desire has been submerged, and accordingly it is through language that it is to be recovered, in this view. The language of this enterprise is to be a language of the body, an *écriture féminine* outside patriarchal discourse which has the ability to express women's diffuse, non-phallic sexuality, their *jouissance*. It rejects the oedipal symbolic world of the father and signals a return to the pre-oedipal semiotic world of the mother, a state of blissful pre-verbal immediacy. According to some critics (Kristeva, for example), men too can produce such a discourse; others (such as Irigaray) insist on the biological specificity of women's writing by women. In any case, the project is the radical disruption and subversion of phallocentric male logic in favor of a fluid, plural, far-reaching, body-centered female logic which leaves room for the expression of female desire. This project remains largely abstract and intellectual, however, and English-speaking feminists have posed objections to it on these and various other grounds. Ann Rosalind Jones points out that French theory is neither body-centered (it partakes of a "literary self-consciousness that goes far beyond the body and the unconscious") nor universal (she queries whether "one libidinal voice, however non-phallocentrically defined, can speak to the economic and cultural problems of all women," 96–98).

In any case, both French- and English-speaking feminists recognize that female desire must be spoken, and that language is the key to its utterance, either in the form of an entirely new language or in a new approach to phallocentric discourse. Margaret Homans, whose work is a good example of the latter, agrees with Irigaray that female sexuality is unspeakable and speculates further that it is in fact incompatible with the concept of representation, simply because representation depends so heavily on the visual: "A culture that privileges the phallus . . . also privileges sight, because it is only by visual criteria that women's bodies can be said to be missing something" ("Syllables of Velvet" 572–73). In *Bearing the Word* Homans opposes the "literal" maternal to the "figurative" symbolic, and illustrates how women writers (Virginia Woolf, for example) are able to express female desire and sensibility by means of the former, using the male lexicon not only for its logical meaning but also for its soothing sound qualities, its sensual maternal "presence."[11] Similarly, in "Syllables of Velvet," Homans shows how Emily Dickinson and Christina Rossetti replace "the painful plot of [male] desire" with a "plotless and joyous intersubjectivity" by privileging metonymy (in which there is "no subject and no object because language has given up its claim to referentiality and therefore to objectification") over metaphor (which "measures the distance between a female object of desire and a desiring male subject"). Such writers also privilege the tactile over the visual (Homans refers to a Dickinson poem in which "red is a feeling more than a sight") and pleasure over desire itself. This latter relation, in fact, so evocative of Marilyn French's privileging of pleasure over power, is perhaps an important key to the puzzle of female sexuality: it is immediate, of the body and capable of ultimate gratification, as opposed to abstract, cerebral and endlessly deferred. It is removed from the "linear logic of representation and desire" and from the "quest-romance of male desire that put [the woman] in the place of silence" (576–88). It seeks pleasure (with another subject) rather than conquest (over an object), in other words.

Such a female use of language obviously manifests itself much more readily in some genres than in others. Poetry, the stream-of-consciousness novel and *écriture féminine* can move freely outside male rational discourse, to which they constantly refer, and so would seem to constitute appropriate vehicles for the expression of female desire. But what about more clearly representational forms, such as realist cinema and the Victorian novel? Do their formal conventions leave room for a female subject to speak her desire? According to Kaja Silverman, the female voice, like the female body, functions as a fetish within mainstream cinema, and what they both signify is lack. The female voice is closely identified with the female body (and with spectacle, as opposed to narrative) through synchronization, the confinement of the voice that is heard to the image that is seen. The unheard and unseen (and therefore more powerful) spectator, as we have seen, is constructed as male. The male voice, by contrast, can occasionally escape or transcend the diegesis by speaking in voice-over, which "speaks with an unqualified authority" directly to the listener over the heads of the characters. Thus, according to Silverman, "Within dominant narrative cinema the male subject enjoys not only specular but linguistic authority" ("Dis-Embodying the Female Voice" 131), while the synchronized female voice in its most characteristic form would produce "that sound which . . . Hollywood is at the greatest pains to extract [from it], i.e. the cry" (*Acoustic Mirror* 39). And this cry is frequently (as in *Peeping Tom*, the movie Silverman is discussing at this point) a cry not of desire but of pain. Objectified both visually and aurally, the heroine of realist cinema is not even a speaking subject, much less a subject of desire.

And what of the heroine of the Victorian novel? Is it possible to conceive of her speaking in an authentic language of desire? First of all, as Rosalind Coward points out, she often does not speak at all. She is "profoundly silent," representing "the soft and understanding aspects of humanity" through her appearance alone (177). The good woman is silent as well as beautiful. Such heroines, while they represent sexuality itself, are mute about their own desire, and confronted with male desire, they blush and fall silent. They may well have desire, but their construction as (good) female characters preludes its verbal expression; the language of desire is masculine. John Kucich's analysis notwithstanding,[12] this repression is unlikely to be anything but harmful, a fact that is acknowledged in the Victorian novel form by the "hysterical" behavior frequently exhibited by passionate heroines (Maggie Tulliver, Jane Eyre and Lucy Snowe come to mind). Coward, commenting on such behavior on the part of the latter, avers that "derangement and hallucination are responses to the burden of interiority placed on the heroine by the novel form, responses to the speaking silence of the female figure" (178).[13]

In discussing the language of desire in the Victorian novels I have chosen, then, I shall look carefully at silences as well as words. The silences of the text, of the narrator and of the female characters in each novel will undoubtedly be germane to questions of female subjectivity and desire. That which is omitted, elided, glossed over, resolutely not mentioned, discreetly ignored, deliberately shunned, is in this case of primary importance. And in the language that is used, can any female voices be heard? To what extent are female characters permitted to speak their desire? When they do speak, what do they say, and to whom do they say it? Are they listened to? How are they silenced, and by whom? If they could speak freely, what might they say? To what extent do any of these texts partake of non-phallocentric forms of language, and to what interpretive audience are they addressed? To which gender does the narrator, that powerful "voice-over," seem to belong? Female desire remained largely "unspeakable" in the nineteenth century. But again, it is a question of degree: to the extent that each novelist pushes against this convention, to the extent that she or he leaves room for at least the possibility of a desiring subjectivity that is distinctively female, we can at least applaud the attempt, which is one of the things I propose to do in the present study.

THE ENACTMENT OF DESIRE

This heading encompasses the previous two, in that a female subject who exercises either the look or the language of desire obviously enacts, or at least expresses, her own desire. And, of course, there are various methods and degrees of enactment: as well as looking and speaking, it can include feeling, thinking and acting itself. The key questions in this regard concern the portrayal of female characters within the novels I shall discuss and the degrees of autonomy they are granted. Are they, in Josephine Donovan's terms, "seats of consciousness" (52)? Are they portrayed as adult rather than infantalized, as active rather than passive, as Self rather than Other? In other words, are they constituted as subjects, as opposed to objects, in the novels they inhabit? To the extent that they are, we can examine them as subjects of desire; if they are completely objectified to begin with, we obviously cannot hope to construe them as agents of a desiring subjectivity. As we have already seen, a mature female sexuality is incompatible with the passive infantalized object of the domination/submission dyad.

About those women characters who do partake of varying degrees of subjectivity, however, we can ask several questions germane to the existence, extent and authenticity of female desire. To what degree are such characters permitted to feel, and to act on their feelings? Do their feelings empower them or weaken them in erotic encounters and negotiations with the males in each novel? Are such feelings a source of pleasure or of pain? We can already anticipate that the margin of room for the expression of authentic female desire in the Victorian novel will be quite narrow, simply because of what we already know about the sexual ethos of the nineteenth century. Grundyism was firmly in place by mid-century, William Acton assured his readers of women's sexual passivity shortly thereafter,[14] and the cult of the "virtuous woman" (in which, as Carol Thurston points out, women found themselves in "the paradoxical situation of being at the same time defined solely in relation to their gender and denied the right to a natural, self-controlled sexuality," 36) was in full flower during the latter part of the period. Openly expressed sexuality was considered a sign of madness in women, as Elaine Showalter movingly points out in *The Female Malady* (and it is significant that the two categories I have already examined, sight and speech, were key indicators of such madness: women could be considered insane if they paid too little or too much attention to their appearance—the latter was labeled "intense vanity"—or if they spoke too little or too much).

It was an era of amazing misogyny, in which somatophobia acquired the status of a positive virtue, the "higher" nature wishing to eradicate the "lower" altogether. Women were to signify the former unambiguously; any display of their "lower" selves elicited severe disapprobation, such as Robert Buchanan's famous diatribe against Rossetti in "The Fleshly School of Poetry": "Females who bite, scratch, scream, bubble, munch, sweat, writhe, twist, wriggle, foam, and in a general way slaver over their lovers, must surely possess some extraordinary qualities to counteract their otherwise most offensive mode of conducting themselves. . . . In reading such books as this, one cannot help wishing that things had remained for ever in the asexual state described in Mr. Darwin's great chapter on Palingenesis" (343).

Such sanctions against sexuality itself were indeed formidable, and resulted in strange compensatory behavior both in literature and in life. Early feminists like Mary Wollstonecraft advocated what Kathleen Blake calls "feminist asceticism" even though they defended healthy physicality for women, simply because the erotic denoted so much abasement (Blake sees Gissing's Rhoda Nunn and Hardy's Sue Bridehead as literary expressions of this concept). Novelists, unable to deal with their characters' sexuality in any straightforward way, resorted to all manner of displacement. Family relationships in particular were seen as non-erotic and "safe" and were therefore paradoxically eroticized; Nancy Armstrong and Leonard Tennenhouse note that "with remarkable regularity, the best possible relationships to be achieved in [Victorian] fiction turn out to be inferior substitutes for an original mother or father" (14). Dickens, despite his ridicule of "Podsnappery" and the blush on the cheek of the young person, is a primary example of this tendency, as we can see in his handling of the erotic cross-currents among Bella Wilfer, John Harmon and Bella's father in *Our Mutual Friend*, for example.[15] It is interesting to note that these ostensibly non-sexual relationships (including female friendships as well as parent-child and brother-sister connections) are the only relationships in the Victorian novel that specifically include touching as part of the connection. Fictional lovers do not usually touch each other, at least not until the end of the century, whereas the disproportionate amount of fondling that occurs among families and female friends would be termed incest or lesbianism if it occurred in a modern novel.

Sex itself was dangerous, and women represented sex; small wonder that the whole century, as Charles Bernheimer points out, participated in Huysmans's hysterical misogyny. French novelists, for all their greater freedom to express the physical, still represented it as disgusting, and their novels (Zola's, for instance) were really no more erotic than the English as a result. In fact, the repressed urges and dislocations in the Victorian novel, the pressure of the unspoken, resulted in a peculiar sort of chaste titillation, a fact which Des Esseintes, the decadent hero of Huysmans's *A Rebours* (1884), discovers to his chagrin when he attempts to calm his nerves by reading Dickens:

The Englishman's works produced the opposite effect from what he had expected: his chaste lovers and his puritanical heroines in their all-concealing draperies, sharing ethereal passions and just fluttering their eyelashes, blushing coyly, weeping for joy and holding hands, drove him to distraction. This exaggerated virtue made him react in the contrary direction; by virtue of the law of contrasts, he jumped from one extreme to the other, recalled scenes of full-blooded, earthy passion, and thought of common amorous practices such as the hybrid kiss . . . where the tongue is brought into play. (109)

Humorous as Des Esseintes's discomfiture is, it encapsulates exactly the suppressed eroticism of the nineteenth-century novelistic imagination, which must be taken into account in any discussion of female desire in the nineteenth-century novel.

Indeed, it is difficult to imagine what room could possibly be left in such a scenario for the enactment of female desire. Not surprisingly, female characters in these novels tend to be characterized by their passivity: their typical "activity," like that of the film heroines discussed by Mary Ann Doane, is waiting. Waiting—not acting, failing to act, suppressing the urge to act—is so prevalent among fictional females in the nineteenth-century novel, in fact, that Kathleen Blake presents it as a ruling literary motif in *Love and the Woman Question in Victorian Literature: The Art of Self-Postponement*. And such waiting is inevitably painful, as we saw earlier in the narrator's admonishment about Caroline Helstone's self-imposed thwarting of her impulses toward Robert Moore in Charlotte Brontë's *Shirley*. Such thwarting, we are told, consists of "sealing the lips, interdicting utterance, commanding a placid dissimulation: a dissimulation often wearing an easy and gay mien at first, settling down to sorrow and paleness in time, then passing away and leaving a convenient stoicism. . . . It should be bitter. . . . Sweet mild force following acute suffering, you find nowhere" (105–6). Yet waiting and suffering are what the "normal" Victorian heroine does best, particularly if the suffering is aesthetically pleasing. Small wonder that, as Doane puts it, "Femininity within a patriarchal culture is always constituted as a pathological condition" (36).

However, just as female characters can appropriate the look or the language of desire to some extent, they can also be permitted various degrees of enactment. Such enactment of female desire may be quite subtle, and possibly indirect; the displacements of desire will obviously be important in this regard, and "action" will need to be broadly interpreted. Given the parallels I have noted between the other representational arts and literature, my study (and literary criticism generally) can undoubtedly benefit from the theory and discoveries of these extra-literary areas. Film criticism, in particular, has made a concerted effort to locate a female subject of desire within the realist genre, with interesting results. As feminist readers of realist novels, we should share the film critics' suspicion of both representation and narrative. The latter is especially important in any critique of ideology, as narrative "becomes suspect in a feminist critique due to its construction of an exclusive world view, an illusory realm complete with closure and invisible seams. The feeling of wholeness and authenticity makes it all the more difficult to detect ideological exclusions or inclusions" (Gentile 81–82). The "feeling of wholeness and authenticity" which makes the reading of Victorian novels so pleasurable is to be queried at all times. We are to become resisting readers, as the overt message of a novel may be quite different from its unstated (and therefore more powerful) ideological assumptions. Even professed feminist novels may thus be deeply—perhaps unwittingly—conformist; Hardy's *Tess of the d'Urbervilles* is a good example of this, as I shall show. And the formation and perpetuation of ideology that takes place in novels, the stories that culture tells itself about itself, are immensely important to human reality, as Flaubert's Emma Bovary bore striking witness in 1857. If erotic relationships are ever to change (and our world along with them), they will only do so within ideology, as new ways of being are envisioned.

The re-reading of the realist novel, the refusal to be beguiled by its symbiotic dream of erotic wholeness within a sexual hierarchy, is a small but important part of such a task. The goal of mutual subjectivity has not yet been attained even in the twentieth century; but any attempts by nineteenth-century novelists to create at least the possibility of a female subject of desire mark progress toward this goal. In my re-readings of Charlotte Brontë, George Eliot and Thomas Hardy, therefore, I shall not hope to encounter a fully fledged female subjectivity. Rather, I shall attempt to trace the movements, however slight, toward a seeing, speaking, desiring female subject within the work of these novelists and within the century.

NOTES

1. Readers already familiar with feminist criticism in these areas may wish to turn to Chapter 2, bearing in mind that my definition of female subjectivity includes active participation in the look, the language and the enactment of desire.

2. George Moore's *Esther Waters* and *A Drama in Muslin* and George Meredith's *The Egoist*, for example, seem to me to be as disruptive of patriarchal norms as many female-authored texts of the century. This is not to deny the force of the distinction between women's writing and male writing which informs much superb feminist criticism (Gilbert and Gubar's or Nancy Miller's, for instance).

3.   The subject-position of the woman in what Peter Brooks calls "Freud's Masterplot"—the oedipal narrative of male desire—is wonderfully complex, as Nancy Miller and Teresa de Lauretis, for example, have illustrated. Such complexities of plot and narrative, while I find them intriguing, are beyond the scope of my present study, which focuses primarily on questions of female subjectivity as a function of more local effects (sight, speech, action) of narrative discourse.

4.   Feminist critiques of pornography, in particular, evince an immense sadness and longing as well as rage. Andrea Dworkin's article "Pornography and Grief" is a good example, as are the musings of Robin Morgan ("There is something in men, surely, that wishes to be known and loved for itself, something purely human. . . . And there is something in women that also wishes deeply to be known and loved for its human self," 122) and of Susan Griffin, whose entire book *Pornography and Silence* evokes a wrenching sense of loss: "Through all pornography . . . we can find a different vision of the world, glimmering, just out of reach, at times not even visible, but always present—this silenced presence of the idea of a marriage between spirit and matter, the forgotten knowledge that culture might embody nature for us rather than deny her" (71).

5.   It is perhaps clear by now that my definition of desire includes neither homoerotic nor autoerotic desire. I do not deal with the former simply because it does not figure largely in the erotic ambience of the canonical novels I have chosen to discuss; and I do not deal with the latter because of its oblique relation, at best, to questions of erotic domination within patriarchal ideology.

6.   See Beth Newman for an application of gaze theory to *Wuthering Heights*, for example. For a detailed comparison of the narrative elements of fiction and film, see Seymour Chatman.

7.   For a fully theorized account of beauty in the Victorian novel, see Lori Lefkovitz's detailed discussion in *The Character of Beauty*.

8.   Juliet Mitchell speaks of the female novelist as an "hysteric," for example (289), and Mary Ann Doane uses the same term to characterize female protagonists of the women's films of the 1940s (see her "Medical Discourse" chapter). On a more literal level, several studies have demonstrated how women's actual speech patterns reflect this difficulty, in the form of indirection, tentativeness, hesitancy and excessive deference to the (male) listener (see n. 9).

9.   For a discussion of this point, see Chapter 6 in Andrea Nye, whose bibliography includes a variety of linguists interested in gender differences.

10.   For a discussion of confession, see Foucault, Vol. 1, 59–69.

11.   See, for example, Homans's brilliant analysis of Mrs. Ramsay's speech to her children in *To the Lighthouse (Bearing the Word* 17–18).

12.   Kucich sees repression as positive, "a nineteenth-century strategy for exalting interiority." Kucich's analysis, while interesting and insightful, tends to extol the very "virtues" which are the hallmarks of the defensive, falsely differentiated male psyche: Victorian repression, he claims, "preserve[d] the sense of a self-conflictual, self-divided interiority," "heighten[d] and vitalize[d] emotional autonomy," "produced a self that was . . . self-sufficient and . . . antisocial," and "could . . . heighten a sense of the self's importance"; in short, it was "a controlled instrument of individuality, . . . a technique for defining oneself both internally and in opposition to others" (2–4). It is difficult to imagine the female psyche, especially in its quest for mutual subjectivity and "self-in-relation" that I have been

discussing, as being in tune with such goals. And given the rebellion of Charlotte Brontë's heroines against the extreme pain Victorian repression causes them (evidenced by the lengthy tirade in *Shirley* I have already quoted, for example), the application of Kucich's theory to her novels seems particularly problematic.

13. It is interesting to note that silenced males also exhibit hysterical symptoms; Elaine Showalter describes shell-shocked soldiers in wartime as "silenced and immobilized and forced, like women, to express their conflicts through the body. Placed in intolerable circumstances of stress, and expected to react with unnatural 'courage,' thousands of soldiers reacted instead with the symptoms of hysteria" (*Female Malady* 171).

14. Acton, a nineteenth-century physician, is famous for pronouncements such as the following—"The majority of women . . . are not very much troubled with sexual feeling of any kind. . . . As a general rule, a modest woman seldom desires any sexual gratification for herself. She submits to her husband, but only to please him"—complete with direct allusions to the motives behind such insistence: "No nervous or feeble young man need, therefore, be deterred from marriage by any exaggerated notion of the duties required from him" (*The Functions and Disorders of the Reproductive Organs*, 4th ed., 1985, qtd. in Jalland and Hooper 234).

15. For further discussion of Dickens's erotic ambivalence, see Barickman et al., 43–44.

2

❖ ❖ ❖

CHARLOTTE BRONTË

Robert Keefe sees a progression in Charlotte Brontë's work from possession (in *The Professor*) through innocence (in *Jane Eyre*) and emptiness (in *Shirley*) to exile (in *Villette*). Tracing Brontë's creative impulse to what Keefe considers to be "the single most important event" in her life, the death of her mother when she was a child, Keefe, like many other critics, sees in the novels a pattern of increasing abandonment. I see a wholly different pattern of progression in these remarkable novels, a pattern that moves from domination of self and others in *The Professor* to conventional male/female erotic domination in *Jane Eyre* to a questioning of this fantasy in *Shirley* to a qualified, negotiated emotional equality in *Villette*. In fact, of the novelists I shall discuss, Charlotte Brontë comes the closest to creating a female subject of desire, so that I was initially tempted to proceed, as Dianne Sadoff does in *Monsters of Affection*, in an anti-chronological order, beginning with Hardy and concluding with Brontë. Sadoff does this type of chronological juggling because she is concerned with Freudian progressions, from primal scene metaphors in Dickens to seduction metaphors in George Eliot to castration metaphors in Brontë. Sadoff is concerned in particular with fatherhood and, while her analysis is valuable and insightful, it leaves room for further analysis. In fact, while parental love and abandonment are undoubtedly important to Charlotte Brontë's work, neither Keefe's mother-love nor Sadoff's father-love tells the whole story, as I shall show in the following chapter.

The desire for the mother and the desire for the father are both subsumed in the desire and need of mature adult male-female relationships in many novels, and particularly in those of the Victorian period. If such desires are closer to the surface, more obvious and accessible, in Brontë's novels it is because her analysis of such relationships is both penetrating and honest. Her understanding of erotic domination and submission is acute, and her grappling with it in the novels is brilliant. In these four works, the reader can trace a bloodstained path, the path of hard-won feminist understanding. It is because she knew and felt the magic of domination and submission so keenly that she was able both to create the quintessential erotic domination/submission fantasy (in *Jane Eyre*) and to progress beyond it to what comes the closest to an equal subject-subject interaction (in *Villette*) in any of the novels I examine, and possibly in the nineteenth-century novel generally. Fully aware of both the enticement and the pain of the woman's position in the erotic domination fantasy, Charlotte Brontë created both implied authors and implied readers who are female. Virtually all important feminist issues occurred to her, and are wrestled with in her novels; she displays an acute awareness not only of practical and material inequities, but, more importantly for the purpose of my analysis, of emotional inequities in sexual relationships within patriarchy.

Charlotte Brontë's novels are novels of passion, of waiting, of frustration, and—as closely as this can be achieved in a patriarchal society—of female desire. Brontë's heroines, unique among their nineteenth-century sisters, are by and large physically plain, a quality that removes them at once from the usual objectification of beautiful women. That this was more than simply a wishful autobiographical trait (enabling the plain woman to be romantically successful in literature if not in life) is indicated by the remark Brontë made to her sisters that their habit of making their heroines beautiful as a matter of course was "morally wrong" (Gaskell 259). Her heroines' plainness eliminates or thwarts the voyeurism that is normally shared by the narrator and the implied (male) reader as soon as a woman character appears in a novel, and focuses the reader's attention on other aspects of such characters.

Even more remarkably, Brontë's heroines own the look of desire in a way that is seldom encountered in the Victorian novel (Kate Millett refers to Brontë as "perhaps the first woman who ever admitted in print that women find men beautiful," 198). In *Jane Eyre* and *Villette*, and to some extent in *Shirley*, it is the male characters whose appearance is described with aesthetic appreciation and in loving detail. Male beauty is a reality in these novels for both the heroines and the reader, and it is the female gaze which is the gaze of desire and ultimately of judgment. To a lesser extent, the language of desire is also "owned" by Brontë's heroines, at least sporadically, although it is more often displaced into metaphor, often violent metaphor. As for the enactment of desire, this (not surprisingly) is beyond the reach of most of Brontë's female characters, just as it is beyond the reach of the nineteenth-century heroine generally. But at least Brontë's heroines protest vehemently against their enforced passivity, inwardly if not overtly, and their waiting—the quintessential activity of the woman in the conventional love relationship—is endured only reluctantly. Jane Eyre and Lucy Snowe (and to some extent Caroline Helstone and Shirley Keeldar) have adult needs and desires; they are in no sense "innocent" in the way that many later Victorian heroines were to be, and, to their credit, they would have made poor angels in the house.

In Charlotte Brontë's novels we can see female subjectivity struggling to be born and protesting bitterly against the conventional restraints that prohibit such a birth. They are remarkable books, and in them we can trace Charlotte Brontë's progression far beyond her time in her fearless exploration of the emotional power dynamics of male-female relationships.

THE PROFESSOR

The Professor is a strange novel. Unique among Brontë's novels (and among the novels I shall be discussing), it has a first-person male narrator. This on its own, however, is not particularly remarkable; what is decidedly unusual is that this narrator, one William Crimsworth, is eminently unlikable as well as unreliable. Heather Glen, in her introduction to the Penguin edition, sees *The Professor* as a fictional example not of confessional autobiography but of "the exemplary biography of the self-made man" (10), and I think Crimsworth's unlikability is directly related to this somewhat fine distinction (as well as to his negativity, as Glen contends). For Crimsworth does not exactly "confess" to the reader, at least not in a way that makes us sympathize with him; in fact, as Glen points out, "Explicit withholding is characteristic of Crimsworth's narrative. . . . Instead of assuming and creating an intimacy between narrator and reader . . . it enacts those refusals and evasions that operate within the world it describes" (294 n.2 ch.3). Crimsworth tells us things, describes events, and even interprets them; but we do not like him for it, nor do we necessarily believe him. If we consider this for a moment, we can see that it is an unusual and difficult achievement, since our instinct as readers is to "side with" a first-person confessional narrator (even though, as Ruth Johnston reminds us, such identification mechanisms are necessarily limited and fallible) and to believe her/him as well, particularly in the absence of overt manifestations of unreliability. Brontë's portrayal of Crimsworth displays none of the latter, nor is there enough distance between the narrator's younger self and his older self to suggest an entirely ironic reading of him; the "curious disjunction between [Crimsworth's] own self-image . . . and the overall effect of his narrative" (11) which Glen discerns arises from a subtler source, namely his gender.[1] Just as the reader—namely, the male reader—takes Moll Flanders's or Becky Sharp's narrative with a grain of salt, simply because it is by or about a woman, Brontë invites her reader—who is, it would seem, a female reader—to stand aside from Crimsworth's point of view. And just as Moll's or Becky's foibles are distinctively female (or so their authors imply), Crimsworth's are distinctively male. "Foibles" is perhaps the wrong word for Crimsworth's oddities, however; "neuroses" might be more appropriate.

The Professor is a disturbing book. Glen sees it as "unpleasant and oddly disquieting" and finds in Crimsworth's story "something oddly disagreeable, even repellent" (7). She is right in seeing this unpleasantness as an important clue to the novel, but her excellent discussion of the negativity in the novel's language leaves several mysteries unsolved. Why Brontë creates such an unpleasant narrator is a vastly interesting question, which I shall attempt to answer in the following pages. It has something to do with sex, that much seems clear; Glen senses a "barely suppressed violence, a peculiarly sadistic sexuality" (11) in the novel. I shall argue that this violence and sadism have a coherent and explicable origin, namely Crimsworth's psychological stance in regard to the female Other. *The Professor* is in fact a novel of domination, of false differentiation and its concomitant defensiveness, of fear of the feminine and the resulting obsessional need of the male to control both Self and Other.[2]

Seen in this way, the disparate and puzzling elements of the novel fit together and make a kind of psychological sense that testifies to Brontë's uncanny, almost modern understanding of erotic relations. That this understanding was almost certainly unconscious and instinctive (as we can infer from the murkiness and dislocations in the novel, the occasional banality of the surface narrative in comparison to the troubled undercurrents) does not make it any less profound. Seen as a conventionally defended male, Crimsworth is not such an enigma. His narrative stance toward the reader—a stance of withholding, of secrecy—simply echoes the stance of the dominant member of the domination/submission hierarchy in relation to the female Other. From this point of view the curious digressions centering on his mother and on Hunsden no longer seem so puzzling, and the overall project or message of the book seems less opaque.

Crimsworth's overwhelming need for control is the motivational force that drives the narrative; it is a tale not of love or sex or affection but of power. Like any falsely differentiated male, Crimsworth is compelled to exercise control over everyone and everything he can, including himself (and imagines that everyone else does likewise, remarking that "human beings—human children especially, seldom deny themselves the pleasure of exercising a power which they are conscious of possessing, even though that power consists only in a capacity to make others wretched," 132); and, also like any other controlling subject, he resents the compulsion: when "Reason" orders him not to kiss Frances good-bye, he remarks, "I obeyed, but I swore rancorously to be avenged one day" (176). The violence created by the juxtaposition of "rancorously" with "swore," which plays on the dual meaning of the verb, is typical of the violence such a struggle engenders throughout the novel. It is often submerged in metaphor, as it is in this case, but it is omnipresent and ominous, adding immeasurably to the volcanic uneasiness of the work as a whole. The muttering unrest that the reader senses rather than comprehends is a result of forces within the main character, forces not in equilibrium but in precarious tension, as Crimsworth is driven yet hates what drives him. As Glen points out, "If [*The Professor*] is a tale of 'self-control,' it is one in which 'self-control' is exposed as a process of radical, indeed violent, self-division," a self-division that is "the reverse of 'integrity' or individual wholeness," resulting in a "seething drama of denied impulse" (21–22).

Not surprisingly, given what we know of the controlling power inherent in the seeing/seen dyad and of the objectifying and distancing power of the gaze, the primary mode of interaction in *The Professor* (as Sadoff points out, *Monsters* 128) is looking. Battles are fought with the eyes, much speaking is done with the eyes, information is obtained through spying, and Crimsworth endlessly describes what he sees, which generally happens to be women. To say that it is a voyeuristic novel is too simple, as what is presented is a whole etiology of looking, and, more significantly, the scopophilic pleasure usually associated with voyeurism is entirely absent. If twentieth-century feminist filmmakers could create such an effect—a movie about voyeurism stripped of voyeuristic pleasure—they would undoubtedly hasten to do so.

The abrasive power of the look is amply illustrated in the conflict between Crimsworth and Zoraïde Reuter, the directress of the school where Crimsworth works and to whom he is initially attracted (and who then becomes attracted to him, after he abruptly loses interest in her as a result of his discovery that she is going to marry M. Pelet, an older teacher at the school). Needless to say, the battle between them is a sexual battle, and begins even before Crimsworth's discovery. In one of their earliest conversations Crimsworth reports that Mlle. Reuter's eye, "astute, penetrating, practical, shewed she was *even with me*" (89, my italics). He also notes a discrepancy between what she says and how she looks at him: "While her lips uttered only affable common-places, her eyes reverted continually to my face. Her glances were not given in full, but out of the corners, so quietly, so stealthily." Crimsworth fears this female look (which he often perceives as stealthy, as he does in this passage) because of its power to glean information about him ("I perceived soon that she was feeling after my real character"). His fear amounts to paranoia, causing the reader to question the validity of his perceptions, especially when his interpretation breaks out into violent metaphors, as it does when he imagines that Mlle. Reuter was "hoping in the end to find some chink, some niche, where she could put in her little firm foot and stand upon my neck—Mistress of my nature." The image of domination gives the clue to the real basis for Crimsworth's fear of this gazing female, and his very next sentence affirms it by denial: "Do not mistake me, reader, it was no amorous influence she wished to gain" (89). As Glen shrewdly reminds us, "To deny an intention is to reveal its unconscious presence" (22), and Crimsworth's narrative displays this type of negative affirmation countless times in the course of the novel, usually in a sexual context. Describing one of his female students in a later scene, for example, he says, "In passing behind her bench I have remarked that her neck is grey for want of washing, and her hair, so glossy with gum and grease, is not such as one feels tempted to pass the hand over, much less to run the fingers through" (99). The suggestion is thus simultaneously planted and denied, the word "tempted" pointing clearly to its genesis. The effect of such denials is cumulative, and helps to explain Crimsworth's somewhat vague unreliability as a narrator; quite simply, we do not believe him overall, even though individual instances (such as those given) are unarguable.

To return to Crimsworth's ocular battle with Mlle. Reuter, however, the scene concludes, as he imagines, to her advantage: "I met her eye too in full—obliging her to give me a straight-forward look; this last test went against me, it left her as it found her, moderate, temperate, tranquil; me it disappointed" (90). He is disappointed because in order to "win" the battle of the gaze he needs both to force her to look at him and to discomfit her by doing so. As feminist critics have noted, in the seeing/seen dyad the female is neither to initiate the look nor to return it, at least not so cooly as Mlle. Reuter does. Crimsworth wishes to assert his superiority over her, and her looking back at him denotes equality.

After Crimsworth discovers that Mlle. Reuter, far from desiring him, has amorous intentions toward M. Pelet, the battle between them is joined, at least on his part, in an escalated form. When Mlle. Reuter's "eye" demands to know why his manner toward her has changed, Crimsworth "answers" her in the following fashion: "Meeting her gaze full; arresting, fixing her glance, I shot into her eyes from my own a look, where there was no respect, no love, no tenderness, no gallantry, where the strictest analysis could detect nothing but scorn, hardihood, irony; I made her bear it, and feel it.... I would not relieve her embarrassment" (113–14). The viciousness of this (punctuated by the word "shot") makes it seem more like a rape than a glance, and it is often the case that the "penetrating glance" in this novel is not only sexual but sadistic. As in real rape and in the pornographic imagination generally, the underlying motives are violence and humili-ation (he enjoys her "embarrassment") rather than satisfaction; the worst thing that the "strictest analysis" could detect in Crimsworth's glance presumably would be any hint of affection or tenderness.

Crimsworth is not the only character in the novel who regards the glance as a weapon. M. Pelet—whose approach to women is more openly porno-graphic than Crimsworth's—notices Mlle. Reuter's eyebrows, in which he detects "du chat dans l'un et du renard dans l'autre," nicely submerged suggestions of bestiality. He describes her look in great detail: "The eye-lid will flicker, the light-coloured lashes be lifted a second, and a blue eye, glancing out from under the screen, will take its brief, sly, searching survey, and retreat again." This description is part of a fairly salacious conversation in which the two men discuss women, and is followed by Pelet's teasing speculation that "I am mistaken if she will not yet leave the print of her stealing steps on thy heart, Crimsworth" and Crimsworth's vehement denial: "Confound it—no! My heart is not a plank to be walked on" (94). The twisting of the metaphor to expose its most violent connotations is characteristic both of the language of the novel and of Crimsworth's fearful and defensive attitude toward the female Other.

Mlle. Reuter is not the only female whose gaze Crimsworth sedulously avoids and disapproves of. Aurelia, the student with the dirty hair, "launches at [him] all sorts of looks, languishing, provoking, leering, laughing," although he is "quite proof against this sort of artillery" (99), and another student, Adèle, has a "gaze ever waiting for [his] and it frequently succeeded in arresting it" (100). The battle imagery—"launching," "artillery," even "arresting"—is typical of all such encounters, and Crimsworth makes it clear that such brazen looking by the female is part of the reason he finds his students so disgusting. In a mass, they talk to him "with their eyes, by means of which organs they could . . . say very audacious and coquettish things" (118). Frances, on the other hand, launches no such looks in his direction, at least not when there is the possibility of a sexual exchange; when he writes "Bon" on her first assignment, she "did not lift her eyes; she could look at me, it seemed, when perplexed and bewildered, but not when gratified; I thought that scarcely fair" (124). Crimsworth is "secretly" pleased by this. The coy, facetious tone of the latter observation—"I thought that scarcely fair"—is obvious, particularly in comparison to the violence of his language when the female does return his look.

Given the importance of looking, it is not surprising that Crimsworth courts Frances almost exclusively with his eyes. The understanding between them is measured in terms of their ability to "read" each other's thoughts and feelings in a series of seemingly mutual gazes. When Frances's students disobey her, Crimsworth "read in her eye pain that a stranger should witness the insubordination" (125); when he omits to mention her *devoirs* with the rest, he "endeavoured to decipher in her countenance her sentiments at the omission" (135); when he encounters her at the graveyard he reports that "amazement had hardly opened her eyes and raised them to mine, ere Recognition informed their irids with most speaking brightness. . . . I loved with passion the light of Frances Evans' clear hazel eye when it did not fear to look straight into mine" (168); when he visits her in her fireless flat, "her eye . . . instantly sought mine, which was just then lingering on the hearth; I knew she read at once [my] inward ruth and pitying pain" (172). In fact, Frances is the appropriately modest object in the seeing/seen dyad. She occasionally "reads" Crimsworth's eyes and looks back at him, but she never appropriates the look of desire, nor does she always receive it comfortably. When she has cleared away the meal she and Crimsworth have shared, he reports that "she betrayed . . . a little embarrassment; and no wonder, for indeed I had unconsciously watched her rather too closely; followed all her . . . movements a little too persever-ingly with my eyes. . . . Her colour . . . rising, rather than settling with repose and her eyes remaining downcast, though I kept waiting for the lids to be raised that I might drink a ray of the light I loved. . . . I must cease gazing and begin talking" (174–75).

As it happens, Crimsworth never ceases gazing throughout the novel, and his gaze is consistently sexual. Even his description of his own reflec-tion in the mirror focuses on his ability (or lack of it) to attract sexual attention; he sees "something young, but not youthful, no object to win a lady's love, no butt for the shafts of Cupid" (77). Even this standard mythological reference is imbued, however faintly, with Crimsworth's sexual fears in the words "butt" and "shafts," we may note. In other scenes his fears verge on paranoia. When he is invited to have tea with old Madame Pelet, for instance, his first thought is one of sexual panic: "Surely she's not going to make love to me. . . . I've heard of old Frenchwomen doing odd things in that line. . . . They generally begin such affairs with eating and drinking, I believe." Although he realizes that this is only a "suggestion of [his] excited imagination," the worry persists ("The first view of her seemed to confirm my worst apprehensions") until he discovers that Madame Pelet's friend, old Madame Reuter, is to take tea with them too. Even then, his sexual disgust remains as a kind of prim superiority toward the old women and their habits. He notes that British granddames would "recoil" from them as "absolutely disreputable," that Madame Reuter has "a twinkle and a leer in her left eye" and that "they ate . . . with no delicate appetite." He declines with disapproval their *petit verre* ("what I thought, rather a stiff tumbler of punch") and continues to be suspicious of them throughout the conversation (71–73). Crimsworth's prudery and castration fears, while extreme, are entirely believable.

In fact, Crimsworth epitomizes the conventional male subject of desire, in that he is infinitely tantalized, yet infinitely repelled, by women. The boarded-up window in his room is the most overtly voyeuristic device in the novel, and his attitude toward it is the reader's first clue to his untrust-worthiness as a narrator. When M. Pelet leaves him alone in his room, he tells us, "The first thing I did was to scrutinize closely the nailed boards, hoping to find some chink or crevice . . . and so get a peep at the consecrated ground." To "peep" is exactly what he is doing, and "consecrated" under-lines the impression of feminine mystery. He is "astonished" at how disap-pointed he feels when he finds no such feminine "chink or crevice," and the putative reasons he gives for this strike the reader as a trifle dis-ingenuous. "I thought it would have been so pleasant to have looked out upon a garden planted with flowers and trees" is his first explanation, and his next is not much better—"so amusing to have watched the demoiselles at their play—to have studied female character in a variety of phases." What really tips us off as to his scopophilic intent, however, is the last, seemingly casual, touch he adds to the scenario: "myself the while, sheltered from view by a modest muslin curtain" (65). The "modest" curtain shields not the girls but himself from view, enabling him to see without being seen, the stock requirement of the voyeur.

Appropriately, Crimsworth is the first of a long line of spies in Charlotte Brontë's novels. He sees from his window Mlle. Reuter and M. Pelet walking in the garden, "arm in arm, or hand in hand (I forget which)" (109–10) and hears their marriage plans. It is unlikely that he would "forget" how the couple was joined, given the importance of the scene; and his curt dismissal of his own feelings does nothing to elicit the reader's sympathy. He summarily reports that "something feverish and fiery had got into my veins which prevented me from sleeping much that night" (111). He does not name the jealousy, nor does he admit it in the course of the following events; he merely punishes Mlle. Reuter in the ways I have already noted.

Crimsworth's occupation allows him to spy much more extensively and deliberately than he does in the discovery scene, however. From the first time he meets with his students, when he is overcome by the vision of female plenitude ("Good features, ruddy, blooming complexions, large and brilliant eyes, forms full even to solidity seemed to abound. . . . I was dazzled, my eyes fell, and in a voice somewhat too low, I murmured," 84), Crimsworth's imagination centers almost exclusively on his nubile young students. He gives detailed portraits of at least six of these—Eulalie, Hortense, Caroline, Aurelia, Adèle and Juanna—and M. Pelet (luckily more concisely) also describes the first three, so that the novel seems saturated with descriptions of women. Because of his fear and discomfort, Crimsworth exercises the power of the look with a vengeance.

The way in which he exercises it is classically voyeuristic, verging on pornographic. He describes not persons but parts, in true fetishistic fashion: eyes, lips, teeth, hair, bustlines, all come under his appraising scrutiny, deluging the reader with endless dismembered details. To give just one example, we read of Aurelia Koslow that "she is of middle size, stiffly made, body long, legs short, bust much developed but not compactly molded, waist disproportionately compressed by an inhumanly braced corset, dress carefully arranged, large feet tortured into small bottines, head small, hair smoothed, braided, oiled and gummed to perfection, very low forehead, very diminutive and vindictive grey eyes, somewhat Tartar features, rather flat nose, rather high cheek-bones yet the ensemble not positively ugly, tolerably good complexion" (98–99). As a male, Crimsworth easily adopts the prerogative of the controlling look, appraising these females as sexual objects as a means of asserting his sexual superiority and of containing his fears of them. Such descriptions become tedious, degenerating into mere lists of female parts, but that is precisely in character: to the pornographic imagination there is pleasure in quantity as well as in repetition.

Crimsworth's psyche also displays a classically violent split between notions of the good (virginal) woman and the bad (sexual) woman. He initially espouses the fantasy of the purity of his charges; before he sees them, he looks at his boarded window and thinks that he will "at last see the mysterious garden: I shall gaze both on the angels and their Eden" (76). What he really wants to see, as his metaphor makes clear, is not angels but Eve, although he continues to lament the absence of "some gentle virgin head, circled with a halo, some sweet personification of Innocence, clasping the dove of peace to her bosom" (102). The reality of his students, far different from this, disgusts him, and his descriptions of them (like the one of Aurelia) exude a combination of sexual fascination and repugnance. His fevered imagination sees a sexual dimension in every aspect of every student. Of Caroline he remarks, "How, with the tintless pallor of her skin and the classic straightness of her lineaments, she managed to look sensual—I don't know—I think her lips and eyes contrived the affair between them and the result left no uncertainty on the beholder's mind," and he tells us that Eulalie "raised her unmoved eye to mine and seemed to expect . . . an impromptu tribute to her majestic charms" while Hortense "regarded me boldly and giggled at the same time" (86). These are clear instances of projection; Crimsworth perceives sexual threats everywhere. He is particularly alarmed and repulsed when he detects any active desire in the women's actions, which he instantly denounces as "unwomanly." When he eavesdrops on the girls at play through the boarded-up window in his room, for example, he hears "not quite silvery, in fact . . . too-often brazen sounds. . . . Not to mince matters—it really seemed to me a doubtful case whether the lungs of Mlle. Reuter's girls or those of M. Pelet's boys were the strongest and, when it came to shrieking, the girls indisputably beat the boys hollow" (66). As he sees and hears more of them, his disgust increases; instead of the "vague, slight, gauzy, glittering" notion of the female character he once had, he finds it to be "a palpable substance enough; very hard too sometimes, and often heavy—there was metal in it, both lead and iron" (97). This material reality dismays him, and his dismay is sexual: "How was it . . . that scarcely one of those girls having attained the age of fourteen could look a man in the face with modesty and propriety? An air of bold, impudent flirtation or a loose, silly leer was sure to answer the most ordinary glance from a masculine eye. . . . They had all been carefully brought up, yet was the mass of them mentally depraved" (98). Given what we know of Crimsworth, it hardly seems likely that his glance was ever "ordinary," and the mental depravity he mentions attaches itself only rather dubiously to the students. Crimsworth's descriptions inevitably descend to bestial imagery: he sees a "panther-like deceit" about

Adèle's mouth and reports that Juanna "made noises with her mouth like a horse, . . . ejected her saliva, [and] uttered brutal expressions; . . . she got up and sustained a swinish tumult" (101).

Crimsworth's fear and hatred of women culminate in his bout of hypochondria, which (significantly) occurs just after Frances has agreed to marry him. He personifies hypochondria as a hag, "taking me entirely to her death-cold bosom, and holding me with arms of bone" (228). He does not understand why he should be accosted by this apparition when his desires, "folding wings, weary with long flight, had just alighted on the very lap of fruition, and nestled there warm, content, under the caress of a soft hand," but perhaps the reader does. No matter how comforting the metaphor, his sexual repugnance is unlikely to disappear with his marriage (and indeed this turns out to be the case), an ominous reality underlined by his final analogy: "I repulsed her, as one would a dreaded and ghastly concubine coming to embitter her husband's heart towards his young bride" (229). Crimsworth cannot escape the need to dominate and the fear of the Other that it masks; he is irretrievably enmeshed in the fantasy of erotic domination, which will create undesirable and insurmountable distances in his marriage.

Crimsworth's pornographic mind-set is reinforced by that of M. Pelet, the other male in the novel in the titillating position of "master" to large numbers of female students. Initially described in a way that reinforces Crimsworth's priggish notion of his own morality ("I suspected a degree of laxity in his code of morals. . . . I hated his fashion of mentioning Love, I abhorred, from my soul, mere Licentiousness," 70), Pelet describes with relish three of Crimsworth's students:

Lovely creatures, all of them—heads for artists—what a group they would make, taken together! Eulalie . . . with her smooth braided hair and calm, ivory brow, Hortense with her rich chestnut locks so luxuriantly knotted, plaited, twisted, as if she did not know how to dispose of all their abundance, with her vermilion lips, damask cheek and roguish, laughing eye—and Caroline de Blémont! Ah, there is beauty! . . . What a cloud of sable curls about the face of a houri! What fascinating lips! What glorious black eyes! (95–96)

This rendition is illuminating in several respects. Purely appreciative, it evinces none of the repugnance that permeates Crimsworth's own descriptions of the women. In fact, it is much closer to conventional nineteenth-century heroine descriptions. The artistic framing ("heads for artists; what a group they would make, taken together") provides an acceptable aesthetic focus for the detailed description of physical features, but the context reveals the thinly disguised sexual delectation of all such descriptions. Such an appraisal reeks of control, and dominance is its motivation, as Pelet's later comment makes clear: "A . . . fellow like you might make himself the *master* of the hand, heart and purse of any one of the trio" (96, my italics).

If anything, Pelet's open lasciviousness is less offensive than Crimsworth's prurient prudishness, which sneers as it appraises; between them they represent a wide spectrum of the dominant male gaze which seeks to define and control.

Crimsworth's attraction to Frances, an exception to such an attitude and an apparent anomaly in one so negative toward most of the females he encounters, is in fact a coherent and understandable response of such a psyche. Significantly, he does not notice her appearance at their first meeting ("I had never stopped to scrutinize either her face or her person, and had but the most vague idea of her general appearance," 117), in telling contrast to his detailed observation of the other students. Later, however, as he becomes more involved with her, he expounds on the improvement in Frances's looks. Now that she is happier,

a clearness of skin, almost bloom—and a plumpness almost embonpoint softened the decided lines of her features. Her figure shared in this beneficial change—it became rounder and . . . one did not regret (or at least *I* did not regret) the absence of confirmed fullness, in contours, still slight, though compact, elegant, flexible—the exquisite turning of waist, wrist, hand, foot, and ancle [*sic*] satisfied completely my notions of symmetry, and allowed a lightness and freedom of movement which corresponded with my ideas of grace. (147–48)

A number of points emerge from this description. First of all, Frances's appearance is non-sexual, and therefore non-threatening, particularly in comparison with that of the other brazen, buxom students who appall Crimsworth so much (even much later, after they are engaged, he describes her as "looking . . . more a woman to respect than to love," 234). Also, his appreciation of her is safely aesthetic rather than erotic, or so Crimsworth thinks in stressing his lack of regret for her "absence of confirmed fullness" (another excellent example of negative affirmation). He carefully objectifies her, and is pleased that she conforms to his aesthetic ideals, his "notions of symmetry" and "ideas of grace." In fact, the passage is centered much more on him than it is on her, and it is clear that the delight he feels is the satisfaction of the controlling subject in the presence of a controllable object: "To speak truth, I watched this change much as a gardener watches the growth of a precious plant" (148).

The graveyard scene emphasizes the notion of control, both his control over her ("I loved her, as she stood there, penniless and parentless, for a sensualist—charmless, for me a treasure, my best object of sympathy on earth, thinking such thoughts as I thought, feeling such feelings as I felt, my ideal of the shrine in which to seal my stores of love," 168–69) and—just as importantly—her control over herself. She is an "object," a "shrine," and unlike the other students, Frances will not enact her own desire but will be content to remain the passive recipient of Crimsworth's. "Personification of . . . self-denial and self-control—those guardians . . . of the gift I longed to confer on her—the gift of all my affections. . . . I knew how the . . . dangerous flame burned safely under the eye of reason. . . . I had seen reason reduce the rebel and humble its blaze to embers" (169). The "dangerous flame" of passion must be controlled at all costs, and Frances is therefore perceived by Crimsworth as the perfect partner, as she is neither too passionate nor too beautiful (although later, in the engagement scene, Crimsworth admits that he "derived a pleasure purely material from contemplating the clearness of her brown eyes, the fairness of her fine skin, the purity of her well-set teeth, the proportion of her delicate form; and that pleasure I could ill have dispensed with," 227).

It is no wonder that Crimsworth finds Frances an ideal mate: she is controllable, she is self-controlled, she is miraculously transformed into a desirable female object under his care and guidance. To this is added the finishing touch of competition and "triangular" desire when Hunsden approaches Frances favorably. An apparent conundrum in the novel, the character of Hunsden is a brilliant conception in the psychic economy created by Brontë. Critics have speculated widely as to his significance, noting his ambiguous sexuality, his possible homosexuality and his ties both to Crimsworth's mother and to Frances (some have even speculated that he is Victor's father). Certainly he fits with Cimsworth's patriarchal distrust and devaluation of the feminine: as the mediator of Crimsworth's desire he becomes the significant other male in the homosocial rivalry for Frances's affections, and as such a suggestive homosexual aura surrounds him as he is described by Crimsworth. Their teasing banter, always a sign of intimacy in Brontë's work, causes him to seem closer to Crimsworth, and certainly more equal to him, than Frances ever does. Crimsworth reports that he has "small, and even feminine . . . lineaments" and that he has "now the mien of a morose bull and anon that of an arch and mischievous girl," and speculates that "as to his good looks, I should have liked to have a woman's opinion on that subject; it seemed to me that his face might produce the same effect on a lady that a very piquant and interesting, though scarcely pretty, female face would have on a man" (35). The latter is almost exactly the effect, of course, that Frances has on Crimsworth, and the convoluted gender reversals of the passage (Hunsden's face would have the same effect on a lady—and has on Crimsworth—that a similar female face would have on a man) create the impression of an oblique sexual relationship between the two men. This is further reinforced by the look they exchange during their conversation about Crimsworth's future—" 'Oh I see!' said he, looking into my eyes, and it was evident he *did* see right down to my heart" (51)—and by the wrestling scene, which significantly occurs just after Hunsden has met Frances for the first time and flirted mildly with her. Crimsworth reports, "He swayed me to and fro; so I grappled him round the waist; it was dark; the street lonely and lampless; we had then a tug for it, and after we had both rolled on the pavement and with difficulty picked ourselves up, we agreed to walk on more soberly" (243). Such a scene, with its grappling in the dark, is just as evocative as (if more concise than) D. H. Lawrence's more famous wrestling scene in *Women in Love* written more than fifty years later.

Hunsden's association with the portrait of Crimsworth's mother is another profound subtlety, pointing silently to the first woman Crimsworth presumably had any difficulty with. When he first discovers the portrait, Crimsworth is "sorry it was only a picture" (14), and when he feels excluded from the party at Crimsworth Hall (particularly by his brother, around whom there is "a group of very pretty girls," 23), he seeks the portrait for comfort: "I gazed long, earnestly; my heart grew to the image. My Mother, I perceived, had bequeathed to me much of her features and countenance—her forehead, her eyes, her complexion" (24). There is a blurring of gender distinctions—he goes on to compare his feelings to those of "fathers [who] regard with complacency the lineaments of their daughters' faces"—and then Hunsden, significantly, makes his first appearance. It is impossible to name exactly the connections among Crimsworth, his mother, Hunsden, and Frances, as Brontë leave them submerged and unstated; but they are there nevertheless, beneath the surface of the novel, adding a powerful and troubling dimension to the surface events. At the end of the novel, Frances as a mother "abandons" Crimsworth to care for their child, and Hunsden is still there, like a "hovering hawk" (267) from whom Victor seems to need protection.

The Professor, then, is a novel of domination. Well does Charlotte Brontë understand the dynamics of control inherent in most erotic relationships. When Crimsworth is no longer in love with Mlle. Reuter (and therefore no longer in her control), he notes that he can begin to control her: "Her manner towards me had been altered ever since I had begun to treat her with hardness and indifference; she almost cringed to me on every occasion. . . . This slavish homage, instead of softening my heart, only pampered whatever was stern and exacting in its mood" (129). As one partner backs away, the other draws near; and it is the partner who loves less who invariably has more control. The most often-quoted passage in the novel, in fact, embodies this truth:

I had ever hated a tyrant, and behold the possession of a slave, self-given, went near to transform me into what I abhorred! There was at once a sort of low gratification in receiving this luscious incense from an attractive and still young worshipper and an irritating sense of degradation in the very experience of the pleasure. When she stole about me with the soft step of a slave—I felt at once barbarous and sensual as a pasha—I endured her homage sometimes, sometimes I rebuked it—my indifference or harshness served equally to increase the evil I desired to check. (184)

This is a nearly perfect rendition of the domination/submission relationship, with its master-slave, sadomasochistic imagery and air of combative eroticism. Crimsworth employs this same strategy in his attempt to attract Frances: "Motioning her to rise, I installed myself in her place, allowing her to stand deferentially at my side, for I esteemed it wise and right in her case to enforce strictly all forms ordinarily in use between master and pupil; the rather because I perceived that in proportion as my manner grew austere and magisterial, hers became easy and self-possessed" (138). Charlotte Brontë remains painfully aware of this perverse dynamic throughout her career; it is the basis for both Jane Eyre's and Lucy Snowe's gigantic efforts of renunciation and self-control. For self-control facilitates control of the Other, whereas a lack of self-control enables the Other to control the Self, usually contemptuously. Pride becomes a matter of power in such a scenario, and each participant is compelled to treat the other as an adversary.

Several critics have seen *The Professor* as a story of success with a conventionally happy ending. But the success, easily enough achieved on the surface, is qualified by the constant watchful tension within Crimsworth; it is as though he can never relax his control for fear of being overwhelmed and controlled himself. He struggles with his own feelings for Frances, for example, until one day they overcome him, at which point he reflects, "There are impulses we can control; but there are others which control us, because they attain us with a tiger-leap and are our masters ere we have seen them. . . . Whereas, one moment I was sitting solus on the chair near the table, the next, I held Frances on my knee, placed there with sharpness and decision, and retained with exceeding tenacity" (222). The violence of the struggle is reflected in the violence of the language ("tiger-leap," "sharpness," "decision," "tenacity"), and Frances's implied response, as opposed to her overt response, is correspondingly fearful: she is "as stirless in her happiness as a mouse in its terror" and "scarcely lifted her head" (224). After this "victory," during which they become engaged, Crimsworth reflects, "There is something flattering to a man's strength, something consonant to his honourable pride in the idea of becoming the providence of what he loves—feeding and clothing it, as God does the lilies of the field" (225). The exultant tone of this betrays the real source of his pleasure, which has little to do with love for Frances: she is "what he loves," an "it," at best a flower, while he is the all-powerful god-like provider. And their "success," their happy marriage (to which Brontë devotes an unusually long section of the novel, eschewing the conventional "happily ever after" ending), is imbued with this same sense of Crimsworth's dominance. At one point Frances is actually overcome with something that seems to be ardor, but this occurs in the midst of her reflections of relief at not being an old maid and is more likely a spasm of gratefulness (" 'I'm not an old maid. . . . I should have been though but for my master. . . . I have been Professor Crimsworth's wife eight years and what is he in my eyes? is he honourable, beloved—?' She stopped, her voice was cut off—her eyes suddenly suffused. She and I were standing side by side; she threw her arms round me and strained me to her heart with passionate earnestness," 256). Even Crimsworth's relationship with his son, Victor, is one of control, and of violent control, as the dog-shooting incident illustrates.

All in all Crimsworth remains a violent and troubled consciousness, a regrettable but fitting end for the dominant male subject. In *The Professor* Charlotte Brontë creates a remarkable portrait of a falsely differentiated male ego for whom control has become a fetishistic obsession. Better than possibly any other English novel, it reveals the psychic reality of the "subject" side of the subject/object dyad and finds it to be painfully restrictive. Remarkably, Brontë seems to be aware that neither the male subject nor the female object in this configuration can attain true subjectivity.

JANE EYRE

Jane Eyre is arguably the most erotic English novel written in the nineteenth century. Emily Brontë's *Wuthering Heights*, another obvious contender, is passionate rather than erotic, a rather fine distinction having to do with the latter's emphasis on merging and the supernatural as opposed to domination and reality. In *Jane Eyre* we have the quintessential Harlequin Romance, the love story of conflict, misunderstandings and seemingly insurmountable obstacles, complete with a dark Byronic hero who turns out to be capable of great tenderness toward the heroine, who reaps her reward in the end in the form of marriage and a child. Jean Wyatt's article "A Patriarch of One's Own" discusses this aspect of the novel very cogently, pointing out the ambivalence inherent in Jane's contradictory "passionate assertion of autonomy . . . and passionate commitment to romantic love" (213), which according to Wyatt appeals to readers so much because it reflects their own conflicting wishes and their desire to "have it all." *Jane Eyre* also fits well with Dianne Sadoff's analysis of what she sees as "Brontë's repeated subject-matter: a woman's desire and its object, the figurative father." As Sadoff points out, "The dialectic of master and slave threads its way through Brontë's texts; she is thrilled and repulsed by it" (*Monsters* 130, 119).

Jane Eyre indeed partakes of the master-slave dialectic, insofar as it is a novel of erotic domination. Unlike *The Professor* it is related, as are Brontë's later novels, from the female's point of view; also unlike *The Professor*, it explores the "positive" aspects of the domination/submission fantasy and makes them seem infinitely desirable. Although Brontë introduces some important modifications to the prevailing fantasy, I do not think, as Sadoff does, that she is seeking "to redefine the terms of mastery, to invert male and female" (119). Rather, I think that in *Jane Eyre* Brontë leaves intact the basic structure of male domination and female submission—which she understands only too well, as we can see from *The Professor*—but plays and explores within it, indulging in one final fling her Angrian love of romantic fantasy at the same time that she gives a startlingly insightful portrayal of the female's part in such fantasy. It represents pure wish-fulfillment, as her later novels make clear, and its overall effect, as I mentioned at the outset, is undeniably erotic.

Jane Eyre's eroticism is heightened by Brontë's profound understanding of the oedipal needs that are subsumed in the master-servant relationship, and by the enormous amount of physical touching that goes on in the novel (which no doubt fed the censure of contemporary critics and caused Brontë to retreat from such displays of physicality in her subsequent novels). Given the stock powerful male/powerless female scenario, it may seem unusual to ask whether Jane could be construed as a female subject of desire. What is even more unusual is the answer, which is "almost." She displays the look, and occasionally the language, of desire; she unabashedly feels desire; and her actions, while extremely oblique, are at least directed toward the fulfillment of this desire. Perhaps most importantly, she is not a conventional object of desire. Her character is not objectified in the way that those of most Victorian heroines are, in that she is not beautiful. She is also much less passive than many nineteenth-century heroines; basically, she has intelligently assessed the combat inherent in the domination/submission relation, and plays to win, yielding to her passions (and Rochester's) only when she knows her future is secure. *Jane Eyre* is the impossible dream, the Cinderella story, with some important differences.

I would like to begin my discussion with what is possibly the most outstanding of these differences, the startling fact of a plain heroine. From the opening chapters, when Abbot, the maid, remarks that "one really cannot care for such a little toad as that" (26), Jane's lack of beauty is made very clear. Nor is this a misperception on her part, as such premature judgments are in the case of Maggie Tulliver, who turns out to be simply an unconventionally beautiful woman, or even of Frances Henri, whose initial plainness is transformed by love (although when Rochester tells her he loves her Jane too "looked at [her] face in the glass, and felt it was no longer plain," 259). Brontë does not try to introduce the quality of beauty by the back door, as it were, and maintains her heroine's plainness even as Jane participates in one of the most romantic love affairs in the history of the English novel. This is partly achieved through the construction of the character of Rochester, who, unlike the puerile Crimsworth, means what he says when he disavows an interest in female beauty. This disavowal is made believable in the context of Rochester's previous love affairs; since his first flirtation with Céline Varens, the French dancer, he has had two other mistresses, whom he describes to Jane as "both considered singularly handsome. What was their beauty to me in a few weeks? Giacinta was unprincipled and violent. . . . Clara was . . . heavy, mindless: . . . not one whit to my taste" (315).

The "normal" cathexis surrounding the beautiful heroine, then, is entirely absent in *Jane Eyre*, and the reader is firmly prevented from objectifying Jane either aesthetically or sexually. It is not that the importance normally attached to female beauty goes unacknowledged; Jane predictably longs to be beautiful: "I ever wished to look as well as I could, and to please as much as my want of beauty would permit. I sometimes regretted that I was not handsomer: I sometimes wished to have rosy cheeks, a straight nose, and small cherry mouth; . . . I felt it a misfortune that I was so little, so pale, and had features so irregular and so marked." The reason for these longings—the prerequisite of beauty in order to be loved—while unstated, is understood: "And why had I these aspirations and these regrets? It would be difficult to say: I could not then distinctly say it to myself; yet I had a reason, and a logical, natural reason too" (99).[3]

The events of the novel, of course, belie this reason roundly, as Brontë illustrates the possibility of male attraction without female beauty. The result is a novel that is much less scopophilic, in the usual sense, than most nineteenth-century novels.[4] The act of looking is de-emphasized; there are a few instances in which eyes speak and one occasion on which Rochester seems "to dive into [Jane's] eyes" (134), but on the whole touch is substituted for sight, a significant development which I shall discuss in more detail presently. Correspondingly, there are few instances of spying in *Jane Eyre* (Rochester eavesdropping on Céline and her lover on the balcony and Rochester observing Jane in the fortune-telling episode are the most obvious) in contrast to Brontë's other novels, which are riddled with it. Overall, these absences combine to create an absence of voyeurism in the usual sense; the cosy, unnoticed conspiracy in which the narrator and the reader usually collaborate in the appraisal and delectation of the female characters is rendered virtually impossible. There are some conventional passages of heroine description—Miss Temple, Blanche Ingram and Rosamond Oliver are all described in the usual amount of dismembered detail—but such passages are so peripheral to the main narrative that they are capable of exciting very little aesthetic or erotic interest. By implication, the reader, the novel's tacit interpretive audience, is female.

In fact, the activity of looking in this novel is—astonishingly—directed toward the male rather than the female in a reversal of the usual scopic economy. While Blanche Ingram sees "loveliness [as] the special prerogative of woman—her legitimate appanage and heritage" and scoffs at the notion of male beauty ("As if a man had anything to do with beauty!" 181), Jane as narrator (and by extension we as readers) experiences extreme fascination in looking at Rochester: "My eyes were drawn involuntarily to his face: I could not keep their lids under control: they would rise, and the irids would fix on him. I looked, and had an acute pleasure in looking,—a precious, yet poignant pleasure; pure gold, with a steely point of agony: a pleasure like what the thirst-perishing man might feel who knows the well to which he has crept is poisoned, yet stoops and drinks divine draughts nevertheless" (176). This is amazingly frank for a nineteenth-century novel. There is no doubt that Jane's "acute pleasure" in looking is sexual, and that it assuages a great need, as we can see from the "thirst" metaphor (an appropriately physical metaphor, and a precursor of the numerous hunger and thirst metaphors in *Shirley* and *Villette*). Such pleasure is also danger-ous, as evidenced by the "steely point" and the poisoned well, because at this point in the novel she does not think Rochester will ever return her love. She carefully makes it clear that his looks do not appeal to her aesthetically—"My master's colourless, olive face, square, massive brow, broad and jetty eyebrows, deep eyes, strong features, firm, grim mouth . . . were not beautiful, according to rule"—but rather erotically: "but they were more than beautiful to me: they were full of an interest, an influence that quite mastered me,—that took my feelings from my own power and fettered them in his. . . . He made me love him without looking at me" (176–77). There is a slippage here, a divergence from the conventional exercise of the look of desire by the conventional male subject, in that instead of mastering Rochester by her gaze Jane finds herself mastered, first by the power of the gaze itself ("an interest, an influence that quite mastered me") and finally by Rochester ("He made me love him without looking at me"). Jane is doing the looking and yet Rochester has the power, a reversal of the usual power dynamic of the seeing/seen dyad which underlines the unconventional aspect of the woman-as-(gazing)-subject.

Rochester as aesthetic object is also atypical. After each of her lengthy descriptions of him, Jane stresses the fact that he is not conventionally handsome. The very first time she encounters him (when his horse slips on the ice), she remarks,

Had he been a handsome, heroic-looking young gentleman, I should not have dared to stand thus questioning him . . . and offering my services. . . . I had hardly ever seen a handsome youth; never in my life spoken to one. I had a theoretical reverence and homage for beauty, elegance, gallantry, fascination; but had I met these qualities incarnate in masculine shape, I should have known instinctively that they neither had nor could have sympathy with anything in me, and should have shunned them as one would fire, lightning, or anything else that is bright but antipathetic. (114–15)

In fact, with his "dark face," "stern features," "heavy brow" (114), "jetty eyebrows," "square forehead," "black hair," "decisive nose," "full nostrils," "grim mouth, chin, and jaw" (121) and "dark, irate and piercing" eyes (122), Rochester is simply the swarthy Byronic hero, a dark type of Brontë's potent and beloved Zamorna. The emphasis on his lack of conventional "beauty" ensures that no taint of feminine passivity adheres to his portrayal, even though he is so clearly a much-appreciated object of Jane's desire. Indeed, Jane is enamored of his "ugliness" because of the strength it seems to signify:

I am sure most people would have thought him an ugly man; yet there was so much unconscious pride in his port; so much ease in his demeanour; such a look of complete indifference to his own external appearance; so haughty a reliance on the power of other qualities, intrinsic or adventitious, to atone for the lack of mere personal attractiveness, that in looking at him, one inevitably shared the indifference; and even in a blind, imperfect sense, put faith in the confidence. (133–34)

Needless to say, no female, including Jane, could afford such "indifference" to physical appearances; Rochester's stance is far removed from the position of the female object of appraisal who must please aesthetically in order to please sexually. It is not so much his looks which excite Jane, but his power.

In fact, as a romantic hero Rochester is extremely conventional, displaying many of the stock characteristics of the exciting but inaccessible male of many a Harlequin Romance. He is cold, arrogant and imperious ("I did as I was bid. . . . Mr. Rochester had such a direct way of giving orders, it seemed a matter of course to obey him promptly," 131) and often tyrannical ("In my secret soul I knew that his great kindness to me was balanced by unjust severity to many others," 148); he turns out, however, to have hidden sensitivities, discernible only to the heroine ("He had great dark eyes . . .— not without a certain change in their depths sometimes, which, if it was not softness, reminded you, at least, of that feeling," 132); and despite his initial coldness, he turns out in retrospect to have loved the heroine from the beginning (he confesses to Jane that at their first meeting, "when once I had pressed the frail shoulder, something new—a fresh sap and sense—stole into my frame. . . . For a long time, I treated you distantly. . . . I did not then know that [you were] no transitory blossom; but rather the radiant resemblance of one, cut in an indestructible gem. . . . When I stretched out my hand cordially, such bloom and light and bliss rose to your young, wistful features, I had much ado often to avoid straining you then and there to my heart," 317–19). When Jane speaks of leaving him, "his voice and hand quivered; his large nostrils dilated; his eye blazed" (308) in standard Byronic fashion; and when he has been blinded Jane likens him, again stereotypically, to "some wronged and fettered wild-beast or bird. . . . the caged eagle, whose gold-ringed eyes cruelty has extinguished, might look as looked that sightless Samson" (436).

The events of the novel, like these images of male virility, follow a predictable romantic pattern. As in twentieth-century romance novels, Jane's and Rochester's love story is beset with obstacles and misunderstandings, which are miraculously resolved in the end, leading to the reconciliation and happy marriage of the hero and heroine. There is even the obligatory scene (two scenes, actually) in which the powerful hero is brought low by accident or illness and is nursed back to health by the willing heroine, thus rectifying, if only momentarily, the imbalance of power between them. And, without a doubt, *Jane Eyre* is a novel of domination and submission. In fact, the whole erotic ambience of the book hinges on Brontë's profound understanding of the immensely powerful oedipal drives inherent in the master-servant relationship. She deftly rings all the changes on this charged combination, which encompasses all the possibilities of Hegel's master-slave dialectic, Freud's parent-child paradigm and the conventional male-female gender hierarchy. In this novel she does not question the existence or necessity of the fantasy of erotic domination; leaving its boundaries intact she freely explores within them.[5]

Like all love relationships in Brontë's novels, the attraction between Jane and Rochester partakes directly of the forces and energies inherent in the parent-child bond. Like Brontë's other heroines Jane is an orphan, and her adult needs for affection recapitulate the child's need for love and nurturance. This is made especially clear in *Jane Eyre*, in that a relatively long section of the novel is devoted to Jane's childhood. The very first scene of the book is a scene of exclusion from the mother: the three Reed children "were now clustered round their mamma in the drawing-room: she lay reclined on a sofa . . . and with her darlings about her . . . looked perfectly happy. Me, she had dispensed from joining the group" (7). The remainder of the novel is interspersed with troubled imagery relating to maternal nurturance. Jane as a child has a surrogate object, a favorite doll: "Human beings must love something, and, in the dearth of worthier objects of affection, I contrived to find pleasure in loving and cherishing a faded graven image, shabby as a miniature scarecrow. It puzzles me now to remember with what absurd sincerity I doted on this little toy" (28–29). It does not puzzle the reader, however, any more than the female child who recurrently appears in Jane's dreams. The child—and the mother—are both Jane, and although she tells us that "it was a wailing child this night, and a laughing one the next" (222), the one dream that she relates in detail (the one she has before her abortive wedding to Rochester) is one of acute distress, so that our overall impression of maternal nurturance is one of great trouble. Jane thinks of her new self, the "Mrs. Rochester" she will become, as an embryo—"She would not be born till tomorrow" (277)—who is of course born dead; more poignantly, she speaks of her love for Rochester as "that feeling which was my master's—which he had created; it shivered in my heart, like a suffering child in a cold cradle; sickness and anguish had seized it: it could not seek Mr. Rochester's arms—it could not derive warmth from his breast" (298–99). Jane as child, her new self as child, her love for Rochester as child: all significant aspects of character in this novel come to rest in the first source of nurturance, and in Jane's most severe crisis (her decision to leave Thornfield) it is her mother's voice that urges her to "flee temptation." (See Homans, *Word* 89 ff., on Jane's mothering.)

The need for the father in this novel, while more complex, is also grounded in the need for nurturance. The first real kindness that the child Jane experiences comes, significantly, from a nurturing male. After Jane faints in the red room, she "becomes aware that some one was handling me; lifting me up and supporting me in a sitting posture . . . more tenderly than I had ever been raised or upheld before. I rested my head against a pillow or an arm, and felt easy." The arm belongs to Mr. Lloyd, the apothecary, who is instrumental in Jane's removal from the Reed family. When he leaves, Jane feels abandoned: "He departed; to my grief: I felt so sheltered and befriended while he sat in the chair near my pillow; . . . as he closed the door after him, all the room darkened and my heart again sank: inexpressible sadness weighed it down" (19).

This kind of parental nurturing, as much as any overtly oedipal impulse, is an important component of Jane's attraction to Rochester. Jean Wyatt, apropos of Janice Radway's analysis of the "maternal" aspect of the romantic hero, remarks that "although Rochester can never be mistaken for a maternal nurturer, . . . Jane's celebration of marital fusion probably engages readers not only on the level of desire for the father figure, but also as a recovery of the bliss, comfort, and unity of that initial boundary-free connection with the mother" (211). Certainly Rochester's care giving is immensely appealing, to both Jane and the reader; and although much of it is described in patriarchal terms of superiority—Jane wishes to be kept "somewhere under the shelter of his protection, and not . . . exiled from the sunshine of his presence" (249), and Rochester more than once refers to himself as a shepherd and to Jane as "a stray lamb" (281), "one little ewe lamb . . . dear to him as a daughter" (302)—several of Rochester's acts of nurturance have a decidedly "feminine" flavor. When Jane first threatens to leave him, thinking he is engaged to Blanche Ingram, he soothes her as a mother would a child: "Jane, be still a few moments; you are over-excited: I will be still too" (256). Likewise, when they come in from the storm together, he takes off her shawl, shakes the water out of her hair, and later "came thrice to my door in the course of [the storm], to ask if I was safe and tranquil" (259), an act he repeats in his vigil outside Jane's room after she has heard about Bertha: "I undrew the bolt and passed out. I stumbled over an obstacle. . . . I fell, but not on the ground: an out-stretched arm caught me; I looked up—I was supported by Mr. Rochester, who sat in a chair across my chamber threshold" (302).

Perhaps it would be most accurate to assess Rochester's solicitousness as familial, if not exactly maternal. Jane reports that she "felt at times, as if he were my relation, rather than my master," and, like Caroline Helstone when the latter is reunited with her mother, "so happy, so gratified did I become . . . that I ceased to pine after kindred: . . . my bodily health improved; I gathered flesh and strength" (147). Love—which always refers back to maternal love—is life-sustaining, in this and in Brontë's other novels.

But the route to such love is long and tortuous and subject to the complex constraints of the erotic domination fantasy. The very first encounter be-

tween Jane and Rochester is indicative of these constraints and sets the
pattern for what is to follow: he is clearly the master, mounted on a
powerful horse, and she is the servant, making her humble progress on
foot. The erotic titillation of this first scene derives from the transgression
of boundaries. He (who is momentarily helpless) is assisted by her (who is
thus momentarily powerful). More important, though, is the boundary she
flouts in her attitude toward him: she coolly (and dangerously, thrillingly)
disobeys him. "The frown, the roughness of the traveller set me at my ease:
I retained my station when he wanted me to go, and announced—'I cannot
think of leaving you, Sir' " (115). Such "audacity"—such an assumption of
equality, however momentary—on the part of one in such a lowly position
piques Rochester's attention immediately: "He looked at me when I said
this: he had hardly turned his eyes in my direction before." This is *the* erotic
moment of the novel, the moment that sets the tone for what follows. It is
recalled by Rochester later in his retrospective confession of love for Jane:
"Childish and slender creature! It seemed as if a linnet had hopped to my
foot and proposed to bear me on its tiny wing. I was surly; but the thing
would not go: it stood by me with strange perseverance, and looked and
spoke with a sort of authority" (317). Rochester's wonderment is clearly
related to the discrepancy in their positions, to the fact of transgression by
one so far "below" him. Implicit in the word "childish" is Rochester as
figurative father; the linnet metaphorically removes Jane to a different
species; and the "thing" widens the gap to include the distance between
animate and inanimate. The erotic charge comes from the power this
"thing" assumes, its "strange perseverance" in the face of his opposition
and its "sort of authority" over him. The piquancy of this discrepancy—between powerful and powerless—is constantly alluded to throughout the
novel. We are repeatedly reminded of the differences in their ages and sexes
(Rochester says many times that he is old enough to be Jane's father), in
their social status (she refers to herself as his "paid subordinate") and in
their worldly and sexual experience (" 'Strange!' [Rochester] exclaimed. . . .
'Strange that I should choose you for the confidant of all this, young lady:
passing strange that you should listen to me quietly, as if it were the most
usual thing in the world for a man like me to tell stories of his opera-mis-
tresses to a quaint, inexperienced girl like you!' " 144).

What is at work here is a pure form of the domination/submission
dynamic, and Brontë is exquisitely aware of the unequal balance of power
inherent in such a configuration. Whereas Rochester is immensely titillated
by Jane's assumption of a "sort of authority" over him, and whereas he tells
her, "You . . . have power over me, and may injure me: . . . I dare not show
you where I am vulnerable" (219) and "Jane, . . . you master me" (263), the
real power in the relationship indubitably belongs to Rochester. Jane's
strength and independence as a heroine hinge on her recognition of this
inequality and the active steps she takes to mitigate it. After they are

engaged, she admits, "My future husband was becoming to me my whole world; . . . almost my hope of heaven. He stood between me and every thought of religion. . . . I could not . . . see God for his creature: of whom I had made an idol" (277). "Him who thus loved me I absolutely worshipped" (320). Jane admits this with a certain amount of anxiety; Hardy's Tess, more than forty years later, will display the same tendency to idolize the male, but with the narrator's implicit approval. Brontë's novels, with the exception of *The Professor*, center around the female's knowledge that such idolization is dangerous, a tendency to be resisted, controlled, mitigated and above all concealed from the male.

The inequality of the domination/submission relation is tacitly assumed in the interactions between males and females in all of Brontë's novels, and the energies of her heroines are rigorously applied to attempting to right the balance. Their only weapon in such a struggle is distance: they must resist, or appear to resist, the male's advances (and the advances must be made by the male); in order to allay his fears of female sexuality and safely secure his ongoing interest they must become somewhat resistant objects. Jane is fully conscious of this necessity, confiding it freely to the reader: "I saw his face all kindled . . . and tenderness and passion in every lineament. I quailed momentarily—then I rallied. Soft scene, daring demonstration, I would not have; and I stood in peril of both: a weapon of defense must be prepared—I whetted my tongue" (275). The battle imagery ("quailed," "rallied," "peril," "weapon," "defense," "whetted") is common to such descriptions of Jane's interactions with Rochester; she understands that to maintain the male subject's interest, the female object must not be too compliant, must not "give in" too easily or too soon. Crimsworth in *The Professor*, from his position on the other side of the battle zone, displays a similar wisdom, explaining his rejection of one of his female students with the remark that "we scorn what, unasked, is lavishly offered" (99) (even though Crimsworth himself will make lavish offers to Frances and certainly not expect to be scorned—it is only the female who must not "offer").

The necessity for female "reluctance" is also acknowledged by Mrs. Fairfax ("Try and keep Mr. Rochester at a distance: distrust yourself as well as him," 268) and (unwittingly) by Rochester himself as he describes his relationships with his past mistresses: "Hiring a mistress is the next worse thing to buying a slave: both are often by nature and always by position, inferior; and to live familiarly with inferiors is degrading" (316). The "inferiority" is gendered, built into the domination/submission hierarchy. Jane, far more frankly than most nineteenth-century heroines, acknowledges this, rather than any pretext of maidenly modesty, as the reason for her resistance to Rochester's romantic overtures: "If I were so far to forget myself . . . as—under any pretext—with any justification—through any temptation— to become the successor of these poor girls [Rochester's mistresses], he would one day regard me with the same feeling which now in his mind desecrated their memory" (316). She sees full well that in order to maintain her power of attraction over Rochester (the only power available to the object of desire), she must feign reluctance. She thinks, "This is the best plan to pursue with you, I am certain. I like you more than I can say; but I'll not sink into a bathos of sentiment: and with this needle of repartee I'll keep you from the edge of the gulph too; and, moreover, maintain by its pungent aid that distance between you and myself most conducive to our real mutual advantage" (276). Her feelings represent a "gulph" into which she might sink and from which she keeps both herself and Rochester with the "needle" of repartee. She also realizes that her reluctance is what he really, secretly wants. She confides to the reader that her "system" meets with "the best success": "He was kept, to be sure, rather cross and crusty: but on the whole I could see he was excellently entertained; and that a lamb-like submission and turtle-dove sensibility, while fostering his despotism more, would have pleased his judgment, satisfied his common sense, and even suited his taste less" (276). Jane even exults at the efficacy of her method—" 'I can keep you in reasonable check now,' I reflected; 'and I don't doubt to be able to do it hereafter: if one expedient loses its virtue, another must be devised' "—but in the end, after all, it is just an expedient, a measure she is forced to take in order to acquire even a modicum of control in the relationship; and in the end it makes her tired. "Yet after all my task was not an easy one: often I would rather have pleased than teased him" (277). But in pleasing him, she risks losing him. It is her position, as the female object of desire, to yield to the male's active pursuit, but only reluctantly and only when the stakes are high enough. When they are not—as they are not when Rochester is legally unable to marry her—she is forced to deny her own desire completely, paradoxically renouncing her lover in order to keep him.

In *Jane Eyre* Brontë does not (as she will in her subsequent novels) question the necessity or appropriateness of this active/passive, male/female configuration. Instead, she plays within it, exploiting the erotic possibilities inherent in such an unequal match. I have already remarked on the titillation of Jane's verbal audacity toward her lover, the assumption of equality disguised by her deferential "sir" and "Mr. Rochester." Even after he is blinded, her banter continues. He asks her, "Am I hideous, Jane?" to which she responds, "Very, sir: you always were, you know" (443). Such banter is erotic for a number of reasons: it is a crossing of boundaries, resembling the disobedience I discussed earlier; it is incredibly familiar, implying the closeness of equals; and it provides a safe release for the very real aggression inherent in all sexually charged situations. So long as Jane exercises all the power available to her, the relationship flourishes; so long as she controls Rochester by controlling her own feelings, in other words, all is well between them.

Her own feelings, however, prove to be difficult to control, a fact which subtly enhances the eroticism of the novel and at least acknowledges the possibility of the existence of female desire, for the feelings she must control so rigorously are undoubtedly sexual. When she hears of the existence of Blanche Ingram, for instance, Jane "endeavoured to bring back with a strict hand such as had been straying through imagination's boundless and trackless waste, into the safe fold of common sense" (162). The vagueness of "such as had been straying" signals forbidden thoughts, and "imagination's boundless and trackless waste" points to the danger of such thoughts. Most of the time Jane succeeds in her efforts at self-control, which occasionally amount to self-punishment. She "sentences" herself to make two portraits, a beautiful one of Blanche and a plain one of herself, after which she congratulates herself on "the course of wholesome discipline to which I had thus forced my feelings to submit" (164). Such masochism hardly sounds "wholesome," but it is obviously better than losing control and thus losing Rochester's esteem. The desperation with which she attempts this denial of feeling, and the extent of the pain it causes her, are indicated by the violence of one of the recurrent child metaphors: when she contemplates being parted from Rochester, she "then strangled a new-born agony—a deformed thing which I could not persuade myself to own and rear" (246). To repress her emotions so strenuously is to mutilate and destroy a part of her self, a price extorted by the exigencies of the domination/submission configuration.

When Jane does lose some of her rigid self-control it provides an erotic release for both her and the reader: it is as if so much pent-up erotic energy is bound to escape. The impression we get is that, in defiance of all conventional restraints, female desire demands to be expressed; and Jane's expression is through speech. The first time she loses control in this way is when she encounters Rochester by the stile on her return from Gateshead. They chat briefly, and "an impulse held me fast,—a force turned me round: I said—or something in me said for me, and in spite of me:—'Thank you, Mr. Rochester. . . . I am strangely glad to get back again to you; and wherever you are is my home,—my only home' " (248). It is revealing that Jane's speech is almost involuntary: she is impelled to speak by an "impulse," a "force," a "something." Although she uses the language of desire, she is not precisely thereby an active subject, in that she does not control or "own" such language. Speech is nevertheless a major vehicle of release for Jane throughout the novel, right from the early scene in which she denounces Mrs. Reed for her unfairness ("*Speak* I must. . . . Shaking from head to foot, thrilled with ungovernable excitement, I continued. . . . Ere I had finished . . . my soul began to expand, to exult, with the strangest sense of freedom, of triumph, I had ever felt. It seemed as if an invisible bond had burst, and that I had struggled out into unhoped-for liberty," 36–37). These scenes all lead up to the scene in which, in a burst of pent-up emotion, Jane confesses her love for Rochester: "I said this [statement] almost involuntarily; and with as little sanction of free will, my tears gushed out. . . . I sobbed convulsively; for I could repress what I endured no longer: I was obliged to yield; and I was shaken from head to foot with acute distress. . . . The vehemence of emotion, stirred by grief and love within me, was claiming mastery, and struggling for full sway; and asserting a right to predominate: to overcome, to live, rise, and reign at last; yes,—and to speak" (254–55). She speaks under what seems to be extreme duress, and it is her feelings that speak rather than she herself; but at least she does speak, unlike so many of her silent Victorian counterparts. Rochester, of course, is on the side of her feelings, and in yielding to them she yields to him. It is a complex interaction in which he triumphs over her (he actually teases her cruelly with hints about Blanche Ingram until she is "forced" to admit her emotions), resulting in the solid establishment of the domination/submission hierarchy. His teasing is his method of pursuing Jane, and her speaking signifies her yielding rather than her independent expression of desire. Nevertheless, the emotional release of her outburst is so great that she feels great strength as a result of it; she says, "I have spoken my mind, and can go anywhere now" and asserts that "I am a free human being with an independent will; which I now exert to leave you" (256). The entire exchange, while erotically "satisfying"—there is victory on one side and surrender on the other—is an exhausting and difficult struggle for Jane, who has been "made" to speak.[6]

When Rochester speaks, on the other hand, it is a wholly different matter. When he tells Jane about his past, he "proceed[s] almost as freely as if [he] were writing [his] thoughts in a diary" (137), and Jane loves to listen: "I . . . talked comparatively little; but I heard him talk with relish. It was his nature to be communicative" (147). The active male speaks, the passive female listens: it is a pattern that is repeated endlessly in patriarchal culture. Even after their positions are equalized by Rochester's blindness at the end of the novel, it is the male who tacitly owns the language of desire, as Jane anxiously waits for him to ask her to marry him: "I had . . . made my proposal [to stay with him] from the idea that he wished and would ask me to be his wife. . . . But no hint to that effect escaping him . . . I suddenly remembered that I might have been all wrong, and was perhaps playing the fool unwittingly" (440). Even after she is sure of his intentions, she waits for him to state them: "I knew of what he was thinking, and wanted to speak for him; but dared not" (449).

Finally, of course, all is resolved in the ending. The heroine's reward for her strenuous self-control and self-denial is total merging with the male. In the final chapter of the novel Jane tells us,

I have now been married ten years. I know what it is to live entirely for and with what I love best on earth. I hold myself supremely blest— . . . because I am my husband's life as fully as he is mine. No woman was ever nearer to her mate than I am: ever more absolutely bone of his bone, and flesh of his flesh. I know no weariness of my Edward's society: he knows none of mine. . . ; consequently, we are ever together. To be together is for us to be at once as free as in solitude, as gay as in company. . . . To talk to each other is but a more animated and an audible thinking. All my confidence is bestowed on him; all his confidence is devoted to me: we are precisely suited in character; perfect concord is the result. (456)

This is truly a fairy-tale ending, especially in view of Jane's earlier description of marriage. When Rochester is courting her, she tells him that when they are married, "for a little while you will perhaps be as you are now,—a very little while; and then you will turn cool; and then you will be capricious; and then you will be stern, and I shall have much ado to please you: but when you get well used to me, you will perhaps like me again,— *like* me, I say, not *love* me. I suppose your love will effervesce in six months, or less" (262). This strikes the reader—the modern reader, at any rate—as a much more realistic account of the outcome of the permanent union of dominant and submissive: the more powerful male soon tires of the less powerful female, who then has "much ado" to please him. The miraculous reversal of this expectation, of course, is brought about by the genuine leveling of Rochester's position vis à vis Jane's. Blind and dependent on her, he is finally her equal, as she well realizes: "I love you better now, when I can really be useful to you, than I did in your state of proud independence, when you disdained every part but that of the giver and protector" (451). Brontë's awareness demands this drastic reduction in Rochester's power; she realizes the impossibility of such blissful merging on a long-term basis within the constraints of the usual male subject/female object configuration. As it turns out, the traumatic events at the end of the novel ensure that Jane and Rochester need each other and therefore appreciate each other equally, as equal subjects must.

In *Jane Eyre*, then, Brontë comes close to portraying a female subject of desire, even though the novel's eroticism springs from the inequalities of the domination/submission hierarchy. By virtue of the melodramatic plot, Jane indeed gets to have and to keep "a patriarch of her own." This aspect of the novel is pure wish-fulfillment: the female is attracted to the dominant male by virtue of his superior strength, which is then stripped away so that she no longer has to worry about sustaining his interest by keeping him at a distance. All distances are finally removed, and each partner gets to experience an almost maternal merging without any threat of separation— bliss, indeed, but not reality.

Even before the melodramatic resolution, however, Jane demonstrates a fair degree of subjectivity, even though it occurs within conventional limitations. Her differences from the conventionally passive romantic heroine are important, particularly her lack of beauty, her admission of desire for Rochester and her active measures to secure his love (even though the latter largely constitutes a movement away from rather than toward the desired other subject). In several ways *Jane Eyre* is a peculiarly literal, peculiarly woman-centered novel. The use of food and drink to signify love, for example, while it occasionally takes the form of metaphor—as when Jane speaks of having "my morsel of bread snatched from my lips, and my drop of living water dashed from my cup" by the possibility of Rochester's marrying Blanche Ingram (255)—more often occurs literally, avoiding what Margaret Homans would term the "figurative" altogether. One of the most distinctive characterists of Lowood, for example, is the "nauseous mess" of burnt porridge the girls are given to eat (prefiguring the cold porridge Jane will later beg for) as well as the stealing of the smaller girls' bread and coffee by the bigger girls. By contrast, the kindly Miss Temple gives the girls real food, a lunch of bread and cheese for everyone and seed-cake for Jane and Helen Burns.

This privileging of the literal over the figurative is recapitulated in the emphasis on touch as opposed to sight as the primary mode of interaction between Rochester and Jane. As art critics, film critics and semioticians have pointed out, looking (traditionally the male's prerogative) is a distancing and figurative mechanism, turning the looked-at object into a sign to be interpreted. Touch, on the other hand, is generally cited as the preferred female mode of interaction, being more akin to merging than to differentiation. As we have seen, Jane—quite unusually—does her share of looking at the male; Rochester on the other hand looks at Jane, in the traditional fetishistic sense, hardly at all. Instead he touches her, and touches her a lot. He seizes her hand, usually in a "grip of iron," at all the important turns in the plot: after Bertha sets his bed on fire, the first time Mason appears, after Bertha attacks Mason, during their abortive wedding and of course many times after he is blinded. His blindness, of course, is especially conducive to interaction through touch, and Brontë makes the most of this in the mutual caressing that takes place. But even earlier in the novel, in addition to holding her hand, Rochester caresses, kisses and embraces Jane far more than is generally the case in the Victorian novel, and Jane also occasionally caresses him.

All in all, *Jane Eyre* is a standard romantic love story, a tale of erotic domination and submission. But within this mode, Brontë creates a heroine whose characteristics strive toward subjectivity. Jane is almost a female subject of desire, in that she comes close to showing and acting upon her desire for Rochester. She exercises the look of desire, in that she derives pleasure from looking at him; more importantly, her plainness exempts her nicely from the usual mechanisms of female objectification. She does not quite control the language of desire—rather, it controls her—but at least she speaks as opposed to remaining silent. And she enacts her desire as best she can, given her inferior position in relation to the powerful male.

It is no wonder that *Jane Eyre* was and is such a successful novel. As Jean Wyatt points out, it creates an unambiguously female reader, and allows that reader, like Jane, to have it all. Jane gets to be both dependent and independent, to be both nurtured (when Rochester is strong) and nurturing (when he is weak), and to reap the rewards of romantic love (including both merging and motherhood) in the absence of the usual feminine requirements of beauty and passivity. Moreover, she gets to keep all these things forever—truly a fairy-tale ending, and Brontë's last imaginative attempt at so simple a resolution. Her next two novels, *Shirley* and *Villette*, are more complex in their acknowledgment of the difficulties inherent in male-female relationships, and much less romantic.

SHIRLEY

Shirley, the weakest of Brontë's mature novels, reveals her growing awareness that Cinderella stories—such as that of Jane Eyre and Rochester—don't happen. The happily-ever-after conclusion is belied by the tenor of the novel as a whole, which is sad, stressed and uncertain. The weakness of the novel, in fact, consists mainly in this contradiction between the tone and the polemic on one hand and the events and their outcome on the other. It is a novel of painful confusion, in which the characters express a distrust of passion and yet go through the motions of romance and in which the bitter sadness of the polemical statements (such as the violent outburst urging enforced feminine passivity that I quoted in Chapter One) makes the happy love scenes seem forced and unrealistic. Feminists frequently claim *Shirley* as an early manifesto—Margaret Blom calls it "the first major novel of the feminist movement . . . [and] still one of the best" (160)—but its ambivalence precludes such labeling. As Pauline Nestor remarks, it is as unwise "to deny Charlotte Brontë's ambivalence in her treatment of female sexuality in the name of a feminist orthodoxy as it is absurdly ahistorical to brand her works as sexist and regressive" (36).

However we view it, *Shirley* is an intriguing novel for feminists. In it Charlotte Brontë raises all the "right" issues and displays a keen feminist awareness, even if she is unsure of how to resolve such issues. In fact, the blatant contradictions between the polemic and the plot constitute the most interesting aspect of the novel as well as its major weakness. The speculations on old maids, for instance, which are both lengthy and thoughtful, arrive at the conclusion that such women's lives are useful and heroic—but Caroline discovers she could never live such a life. By the same token, we are told that beauty is unimportant—but Robert states flatly that he "won't have an ugly wife." Much is made of the necessity for women's independence and equality—but both Caroline and Shirley desire to be "mastered"; even the ferociously self-sufficient Shirley expresses the dismayingly regressive sentiment that "I will accept no hand which cannot hold me in check. . . . Any man who wishes to live in decent comfort with me as a husband must be able to control me" (551). Like Jane Eyre, *Shirley's* narrator seems to realize that female self-control is necessary in order to secure the male's interest—but Caroline Helstone loses control completely and still gets to marry the man of her dreams. Affection is privileged over passion (Shirley calls passion "a mere fire of dry sticks, blazing up and vanishing," 217, and Caroline says that "love hurts us so. . . . it is so tormenting, so racking, and it burns away our strength. . . ; in affection is no pain and no fire, only sustenance and balm," 264)—and yet both heroines opt for passionate relationships. Marriage itself is denigrated, both by Mr. Helstone ("A yokefellow is not a companion; he or she is a fellow-sufferer," 101) and by Shirley ("[Marriage] is never wholly happy. Two people can never literally be as one," 379)—but the novel ends with two conventionally happy marriages.

There are other interesting feminist speculations in this novel as well. Shirley and Caroline comment on men's attitudes to women, for instance, at some length. Caroline remarks that women are "neither temptresses, nor terrors, nor monsters" (246), even though some men see women as all of these things, and later in the book Shirley says, "Men . . . fancy women's minds something like those of children. Now, that is a mistake. . . . The acutest men are often under an illusion about women: . . . they misapprehend them, both for good and evil: their good woman is a queer thing, half doll, half angel; their bad woman almost always a fiend. . . . If I gave my real opinion of some first-rate female characters in first-rate works, where should I be? Dead under a cairn of avenging stones in half an hour" (352). We can only wonder what "first-rate female characters" Brontë is referring to in particular, but at least we can divine from this passage her opinion of conventional portrayals of women in the novels of the time, novels written (as the passage indicates) by men. There is a similar "modern" aside about Milton—Shirley says, "Milton tried to see the first woman; but Cary, he saw her not" (320)—and other asides about matters such as the interruption of female friendship by the male ("[Robert] keeps intruding between you and me: without him we should be good friends; but that six feet of puppyhood makes a perpetually recurring eclipse of our friendship. . . . He renders me to you a mere bore and nuisance," 263).

None of these matters is taken up or settled in the novel in any satisfactory way. Sort through them as we might, the various "bits" of this novel do not form a coherent thematic whole. Despite its happily resolved love plots, it is a much darker novel than *Jane Eyre*, evincing a pain that does not derive from the story itself. It is a novel of waiting; and no heroines wait more poignantly than Charlotte Brontë's. The part of the novel that is the most vivid, the part that we retain, is the desperate sadness and depression of Caroline's unassuaged need for love, even though that need is satisfied abundantly by the end of the book. We cannot help but think, if we know Charlotte Brontë's life, that her own unassuaged need and fruitless waiting had by this time left their mark on her work, and that her happy ending fails because she herself does not really believe in it. In any case, the

overriding "message" of *Shirley*, insofar as there is one, is the message of
the prevalent mood: that love is painful (you can die from it, in fact), that
marriage is difficult but the alternative is terrible, that women can only wait
passively for love to come to them.

It hardly needs to be demonstrated that there is no female subject of
desire in this novel. Indeed, there is not much real desire; *Shirley* is not a
particularly erotic novel, even in the murky way that *The Professor* is. Even
the independent, somewhat masculinized Shirley is passive when it comes
to love, and is no more a genuine subject of desire than the slightly insipid
Caroline. Supposedly modeled on Emily Brontë, Shirley is created to come
across as spirited and feisty: she has a set of pistols (as Hedda Gabler will
have—and use—several decades later), she separates two mad dogs with
her bare hands, and she "consider[s] [herself] not unworthy to be the
associate of the best of them—of gentlemen" (215). She is essentially an
unconvincing character, however. Her bravado seems artificial and forced,
and her "masculine" attributes seem like play-acting. She asserts, "Shirley
Keeldar, Esquire, ought to be my style and title. They gave me a man's
name; I hold a man's position: it is enough to inspire me with a touch of
manhood. . . . You must choose me for your churchwarden, Mr. Helstone. . . . They ought to make me a magistrate and a captain of yeomanry"
(200).

None of this contributes significantly to Shirley's subjectivity, however,
particularly as she is portrayed in her love-relationship with Louis Moore
as a conventional object of desire. She is beautiful to look at, she longs to
be dominated by a strong man ("the higher above me, so much the better,"
219), and she engages in conventionally coy feminine behavior in her mock
"battle" with Louis Moore in which each tries to force the other to admit to
erotic attraction. It is interesting that this encounter is related entirely from
Louis's point of view, through the extremely clumsy device of a lengthy
journal entry. This has the effect of obliterating Shirley's thoughts and
feelings entirely, so that the reader, like Louis, must infer her desire through
her look, speech and actions (or lack of them).

The "battle" itself is meant to be erotic, an exercise in domination and
submission designed to reveal the characters' deepest feelings. Louis first
attempts to arouse Shirley's jealousy (and to counterbalance his own jealousy over Philip Nunnely) by inventing a tale of emigration to North
America complete with a "savage girl" who would be his slave. It is
understood that Shirley's passivity indicates submission ("She could not
answer me, nor could she look at me: I should have been sorry if she could
have done either," 614). Her much-vaunted "equality" suddenly crumbles
in this scene, and she is described as a fluttering female: "Her cheek glowed
as if a crimson flower, through whose petals the sun shone, had cast its light
upon it. On the white lid and dark lashes of her downcast eye, trembled all
that is graceful in the sense of half-painful, half-pleasing shame" (614). The

strained rhetoric of this does not make it any more convincing, and such rhetoric is characteristic of the entire scene, which seems awkward and melodramatic as a result. Louis, for instance, imagining that he can "read" Shirley's face, attributes to her the following sentiment: "My heart may break if it is baffled: let it break— . . . it shall never dishonour my sisterhood in me. Suffering before degradation! death before treachery!" (615). He also calls her "my leopardess" (623) and takes the greatest pleasure in her "capture." He wants "something to tame first, and teach afterwards: to break in, and then to fondle. . . . To establish power over, and then to be indulgent to" (620). Modern feminists might well recoil in disgust from such a view, as it so clearly delineates the craving for power of the dominant over the submissive, the master over the slave. Nor is this the first time in the novel Louis expresses such a need; earlier, he voices a familiar and pernicious view of erotic attachment, seemingly with the narrator's approval: "I worship [Shirley's] perfections; but it is her faults . . . that bring her near to me— . . . and that for a most selfish, but deeply-natural reason: these faults are the steps by which I mount to ascendancy over her. If she rose a trimmed, artificial mound, . . . what vantage would she offer the foot? It is the natural hill, with its mossy breaks and hollows, whose slope invites ascent—whose summit it is pleasure to gain" (522). Although Louis admits that such a wish to dominate is selfish, he also calls it "deeply natural," indicating Charlotte Brontë's own ambivalence about domination and submission in erotic relationships at this point in her career. It is significant too that his hill metaphor objectifies the female, who becomes an object to be "mounted" and thus conquered.

Basically Shirley's feistiness and independence merely make her a more interesting and challenging creature to be tamed, a variation on the submissive female stereotype. Such feistiness, like coy reluctance, is a satisfactory distancing mechanism that enables the male to conquer his own fears and proceed with the erotic pursuit. One version of the stereotype submits to the male's desire with shy reluctance, the other submits to it with spirited resistance; neither acts upon her own desire. The resistance is just as titillating—or even more so—as the reluctance, as Louis writes in his diary: "I fear I should tire of the mute, monotonous innocence of the lamb; I should erelong feel as burdensome the nestling dove which never stirred in my bosom; but my patience would exult in stilling the flutterings and training the energies of the restless merlin. In managing the wild instincts of the scarce manageable 'bête fauve,' my powers would revel" (525). Apart from its offensive sentiment and blatant objectification, there is something irretrievably theoretical about such a passage. We never experience the erotic in *Shirley* except indirectly; the most vivid moment in the encounter between Louis and Shirley is one of metaphorical displacement in which Louis reminds her, "In the winter evenings, Tartar lies at your feet: you suffer him to rest his head on your perfumed lap; . . . his rough hide is familiar with the contact of your hand: I once saw you kiss him on that snow-white beauty-spot which stars his broad forehead. It is dangerous to say I am like Tartar: it suggests to me a claim to be treated like Tartar" (620).

The scene concludes with much braggadocio on Louis's part ("I scared her; . . . it was right; she must be scared to be won," 621) and much trembling on Shirley's. Finally she "submits" to her captor—not happily, but with much repining. Louis writes, "Pantheress!—beautiful forest-born!—wily, tameless, peerless nature! She gnaws her chain: I see the white teeth working at the steel! She has dreams of her wild woods, and pinings after virgin freedom" (629). The reader, in spite of the vivid metaphor, can only be impatient at such posturing, which is no more convincing when described by the narrator: "There [Shirley] was at last, fettered to a fixed [wedding] day: there she lay, conquered by love, and bound with a vow. Thus vanquished and restricted, she pined, like any other chained denizen of deserts. Her captor alone could cheer her: . . . in his absence, she sat or wandered alone; spoke little, and ate less" (637–38). Here is the language of domination—"fettered," "fixed," "conquered," "bound," "vanquished," "restricted," "pined," "chained," "captor"—which is thoroughly romanticized in such passages. Shirley's supposed resistance simply causes her to be a more glamorous and exotic object of desire than usual. Also, there is no real submission on Shirley's part, since she is under no practical or emotional necessity to resist (or accept) Louis. She has never gone through any of the genuine torment that many of Charlotte Brontë's other characters go through for love, and her capitulation seems routine rather than agonized. Such passages also fail to be erotic. In order for the domination/submission hierarchy to "work," in order to create erotic tension, there must be genuine obstacles and genuine surrender, as Harlequin Romance writers have always been aware. Shirley's "protest," of course, is against marriage, about which the novel purports to be ambivalent; but in the end the flurry of happiness surrounding the two marriages negates the earlier questioning of it.

Caroline Helstone, the other happy bride at the end of the novel, is a more interesting character than Shirley, even though she is so much paler. Her sufferings, unlike those of Shirley, are real, and agonizingly so. She longs for Robert throughout the novel, spends most of her time trying to suppress her feelings, and nearly dies in the attempt in an unnervingly realistic portrayal of depression and decline. By nature passive, she can hardly be designated a subject of desire; rather, she enacts the part of a spurned object of desire, at least until Robert (quite unbelievably) changes his mind about her.

Although Hortense Moore characterizes her as "not sufficiently girlish and submissive," this is precisely what Caroline is, to a degree that verges on the insipid. She is submissive in such a child-like way, moreover, that the erotic possibilities inherent in submission are completely lost. Her inner musings about Robert, presumably calculated to illustrate her goodness, instead reinforce her blandness: "Sometimes I am afraid to speak to him, lest I should be too frank, lest I should seem forward: for I have more than once . . . feared I had said more than he expected me to say, and that he would disapprove what he might deem my indiscretion; . . . tonight . . . he was so indulgent. How kind he was. . . . I would be an excellent wife to him. . . . I would study his comfort, and cherish him, and do my best to make him happy. Now, I am sure he will not be cold to-morrow" (99–100). Such timidity has more than a hint of the dutiful child about it, the child who is anxious to please an unpredictable parent, and as in Charlotte Brontë's other novels, parental and sexual bonds are juxtaposed and inter- twined in intricate and suggestive ways. Robert seems paternal toward Caroline by virtue of his greater sexual experience, for instance (he tells himself that "the phrenzy is quite temporary. I know it very well: I have had it before. It will be gone to-morrow," 96), and there is even a literal "bad father" in the person of James Helstone, Caroline's drunken father, who occasions a startlingly vivid description of child abuse:

She recollected . . . some weeks that she had spent with him in a great town somewhere, when she had had no maid to dress her or take care of her; when she had been shut up, day and night, in a high garret-room, without a carpet, with a bare uncurtained bed, . . . when he went out early every morning, and often forgot to return and give her her dinner during the day, and at night, when he came back, was like a madman, furious, terrible. . . . She knew she had fallen ill in this place, and that one night when she was very sick, he had come raving into the room, and said he would kill her, for she was a burden to him. (102–3)

Such a scene (as disturbing as those of Dickens or Zola) makes it easy to understand that what Caroline really longs for, even in her desire for Robert, is mother-love rather than father-love. Throughout the novel Caroline reiterates her longing for reunion with her mother, and of course it is the melodramatic discovery that Mrs. Pryor is her mother that saves her from death.

The discovery that Robert loves her saves her from another kind of death (depicted with stark clarity in the extended portraits of the old maids in the novel), and it is significant that in a scene near the end of the novel Caroline literally mistakes Robert for her mother. It is evening, and she is looking at "the star of love": As she gazed she sighed, and as she sighed a hand circled her, and rested quietly on her waist. Caroline thought she knew who had drawn near: she received the touch unstartled. 'I am looking at Venus, mamma. . . . ' The answer was a closer caress; and Caroline turned, and looked, not into Mrs. Pryor's matron face, but up at a dark manly visage" (639). This rings true, and is in fact the closest approximation of eroticism that the novel affords, lending credence once again to theories such as those of Adrienne Rich and other radical feminists who claim that the deepest level of erotic longing is for the mother.

In the context of *Shirley*, however, it is far from clear that such maternal/erotic yearning is straightforwardly desirable. Given Caroline's passive dependency, both on her mother and on Robert, her longing seems only to enhance her child-like aspect. Also, maternal merging itself is portrayed ambiguously, in the brief portrait of Mrs. Yorke and her baby: "It is all her own yet . . . ; it derives its sustenance from her, it hangs on her, it clings to her, it loves her above anything else in the world: she is sure of that, because, as it lives by her, it cannot be otherwise, therefore she loves it" (148). This has more than just an undertone of narrative irony, evident in both the language ("hangs on her") and Mrs. Yorke's specious reasoning, suggesting that such "love" is perhaps exploitive as well as nurturing.

Nevertheless, love is portrayed in *Shirley* as necessary to life itself. This is made clear not only in the events of the novel, which portray Caroline being literally rescued from death by love, but also in the recurring metaphor of love as food. From the narrator's harrowing diatribe early in the novel, in which a stone and a scorpion are substituted for the expected bread and egg, love is portrayed as a nourishing, vital substance without which death by starvation will surely follow. When Caroline's tête-à-tête with Robert is interrupted by Shirley, Caroline "suffered . . . miserably: a few minutes before, her famished heart had tasted a drop and crumb of nourishment that, if freely given, would have brought back abundance of life where life was failing; but the generous feast was snatched from her, spread before another, and she remained but a bystander at the banquet" (252). This metaphorical pattern lends poignancy to Caroline's action of leaving a bit of biscuit for the mouse who visits her room while she herself goes "unfed"; and as the story progresses such metaphors increase in vividness and intensity. Of Caroline's sleepless nights we are told, "Life wastes fast in such vigils . . . ; vigils during which the mind,—having no pleasant food to nourish it—no manna of hope—no hived-honey of joyous memories—tries to live on the meagre diet of wishes, and . . . feeling itself ready to perish with craving want, turns to philosophy" (350–51). The religious connotations of the manna and "hived-honey" indicate the spiritual aspect of such a craving for love, at least on the part of the female. Like Jane Eyre (but very much unlike William Crimsworth), Caroline cannot resist making an idol of the one she loves. That males do not do this to the same extent is subtly suggested by a comment Shirley makes to Caroline about literal food: "For ourselves, you see, these choice wines and scientific dishes are of no importance to us; but gentlemen seem to retain something of the naïveté of children about food, and one likes to please them" (275).

Caroline, then, is an unusually helpless and passive heroine for Charlotte Brontë, lacking entirely the rebelliousness of Jane Eyre or Lucy Snowe. She owns neither the look nor the language of desire and remains child-like throughout the novel despite her terrible suffering. Even her beauty seems insipid and immature, despite the frequent references to it by Mrs. Pryor and Martin Yorke. The narrator's first description of her is vague, stressing her manner rather than her features. The opening sentence—"To her had not been denied the gift of beauty" (75)—sets the tone with its double negative, and the rest is simply a list of standard phrases: "Her shape suited her age; it was girlish, light and pliant; every curve was neat, every limb proportionate: her face was expressive and gentle; her eyes were handsome, and gifted at times with a winning beam. . . . Her mouth was very pretty; she had a delicate skin, and a fine flow of brown hair" (75). The overall impression is that of a tidy schoolgirl, and by the end of the novel this has not changed. When she goes to visit Robert, we read that she "tripped up Sarah's stairs . . . , and came down as quietly, with her beautiful curls nicely smoothed; her graceful merino dress and delicate collar all trim and spotless; her gay little work-bag in her hand" (598). "Tripped," "quietly," "nicely," "graceful," "delicate," "trim," "spotless," "gay," "little": Caroline seems to be a model Victorian maiden, and this, rather than her beauty, wins Robert in the end.

True to form for Charlotte Brontë, then, there is surprisingly little desirous looking by the males in *Shirley*. Shirley herself attracts Louis not by her beauty but by her rebellious nature (which is transformed by love into a Caroline-like submissiveness). Caroline, though, like Jane Eyre before her and Lucy Snowe after her, finds her chosen male pleasing to look at. Before Robert turns cold toward her, when Caroline is going to meet him, "she stopped, withdrawing a little behind a willow, and studied his appearance. 'He has not his peer,' she thought; 'he is handsome as he is intelligent. What a keen eye he has! What clearly cut, spirited features—thin and serious, but graceful! I do like his face—I do like his aspect— . . . bonnie Robert!' " (104). This is a precursor of the many scenes in *Villette* in which Lucy Snowe spies and is spied on, and constitutes a covert, surreptitious exercise of the look of desire. Caroline does not look openly at Robert—"At church . . . she rarely looked at him: it was both too much pain and too much pleasure to look" (171)—and she can hardly bring herself to return his look. She repays him for his tutoring with "an admiring and grateful smile, rather shed at his feet than lifted to his face" (77), and at the school picnic "she dared not trust herself to hazard a second glance; for his image struck on her vision with painful brightness, and pictured itself on her memory as vividly as if there daguerrotyped by a pencil of keen lightning" (308). In this novel, as in *Jane Eyre* and *Villette*, it is the female who looks at the male, but not in a way which appreciably enhances the former's subjectivity.

Just as Caroline does not look at Robert, neither does she speak to him. When she finally sees him after a long absence, we are told, "If she had dared . . . she would have declared . . . how she longed to return to [Hollow's Cottage]. . . . Not daring, however, to say these things, she held her peace: she sat quiet at Robert's side, waiting for him to say something more" (250). Such silence and waiting are entirely characteristic of Caroline; needless to say, she is never permitted the language of desire, a fact which is emphasized in the harsh advice of the narrator in one of the most disturbing and intense passages in the novel ("A lover feminine can say nothing. . . . You expected bread, and you have got a stone; break your teeth on it, and don't shriek . . .—the stone will digest. You held out your hand for an egg, and fate put into it a scorpion. . . . Close your fingers firmly upon the gift; let it sting through your palm. . . . In time, after your hand and arm have swelled and quivered long with torture, the squeezed scorpion will die, and you will have learned the great lesson how to endure without a sob," 105).

The literal effects of this erotic muzzling, as they are portrayed in the events of the novel, are just as damaging as the metaphorical digesting of the stone and squeezing of the scorpion; and they also manifest themselves in a kind of starvation, as I have already noted. Indeed, when Caroline finally confesses her love for Robert (after he has safely confessed his love for her), it is this starvation and pining that she confesses rather than desire. "I believed I should never see you again," she tells him, "and I grew so thin . . . I could do nothing for myself— . . . I could not eat" (583).

In fact, Caroline's struggle for self-control—never easy for Charlotte Brontë's heroines—is the most interesting and veracious (albeit the most painful) part of the novel. One of the worst aspects of such self-censure, as in the digesting of the stone and squeezing of the scorpion , is that it is self-imposed. Worse still, the necessity for it is perceived as her own fault: "Robert had done her no wrong: . . . it was she that was to blame. . . . She had loved without being asked to love,—a natural, sometimes an inevitable chance, but big with misery" (106–7). The fertility metaphor here is brilliantly apt—if a woman loves first, she will bear not a child but "misery." "Without being asked to love" is the key phrase: passive as she is, Caroline's passivity is not perfect, and her punishment is the impossible choice she must make. "Now, what was she to do?—to give way to her feelings, or to vanquish them? To pursue him, or to turn upon herself?" There is really only one option open to her, as the narrator points out: "If she is weak, she will try the first expedient,—will lose his esteem and win his aversion; if she has sense, she will be her own governor, and resolve to subdue and bring under guidance the disturbed realm of her emotions" (107).

The remainder of the novel traces in cruel outline Caroline's efforts to "subdue and bring under guidance" her feelings for Robert. It is a grim struggle that makes Jane Eyre's feats of emotional self-restraint seem like child's play; the difference is that Jane knows her feelings are returned, while Caroline is quite sure hers are not. Robert's coolness toward her at the beginning of the novel is real, and her struggle is necessary. The record of her struggle constitutes a painfully accurate portrait of clinical depression. Caroline initially attempts to subdue her longing through ceaseless activity:

Bent on victory over a mortal pain, she did her best to quell it. Never had she been seen so busy, so studious, and, above all, so active. She took walks in all weathers. . . . She came back in the evening, pale and wearied-looking, yet seemingly not fatigued; for still, . . . she would, instead of resting, begin to pace her apartment: sometimes she would not sit down till she was literally faint. She said she did this to tire herself well, that she might sleep soundly at night. But . . . at night . . . she was tossing on her pillow, or sitting at the foot of her couch in the darkness. (185)

Such efforts are beyond the strength of Caroline, and she makes little progress in eradicating her love for Robert. She writes letters to him, which she never sends ("Shame and good sense forbade," 186); she continually watches for a light in his window at the mill ("If, while she gazed, a shadow bent between the light and the lattice, her heart leaped—that eclipse was Robert: she had seen him," 187); and she has to be forcibly restrained by Shirley from rushing to him when he is dealing with the riot at the mill ("'Am I always to be curbed and kept down?' demanded Caroline, a little passionately. 'For his sake, yes. And still more for your own. . . . If you shewed yourself now, you would repent in an hour hence, and so would Robert,' " 347). For the latter restraint, Caroline meekly thanks Shirley ("I promise not to try to see Robert again till he asks for me. I never will try to push myself on him," 348), but both she and the reader recognize her struggle as hopeless. Her depression becomes increasingly pronounced. She cries often, "in a sort of intolerable despair; which, when it rushed over her, smote down her strength, and reduced her to childlike helplessness" (185). She suffers from generalized anxiety, telling Mrs. Pryor, "I think I grow what is called nervous. I see things under a darker aspect than I used to do. I have fears I never used to have—not of ghosts, but of omens and disastrous events; and I have an inexpressible weight on my mind which I would give the world to shake off, and I cannot do it. . . . Is this weakness of mind, Mrs. Pryor, or what is it? I cannot help it: I often struggle against it: I reason; but reason and effort make no difference" (240–41). It is no surprise that she eventually declines into a total collapse in which she is bedridden, (significantly) anorexic and close to death.[7]

As a character, Caroline evokes our pity; as a victim of the enormous inequality of the sexual hierarchy, she elicits our anger. As a woman, Caroline has no "weapons" with which to attract Robert: she is not a raving beauty, she has no great wealth, and perhaps most importantly, she has no other suitors who would enhance her value as a sexual object. Rochester is jealous of Jane's relationship with St. John Rivers, and Louis Moore is jealous of Shirley's relationship with Sir Phillip Nunnely; but Caroline has no obvious "market value" with which to excite Robert's interest. Neither does she have an interesting occupation to immerse herself in, and her thoughts on this matter underline the painful inequality of the male and female positions in regard to love-relationships: "Different, indeed . . . is Robert's mental condition to mine: I think only of him; he has no room, no leisure to think of me. The feeling called love is and has been for two years the predominant emotion of my heart; always there, always awake, always astir: quite other feelings absorb his reflections, and govern his faculties" (172).

Basically, Caroline has no personal power. She is helpless to change her love for Robert, and forbidden by the inbuilt rules of the subject/object hierarchy to act on it. Her role—the female role—is one of waiting, and ultimately she is pathetic, totally dependent on the benevolence of the male subject. When she is visited by Robert "in doubt that it pleased—in dread that it might annoy him—she received the boon of the meeting as an imprisoned bird would the admission of sunshine to its cage: it was of no use arguing—contending against the sense of present happiness: to be near Robert was to be revived" (251). Caroline is the completely submissive heroine, and it is not difficult to see why Robert fails to find her interesting. Indeed, it is his change of heart that seems implausible. Even when he puts his "hypothetical case" to Mr. Yorke, it is summarized in the form of negatives ("Supposing, in short, [she] had been—not cold, but modest; not vacant, but reflective; not obtuse, but sensitive; not inane, but innocent; not prudish, but pure . . . ?" 541). Robert clearly capitulates to his "fondness" for Caroline largely because of what she is not: she is not any trouble, and she is not any threat sexually. Charlotte Brontë indicates this in a nicely telescoped compliment voiced by Robert near the end of the novel: "My mother was a Roman Catholic; you look like the loveliest of her pictures of the Virgin" (606). Caroline is the perfect "virgin mother," safe to worship and to dismiss.

In the end, Caroline takes little part in her own salvation, which comes about as a result of the actions of Mrs. Pryor and Robert, the latter being helped along in his affections for Caroline as a result of both Shirley's refusal of his offer of marriage and his long illness, in which Caroline appears at his bedside to comfort him. (The latter situation, we may note, is a prototype of the one in which so many modern romance heroines "get their man.") It is this passivity and helplessness which cause the conclusion of the novel to seem forced and unrealistic, particularly in light of what Charlotte Brontë demonstrably "knows" about male-female love dynamics—that loss of control, of power, equals the loss of the other person's interest. Caroline voices this wisdom, saying she must leave Robert because "you most wish to retain when you are most certain to lose" (607), but only after he is safely attached to her. Robert's change of heart, finally, seems nothing short of miraculous, both to Caroline and to the reader.

Caroline is not the first Victorian heroine to suffer the pangs of unrequited love, and she is certainly not the last, but she is surely one of the most convincing. As readers, we are permitted none of the aesthetic pleasure that is often associated with the scenario of "suffering beauty"; the graphic realities of Caroline's ordeal preclude that particular escape. Also, rather than observing her suffering from the outside (as we largely do in the case of Hardy's Tess, for example), we experience it from the inside in the form of Caroline's self-torturing thoughts. When Robert and Mr. Yorke walk past without seeing her, for instance, we are given her desperate inner monologue: "Oh! had he but been alone! Had he but seen me . . . , he would have said something; he would have given me his hand. He *does*, he *must* love me a little: he would have shown some token of affection: in his eye, on his lip, I should have read comfort: but the chance is lost. The wind—the cloud's shadow does not pass more silently, more emptily than he. I have been mocked, and Heaven is cruel!" (188–89). Caroline's suffering, if not her desire, is indubitably subjectified; she is not a (beautifully) suffering object, whom we are free to appreciate from a distance, but a (painfully) suffering subject with whom we are asked to identify from within.

Shirley, then, is a strange novel. It is an amalgam of contradictory impulses, representing Charlotte Brontë's longing for happy romantic endings and her growing certainty that they are impossible. Essentially it is a novel of desperate need, of despair. Erotic desire is almost entirely absent from it, in keeping with Brontë's bitter awareness that female desire cannot be expressed and that the smothering of it, even in a mild nature, causes grievous mental and physical harm. When the erotic does resurface, in *Villette*, it is in a changed, more subdued form.

VILLETTE

Charlotte Brontë's final novel encompasses the solution to the central agonizing question posed by her other novels, the question of how a woman can best handle her own desire, given the dilemma of male domination and female submission. In *Villette* there is no fairy-tale ending; Lucy Snowe is Jane Eyre grown up and living in the real world. Neither are there passages of feminist polemic like the ones that are unconvincingly scattered throughout *Shirley*; the feminism of *Villette* is authentically displayed in the events of the novel itself.[8]

The issues posed in the earlier novels are faced head-on. The hopeless longing and lack of power of she who loves "without being asked," in particular, are present in Lucy's attraction to Graham Bretton, and there are the familiar triangles, jealousies and oedipal convolutions as well. There is waiting, there is spying, and there is the ever-present need for self-control, just as there are to varying degrees in *The Professor, Jane Eyre* and *Shirley*. But *Villette* eschews the capitulation to the domination/submission hierarchy displayed by its predecessors, and finds a way for a female character to negotiate a realistic pathway to both love and independence.

This solution is the one that *Shirley* half-heartedly theorizes and then discards, namely the rejection of a hopeless romantic love in favor of a more prosaic and affectionate attachment. Lucy speaks eloquently of the latter, characterizing it not as "the love born of beauty" but "another love, venturing diffidently into life after long acquaintance, furnace-tried by pain, stamped by constancy, consolidated by affection's pure and durable alloy, submitted by intellect to intellect's own tests, and finally wrought up, by his own process, to his own unflawed completeness, this Love that laughed at Passion, his fast frenzies and his hot and hurried extinction, in *this* Love I had a vested interest" (585). "The love born of beauty," Lucy's love for Graham, is precisely parallel to Caroline Helstone's love for Robert Moore, except that Brontë has the courage in *Villette* not to allow the hero to come to the rescue, and gives her heroine the courage not to submit to helpless waiting. Lucy does not merely repress her feelings for Graham, allowing them to destroy her like the clenched scorpion of *Shirley*; she actually lets them go in a symbolic act of burial, freeing herself to love again in a more fruitful way.

The challenge for Brontë in this scenario is to make the second, less passionate attachment seem compelling and desirable, and not merely second best, and to my mind she achieves this with astonishing success. In the end Paul Emanuel seems a richer, more complex and more interesting character than Graham, whose bland good looks and fairly simplistic attachments to his mother, to Genevra, and finally to Polly seem puerile in comparison to the teacher's darker sufferings. The message is that female desire can move beyond romantic submission to a place of greater equality, can be re-directed to encompass reality rather than romantic fantasy. Robert Keefe sees the relationship between Lucy and Paul Emanuel as unequal ("Brontë was never able to portray a fully believable sexual relationship between equals. . . . The problem with Lucy's love for the Belgian teacher can be seen in his very name," 175), but within the context of the Victorian novel, it comes very close to achieving sexual equality.[9] Even if "Imanuel" does mean "God with us," as Keefe points out, there is little evidence in Lucy's attitude toward Paul Emanuel of the deity-worship of Jane Eyre toward Rochester, say, or of Caroline Helstone toward Robert Moore. Indeed, Lucy has to overcome her own initial repugnance for the Belgian before she can appreciate him even as a friend; also, she is not only his student but a teacher as well. Most importantly, Paul Emanuel is portrayed as a flawed character with faults and vulnerabilities of his own, and the interaction between them is clumsy, honest and difficult. There is very little of conquering or submission in it, yet it still seems exciting: a real achievement for Brontë.

The achievement is not without flaws, and follows a tortuous progression, but it represents a real advance in Charlotte Brontë's feminism. Lucy Snowe is a more complex (and more adult) character than Brontë's other heroines, and the emotional difficulties she faces are very real. The novel begins, significantly, not with Lucy's childhood but with her detailed observation of another character's childhood, that of Polly, whom Graham will eventually love. And just as Lucy will later observe Polly's relationship with Graham with a mixture of envy and vicarious pleasure/pain, she observes Polly's relationship with her father with great ambivalence. Of Polly's deep attachment she remarks with annoyance, "This . . . was a one-idead nature; betraying that monomaniac tendency I have ever thought the most unfortunate with which man or woman can be cursed" (14). The events of the novel bear this out, in Lucy's painful curbing of her own monomaniac infatuation with Graham, thus avoiding the curse of hopeless longing to which Caroline Helstone, for example, falls prey.

The stage is also set for Lucy's struggle with her own passionate nature, as witnessed in her irritation with Polly's silent enjoyment of her father's caresses: "It was a scene of feeling too brimful, and which, because the cup did not foam up high or furiously overflow, only oppressed one the more. . . . I wished she would utter some hysterical cry, so that I might get relief and be at ease. . . . She seemed to have got what she wanted—*all* she wanted, and to be in a trance of content" (16–17). The unuttered hysterical cry is of course Lucy's own, at the prospect of never similarly having "all she wanted." The "all" is love, which Lucy does not expect to have because of her lack of beauty (she later speaks bitterly of "that degree of notice and consequence a person of my exterior habitually expects: that is to say, about what is given to unobtrusive articles of furniture, chairs of ordinary joiner's work, and carpets of no striking pattern," 119).

That Lucy is a passionate character, despite her overt diffidence, is made clear in the most violent metaphorical scene in the novel, that of the thunderstorm. She dreads "such accidents of the weather" because they "woke the being I was always lulling, and stirred up a craving cry I could not satisfy. . . . I was roughly roused and obliged to live. . . . It was wet, it was wild, it was pitch-dark. . . . I could not go in: too resistless was the delight of staying with the wild hour, black and full of thunder, pealing out such an ode as language never delivered to man—too terribly glorious, the spectacle of clouds, split and pierced by white and blinding bolts" (134). The language of this is sexual as well as violent ("craving cry," "satisfy," "roughly roused," "wet, . . . wild, . . . pitch-dark," "resistless. . . . delight," "split and pierced"), and the passage would seem to approach Margaret Homans's category of the literal. There is no overt metaphor here; what is being described overtly is the thunderstorm, long before such a technique became a cinema cliché.

The thunderstorm gives rise to a more concrete longing on Lucy's part, which in turn gives rise to an even more violent metaphor of suppression: "I did long, achingly, then and for four-and-twenty hours afterwards, for something to fetch me out of my present existence. . . . This longing, and all of a similar kind, it was necessary to knock on the head; which I did, figuratively, after the manner of Jael to Sisera, driving a nail through their temples. Unlike Sisera, they did not die: they were but transiently stunned, and at intervals would turn on the nail with a rebellious wrench; then did the temples bleed, and the brain thrill to its core" (134–35). Every bit as vividly as the digested stone and clenched scorpion of *Shirley*, this bloody metaphor indicates the pain and mutilation of the repression of desire. There is an important difference, however. While the stone/scorpion image referred to self-mutilation, in this case Lucy's desires are seen as separate from herself, so that the attempted destruction of them (while no less violent) does not at the same time destroy her.

The feelings she must destroy are her feelings for Graham, which largely consist of a conventional romantic feminine desire to submit to his pleasure ("In a strange and new sense, I grew most selfish, and quite powerless to deny myself the delight of indulging his mood," 240). Her desire, in other words, becomes submerged in his, in perfect conformity to the domination/submission hierarchy. She senses this as a temptation, a weakness in herself, however, a "delight" she is "powerless to deny [her]self" even though it must be denied in order for her to be happy. The struggle that follows is similar to Caroline Helstone's ordeal of repression, except that Lucy is more bitter and rebellious, and more intensely self-aware than Caroline was. At first Lucy tries to persuade herself that she is "satisfied with friendship—with its calm comfort and modest hope," as she tells herself after attending a concert with Graham and his mother. But when she has to return to Madame Beck's she is no longer satisfied, as another painful metaphor makes clear. As in *Shirley*, love in *Villette* is portrayed as spiritual sustenance, as food and drink (when Lucy says good-bye to Graham, she "swallow[s] tears as if they had been wine," 285–86). When she dares to hope that he will write to her, as he has promised, Reason, personified as a "hag," a "devil," an "envenomed . . . step-mother" who has often "turned me out by night, in mid-winter, on cold snow, flinging for sustenance the gnawed bone dogs had forsaken," tells her to attach no significance to any letter she does receive from him, and never to express her feelings in any letters she may write him. In rebellion against such a harsh decree, Lucy turns in her mind to "Imagination—. . . our sweet Help, our divine Hope. . . . My hunger has this good angel appeased with food, sweet and strange, gathered amongst gleaning angels, garnering their dew-white harvest in the first fresh hour of a heavenly day" (287–88).

Lucy lives on this "sweet and strange" food for some time, rejecting the "gnawed bone" provided by her Reason, but when she actually receives the imagined letter from Graham, she is able to see the difference—crucial in this novel—between the illusory sustenance provided by her Imagination and the real food of real human response. When she is given the letter, she realizes, "I held in my hand a morsel of real solid joy: not a dream . . .

on which humanity starves but cannot live; not a mess of that manna I drearily eulogized awhile ago—which . . . at first melts on the lips with an unspeakable and preternatural sweetness, but which, in the end, our souls full surely loathe; longing deliriously for natural and earth-grown food . . .—an aliment divine, but for mortals deadly" (299). The relief of the ingestion of "earth-grown food"—concrete expressions of affection as opposed to either reasoned repressions of desire or hopeless imaginary fantasies—is evident in the vividness of the metaphor: "It was neither sweet hail, nor small coriander-seed—neither slight wafer, nor luscious honey, I had lighted on; it was the wild savoury mess of the hunter, nourishing and salubrious meat, forest-fed or desert-reared, fresh, healthful, and life-sustaining." The "earthiness" of this metaphor is perfect: meat, the "wild savoury mess," with its flesh, its blood, is the perfect analogue for sexual love.

As in Charlotte Brontë's other novels, love is needed, with an urgent and very physical need, to nourish the soul. Even the ethereal Polly, when she receives a real love letter from Graham much later in the novel, describes her reaction to it in intensely physical terms: "While I read, . . . every quiver seemed like the pant of an animal athirst, laid down at a well and drinking; and the well proved . . . gloriously clear; . . . I saw the sun through its gush, and not a mote . . . in the . . . golden gurgle" (470). "Quiver," "pant," "gush," "gurgle": the language of sexuality is perfectly embedded in the language of literal appetite. As Rosalind Coward points out, food and drink metaphors in general, with their covert reference to forbidden lusts, tastes, feeding and gluttony, are a peculiarly feminine form of displaced desire (anorexics, for example, may be rejecting real food in favor of the "carrion comfort" of the illusory "manna" Charlotte Brontë describes). It is because of this displacement, which allows for a richer descriptive idiom, that *Villette* is a more erotically complex novel than *Jane Eyre*, for example, in which there is much literal touching (and much literal food) but little use of metaphor. The latter technique provides for a sensuality of language that is as richly suggestive as any in the novel of the time. In *Villette*, food and drink metaphors recur whenever love is thought of, spoken about or enacted, creating a pattern of embedded figuration evincing both linguistic beauty and sexual intensity. Lucy speaks of Graham's voice as "music" which he imparts "as the ripe fruit rewards with sweetness the rifling bee" (454); Lucy chides Paul Emanuel that his spying is "to banquet secretly and sacrilegiously on Eve's apples" (459); Polly's letter to Graham is described as "a morsel of ice flavoured with ever so slight a zest of fruit or sugar" (471); and finally, Lucy says of Paul Emanuel that "he would give neither a stone, nor an excuse—neither a scorpion, nor a disappointment; his letters were real food that nourished, living water that refreshed" (615–16).

The allusion to *Shirley* is apt, for *Villette* finally resolves the issue that lies uneasily submerged in the earlier novel. Caroline Helstone, in much the same position vis-à-vis Robert Moore as Lucy is vis-à-vis Graham— that is, loving "without being asked"—feeds her desire on Imagination's manna, which magically turns into real food (in the form of Robert's love for her) just before she starves to death. The murky message of this concatenation of events, that a woman has no choice but to wait for her love to be returned (and that she may die if it is not), is revised in *Villette* in the only way possible. With the insight of more modern feminists, Charlotte Brontë confronts the issue of female desire in a wholly realistic way, rejecting the unhealthy domination/submission hierarchy in favor of a more equal partnership. It is still the case, within the ethos of *Villette*, that a woman can die for want of a man's love; but it is also true that she can choose to seek sustenance elsewhere.

In order to do this, however, she must jettison her need to submit to the male as well as her idolization of him. With amazing acuity, Brontë has Lucy do this in the enactment of a psychological ritual reminiscent of a funeral, in exactly the same way that modern therapists advocate to mark the conclusion of the grieving process. In this manner Brontë acknowledges the enormous difficulty attached to weaning oneself of the need for the "love born of beauty"—it is like a death. In eliminating the destructive desire to submit (as opposed to merely repressing it, as Caroline Helstone does), Lucy is thus able to save her own life (as Caroline seems helpless to do) and to emerge from the ordeal if not triumphant, then at least stronger and saner. After she buries Graham's letters, she reports, "I had a dreary something—not pleasure—but a sad, lonely satisfaction. . . . I felt not happy, far otherwise, but strong with reinforced strength" (368–70). Charlotte Brontë does not minimize the difficulty of such a struggle, but she also makes it clear that the satisfaction and the strength it brings are real.

And the reward, finally, is real too. The "other love" Lucy finds with Paul Emanuel, "furnace-tried by pain, stamped by constancy, consolidated by affection's pure and durable alloy" (585), proves to be better, incomparably more sustaining and enriching, than her worshipful infatuation for Graham. The latter, the "love born of beauty," is revealed as superficial and power-based, even when it is mutual, as the relationship between Graham and Polly illustrates. Polly agonizes deeply over her reply to Graham's first love letter, understanding only too well that she must curb her natural ardor or risk losing him. She tells Lucy, "I replied briefly, but I did not repulse him. Yet I almost trembled for fear of making the answer too cordial: Graham's tastes are so fastidious. I wrote it three times—chastening and subduing the phrases at every rescript" (471). Here indeed are the old, familiar rules of male desire, so well understood by Brontë: the female must feign reluctance, "chastening and subduing" her response in order to allay the male's fears of feminine desire. A reply that was "too cordial," presumably, would offend Graham's "fastidious" tastes—in other words his fear and loathing of women who fail to tread the fine line between receptive object and resistant object.

Lucy's relationship with Paul Emanuel, by contrast, partakes of no such emotional power-maneuvers. Instead, Lucy is completely at ease in the professor's presence. When he sits beside her during the study-hour, for instance, she remarks, "I did not now sit restrained . . . at his side; I stirred when I wished to stir, coughed when it was necessary, even yawned when I was tired—did, in short, what I pleased, blindly reliant upon his indulgence. . . . Silence is of different kinds, and breathes different meanings; no words could inspire a pleasanter content than did M. Paul's wordless presence" (436). Here indeed is something new in the Victorian novel: a love relationship based on comfort rather than anxiety on the part of the female (who in such situations generally experiences palpitations, agitation, flutterings, pallor and overall physical discomfort). Whether or not this parallels the comfort Charlotte Brontë finally attained in her own marriage we can only speculate; the important thing is that she imagined it, and so successfully. With Paul Emanuel, Lucy never has to perform the delicate balancing act between reserve and enthusiasm that characterizes Polly's response to Graham. Such feminine ploys are in fact scorned by Paul Emanuel, as he tells Lucy after she has accepted a bouquet of violets from him: "It pleased me when you took them peacefully and promptly, without prudery—that sentiment which I ever dread to excite, and which . . . I vindictively detest" (458).

"Without prudery": the essence of Lucy's relationship with Paul Emanuel is the sort of emotional honesty that grows slowly, usually between friends rather than lovers. In fact, Lucy's first impression of him, based largely on his appearance, is unfavorable: "He seemed a harsh apparition, with his close-shorn, black head, his broad, sallow brow, his thin cheek, his wide and quivering nostril, his thorough glance and hurried bearing. Irritable he was" (159). The reader, too, is allowed to see Paul Emanuel's good points only very gradually, while his "irritability" is seen in abundance. Lucy's first admission of affection for him, appropriately, is no love paean but rather a negative assertion. She says simply, "My morning's anger quite melted: I did not dislike Paul Emanuel" (432). How much more authentic this seems than Caroline Helstone's mooning over Robert Moore, or Lucy's own tender speculations about Graham. The confidences Lucy and Paul Emanuel share partake of a similar honesty. When the latter confesses his insecurity (his "modesty," as he calls it) about his attractiveness to women, Lucy reports, "I quite believed him now; and, in believing, I honoured him with a sincerity of esteem which made my heart ache" (457). Later in the novel, after their theological disagreement, she continues to describe their relationship in terms of trust, respect and affection: "The jar was over; the mutual understanding was settling and fixing; feelings of union and hope made themselves profoundly felt in the heart; affection and deep esteem and drawning trust had each fastened its bond" (552).

Such Platonic mutual regard is the basis for the relationship between Lucy and Paul Emanuel, but that is not to say that it is entirely devoid of any elements of domination or submission. They by no means have the sort of lukewarm connection that tends to characterize male-female friendships in the nineteenth-century novel, such as that between Maggie Tulliver and Philip Wakem, for example. The aggression Lucy and Paul Emanuel occasionally experience toward each other lends their relationship a vital erotic spark; the crucial difference between theirs and the usual domination/submission configuration is a more equal distribution of power. It is acknowledged from the outset in *Villette* that power tends to be a masculine trait. Lucy describes the domineering Madame Beck, for instance, as "not wear[ing] a woman's aspect but rather a man's. Power of a particular kind strongly limned itself in all her traits." Lucy goes on to make it clear that "that power was not *my* kind of power" (95), although she does think of herself as powerful, especially in comparison to most other women: "I was not accustomed to find in women or girls any power of self-control, or strength of self-denial" (361).

She exercises her own power (and not only that of self-control) fairly easily in her dealings with Paul Emanuel, whom she describes as "like Bonaparte. He was a man not always to be submitted to. Sometimes it was needful to resist; it was right to stand still, to look up into his eyes and tell him that his requirements went beyond reason—that his absolutism verged on tyranny" (439). Indeed, Paul Emanuel is a believable, appropriately flawed character, falling far short of the requirements for a romantic hero. Lucy candidly marks instances of objectionable behavior on his part, and does not hesitate to chastise him for them. When she learns that he spies on the students in the garden, for instance, she bluntly tells him that "every glance you cast from that lattice is a wrong done to the best part of your own nature" (459). Her attitude evinces none of the feminine fear of displeasing (or losing) the male that characterizes so many other fictional love relationships of the century, including that of Jane Eyre and Rochester. Instead, she is truly at ease, even cavalier, about Paul Emanuel's attempts to dominate her: "I listened to him, and did not trouble myself to be too submissive; his occupation would have been gone, had I left him nothing to 'keep down' " (455). The result is that at the end of the novel, during their engagement scene, Lucy's "homage" to Paul Emanuel seems neither submissive nor weak, but emotionally honest: "He gently raised his hand to stroke my hair; it touched my lips in passing; I pressed it close, I paid it tribute. He was my king; royal for me had been that hand's bounty; to offer homage was both a joy and a duty" (607). There is none of the verbal sparring that often takes place in such scenes (such as that between Shirley

and Louis Moore), in which each of the participants attempts to make the
other "confess" his or her affection first.

In fact, what Lucy attains in her relationship with Paul Emanuel is what
many modern feminists describe as the underlying desideratum of all
sexual relationships, namely mother-love. Without herself taking the position of the needy child (as Caroline Helstone did, for example), Lucy is
nurtured by Paul Emanuel in a way generally regarded as feminine. Even
before they are in love, Lucy describes the professor's heart as "not an
ossified organ: in its core was a place, tender beyond a man's tenderness; a
place that humbled him to little children, that bound him to girls and
women" (425). "Tender beyond a man's tenderness" describes beautifully
what is possibly the most moving incident in the novel, that in which Paul
Emanuel wraps the sleeping Lucy in warm shawls. Later in the novel, the
metaphor used to describe the moment of mutual recognition is, not
surprisingly, maternal: "He took my hand in one of his, with the other he
put back my bonnet; he looked into my face, his luminous smile went out,
his lips expressed something almost like the wordless language of a mother
who finds a child greatly and unexpectedly changed, broken with illness,
or worn-out by want" (599). And later, after she has told him her story, in
a similarly motherly way, "he gathered me near his heart. I was full of faults;
he took them and me all home" (612).

The parent-child paradigm (which functions both ways, we may note—
Paul Emanuel is occasionally child-like himself, causing Lucy to comment,
"Soothe, comprehend, comfort him, and he was a lamb" 479) contributes
its erotic charge to their relationship, carrying it beyond a simple friendship. The familial is also implicated in their interaction earlier in the novel,
when Paul Emanuel asks Lucy to be his "sister." The implied eroticism of
this relation is evident in Lucy's subsequent remark that "I envied no girl
her lover, no bride her bridegroom, no wife her husband; I was content with
this my voluntary, self-offering friend" (510).

The equality of such an exchange is particularly pronounced in contrast
to the other love relationships in the novel, especially that between Polly
and Graham. Their relationship, too, is highly familial, much more overtly
so than that between Lucy and Paul Emanuel, in fact. As a child, Polly
simply transfers her intense feelings for her father to Graham, and they are
the feminine feelings of the need to merge and submit. Lucy observes, "One
would have thought the child had no mind or life of her own, but must
necessarily live, move, and have her being in another: now that her father
was taken from her, she nestled to Graham, and seemed to feel by his
feelings: to exist in his existence" (30). It is hardly surprising that this
relationship later turns into the conventional dominant male/submissive
female arrangement, in which Graham simply takes over the role of Mr.
Home and Polly remains the enchanting child. Indeed, the reader must pay
close attention at times in order to discern which of the two men Polly is

flirting with. When she wants some ale, for instance, "she continued to look up exactly with the countenance of a child that longs for some prohibited dainty. At last the Doctor relented, took it down, and indulged himself in the gratification of letting her taste from his hand" (351). This sort of father-daughter bond is reiterated endlessly in the Victorian novel; Dickens' Bella Wilfer and her father and John Harmon constitute a constellation that conforms exactly to that of Polly and her father and Graham. The true nature of such a bond is revealed by a symbolic incident early in *Villette* in which Polly lies on the carpet at Graham's feet: " 'Little Mousie' crept to his side, and lay down on the carpet at his feet, her face to the floor; mute and motionless she kept that post and position till bed-time. Once I saw Graham—wholly unconscious of her proximity—push her with his restless foot. . . . A minute after one little hand stole out . . . and softly caressed the heedless foot" (38).

Well does Brontë understand the erotic potential of such oedipal arrangements. They are imbued with all the nuances of master and slave, powerful and powerless, and are central to the domination/submission hierarchy that is the "norm" between men and women. The relationship between Graham and his mother is similarly eroticized; he teases her and flirts with her, and tells her, "Mother, you are better to me than ten wives yet" (274). Lucy's relationship with Paul Emanuel, however, represents a new departure, deriving erotic energy from its familial overtones and yet eschewing the familiar father-daughter or mother-son patterns in favor of a more emotionally equal interaction.

This new departure is evident in the look, the language and the enactment of desire in *Villette*, and it is especially evident in view of the contrasts among the various relationships in the novel. The first part of the novel is devoted to "the love born of beauty," the kind of romantic love that Charlotte Brontë's other heroines hoped and waited for. And, as in the previous novels, the "beauty" is male. Lucy herself is plain, a fact that places her at a distinct disadvantage in the matter of sexual negotiations, as she well realizes. Seeing herself in a full-length mirror, she says, "No need to dwell on the result. It brought a jar of discord, a pang of regret; it was not flattering, yet, after all, I ought to be thankful: it might have been worse" (262). Lucy is never the object of the look of desire; in this novel this look is deployed in two directions, initially from Lucy to Graham and then from Graham to Ginevra and Polly. The latter direction gives rise to several stock descriptions of the two women ("Ginevra's dress of deep crimson relieved well her light curls, and harmonized with her rose-like bloom. Paulina's attire . . . made the eye grateful for the delicate life of her companion, for the soft animation of her countenance, for the tender depth of her eyes, for the brown shadow and bounteous flow of her hair—darker than that of her Saxon cousin, as were also her eyebrows, her eye-lashes, her full irids, and large mobile pupils," 388–89), and it also gives rise to a structural aberration in the novel, namely the clumsy adoption by Lucy of Graham's point of view. This continues for several chapters, in which Lucy "sees" Polly through Graham's eyes: "Dr. John had not been unobservant of the fairy's dance; he had watched it, and he had liked it. . . . Again she seemed a child for him" (350–51); "He found the impression true. . . . " (360); "His wish was rather to look than converse" (391). Jarring though this device is, it serves to emphasize Lucy's awareness of Graham's appreciation of Polly's beauty and the fact that she herself will never inspire such appreciation. Like Jane Eyre and Caroline Helstone, Lucy suffers the pain of jealousy in the presence of a beautiful rival (conveniently imaginary, in their cases); unlike them, however, she lets this pain enable her to turn away from the situation, neither competing nor hopelessly longing. Her vicarious sharing of Graham's pleasure in Polly represents an unflinching acceptance of reality, the reality encoded in the domination/submission hierarchy that it is a woman's beauty that causes her to be regarded as an object of desire. The "love born of beauty," she realizes, will never be hers.

But the main focus of the look of desire in *Villette* is the male characters. Lucy describes Graham, particularly, in loving detail: "His profile was clear, fine, and expressive: perhaps his eye glanced from face to face rather too vividly, too quickly, and too often, but it had a most pleasant character, and so had his mouth; his chin was full, cleft, Grecian, and perfect" (116–17). "His well-proportioned figure was not to be mistaken. . . . His uncovered head, his face and fine brow were most handsome and manly" (184). Such a catalogue of physical attributes is a nice parallel to countless such descriptions of female faces and figures in the nineteenth-century novel, and objectifies Graham in much the same way. This is emphasized in Lucy's descriptions of Graham's portrait, which (tellingly) gives rise to as much speculation on her part as Graham himself:

A head, . . . fresh, life-like, speaking, and animated. It seemed a youth of sixteen, fair-complexioned, with sanguine health in his cheek; hair long, not dark, and with a sunny sheen; penetrating eyes, an arch mouth, and a gay smile. . . . Any romantic little school-girl might almost have loved it in its frame. Those eyes looked as if when somewhat older, they would flash a lightning response to love: I cannot tell whether they kept in store the steady-beaming shine of faith. For whatever sentiment met him in form too facile, his lips menaced, beautifully but surely, caprice and light esteem. (213)

Graham is clearly different from Charlotte Brontë's former romantic heroes, Rochester and Robert Moore. He is more feminine—there is none of Zamorna about him—and more dangerously beguiling, as Lucy's asides reveal ("perhaps his eye[s] glanced from face to face rather too vividly, too quickly, and too often. . . . I cannot tell whether they kept in store the steady-beaming shine of faith"). He has beauty but lacks substance; "any romantic little school-girl" might have become enamored of his looks.

Paul Emanuel, on the other hand, as I have already shown, is far from beautiful, a "harsh apparition," in Lucy's words. After she gets to know him, however, he appears to her in a different light: "The little man looked well, very well; there was a clearness of amity in his blue eye, and a glow of good feeling on his dark complexion, which passed perfectly in the place of beauty" (425). Neither Paul Emanuel nor Lucy is objectified through physical beauty, and therefore they stand a much better chance of relating to each other as equal subjects.

The language of desire displays a similar marked contrast between its use in the first part of the novel and its use by Lucy and Paul Emanuel. As I have shown, Polly feels that she must "chasten and subdue" her words to Graham, and Lucy's "Reason" tells her that she must never send any words to him at all. To Paul Emanuel, on the other hand, Lucy speaks as freely as she wishes; when she objects to his spying, for instance, she remarks, "He often lectured me by the hour together—I did not see why I should not speak my mind for once" (458). She is also able to "speak her mind" about her feelings for him. When Madame Beck tries to prevent Paul Emanuel from seeing her, Lucy responds with an urgency that is similar to Jane Eyre's irrepressible impulse to self-expression: "Pierced deeper than I could endure, made now to feel what defied suppression, I cried—'My heart will break!' " (600). And later, when she tells Paul Emanuel about the night in the park, she recounts, "I spoke. All leaped from my lips. I lacked not words now; fast I narrated; fluent I told my tale; it streamed on my tongue" (611). Her speech, however, the actual words themselves, is not so important as the emotional release: "The seal of another fountain yielded under the strain: one breath from M. Paul . . . lifted a load, opened an outlet. With many a deep sob, with thrilling, with icy shiver, with strong trembling, and yet with relief—I wept" (600).

Her weeping is part of the wordless communication that exists between Lucy and Paul Emanuel during the final scenes in the novel. It is a special language, the language of lovers, and a perfect example of the pre-oedipal literal language that Margaret Homans categorizes as female. This fits exactly with the "mother love" with which Paul Emanuel nurtures Lucy; I have already noted his "wordless language of a mother who finds a child greatly and unexpectedly changed" (599), and his speech later mingles with the other comforting natural sounds that Lucy hears: "M. Paul talked to me. His voice was so modulated that it mixed harmonious with the silver whisper, the gush, the musical sigh, in which the light breeze, fountain, and foliage intoned their lulling vesper" (608). Such speech works both ways. When Lucy attempts to thank Paul Emanuel for his gifts, she admits, "I can no more remember the thoughts or the words of the ten minutes succeeding this disclosure, than I can retrace the experience of my earliest year of life" (606), reinforcing the now submerged mother-child metaphor and illustrating that her own speech, as well as Paul Emanuel's, might as well be "wordless." In an eerie anticipation of T. S. Eliot, she later reports, "In such inadequate language my feelings struggled for expression: they could not get it; speech, brittle and unmalleable, and cold as ice, dissolved or shivered in the effort" (607). Such a struggle for honest expression is in direct contrast, we may note, to the word-games played by Polly in her letter to Graham, for example. The latter (following the speech rules of the domination/submission hierarchy) seem in comparison to be a language of pseudo-desire, designed to conceal rather than reveal real feelings. The language of authentic desire in this novel is more exactly a pre-language, and it belongs equally to the male and the female. In her speech, as in her looks, Lucy is just as much a subject of desire as Paul Emanuel.

The enactment of desire between Paul Emanuel and Lucy is similarly mutual. Lucy does a certain amount of anxious waiting to see Paul Emanuel after the scene in the park, but unlike her endless waiting for Graham's letters it has a fruitful conclusion. Also, it is not particularly passive; her action of going to the park in the first place constitutes an active search for truth.[10] And when she finally does encounter Paul Emanuel, she is determined to participate fully in the farewell she anticipates, even though she believes him to be leaving her for someone else: "I could not meet his sunshine with cloud. If this were my last moment with him, I would not waste it in forced, unnatural distance. I loved him well—too well not to smite out of my path even Jealousy herself, when she would have obstructed a kind farewell. A cordial word from his lips, or a gentle look from his eyes, would do me good. . . . I would take it—I would taste the elixir, and pride should not spill the cup" (599). The "drink" metaphor signals sexual desire, and while Lucy is not exactly active here—she "takes" the cup rather than giving it—she is at least determined to participate. The feeling that she conquers is not her own desire, but the jealousy that stands in the way of its expression. As we have seen, the verbal disclosures between Lucy and Paul Emanuel are mutual at this point, and so are their actions. While Lucy's gestures tend to be worshipful, they are not exactly submissive, and they constitute a frank acknowledgment of her own feelings. When she first learns of his gift of her own school, she "hardly knew what to do. I first caressed the soft velvet on his cuff [she is holding his hand], and then I stroked the hand it surrounded" (606). It is after this highly sexual image that she kisses his hand" ("pressed it close, . . . paid it tribute," 607), indicating both her gratitude and her own unabashed desire.

CONCLUSION

In her brief career, Charlotte Brontë attempted, and in good measure achieved, something quite extraordinary: a feminist revision of the domination/submission fantasy. Her feminism, more innate and instinctual than conscious and articulate, resides in her acute awareness of both the power of the erotic hierarchy and its unworkable inequities for both men and women. *The Professor* traces the power and the pain of the domination/submission configuration through the experience of the male subject, while Jane Eyre enacts the wish-fulfillment of the female object who is miraculously transformed into an equal subject by the end of the novel. In *Shirley* the female object's protests against her passive role become too insistent to ignore, disrupting the deceptively smooth conclusion of the novel's events, and in *Villette* a feminist solution is finally offered to the problem, the solution of a nearly mutual subjectivity in erotic relations.

In *Villette* the feminine struggle for self-control begun by Jane Eyre and continued with increasing difficulty by Caroline Helstone has become much more complex than simply the effort not to lose a man through the betrayal of feelings. Jane Eyre plays the game of repression and wins, Caroline Helstone plays it much less successfully and nearly loses (amid much bitter protest in each novel against the necessity for such repression), but in *Villette* we are given a heroine who finally opts out of the game. Lucy Snowe, just as bitterly angry as Jane Eyre or *Shirley's* implied author about the need to squelch the expression of female desire, at first experiences the kind of love (the "love born of beauty") which demands that she stifle her feelings for Graham, which she does by biting her tongue, swallowing her tears and burying her letters from him. But she then goes on to experience a love that is comfortable and nurturing—at its deepest level a kind of maternal love—and which demands no deception or repression in order to survive. This new love is adult and mutual but also, through its oedipal aspects and its hints of aggression, still erotic; its fulfillment in no way constitutes an anticlimax or a substitute for the real thing (as the final union between Hardy's Bathsheba Everdene and Gabriel Oak appears to, for example), even if we choose to believe in the drowning of M. Paul.[11]

Charlotte Brontë courageously explores the complexities of erotic relationships in her work, fearlessly probing both the power and the pain of the male-female domination/submission hierarchy from both the male and the female point of view. Her plain heroines display increasing dissatisfaction with their submissive roles in the erotic hierarchy until finally in *Villette*, her most powerful and most painful novel, Lucy Snowe achieves a relationship in which she becomes, at least tentatively, the authentic subject of her own desire. In the context of the nineteenth-century novel, this constitutes a major achievement.

NOTES

1. Ruth Johnston, for whom temporal structure is a key feature of nineteenth-century realism, finds the distinction between Crimsworth's past and present selves much more significant. Johnston's thought-provoking essay is concerned with the way in which *The Professor* disrupts the usual signifying practices em-

ployed by the realist text in creating its subject as masculine, thus exposing the foreclosure of feminine subjectivity in such texts.

2. In autobiographical terms, this reading points to the possibility of Brontë's subliminal anger at M. Heger's rejection of her, superimposed on the wish-fulfillment of the marriage of master and student.

3. For further discussion of the implications of Jane's lack of beauty, see Annette Federico.

4. For an alternative view of the scopic economy in *Jane Eyre*, see Peter Bellis.

5. Bette London and Pat MacPherson both find this affirmation of patriarchal erotic structures disappointingly conventional. MacPherson persuasively points out that such structures militate against the possibility of female desire ("Jane finds a way to set her own brideprice with complete moral integrity and autonomy.... But she cannot change the marriage market itself.... We reach the limits of *Jane Eyre's* feminism at this point," 34), while London discusses *Jane Eyre* as a "textbook of self-discipline" which "can be read as a nineteenth-century deportment book, offering its readers . . . lessons in the proper forms of feminine conduct" (209).

6. Bette London, on the other hand, sees Jane's outbursts as "masochism's excess: the effect of scrupulous observance of a position of silent self-abnegation" (203).

7. For a wider discussion of this point, see Miriam Bailin.

8. It is also displayed in the novel's enigmatic "heretic" structure, as Patricia Johnson and many other critics have pointed out. Because of its elusive narrator and her ambiguous, unstable relation to her implied audience, *Villette*, perhaps more than any other novel in my study, lends itself to discussions of narrative plurality, fragmentation, doubleness, identity, disclosure and interpretation, as well as to Lacanian and Foucauldian analyses (see Boone, "Depolicing *Villette*," for example). My analysis, more narrowly focused on patterns of erotic interaction among the novel's characters, is tangentially located in relation to this broader discourse.

9. Material inequality, of course, still exists, as Nancy Rabinowitz points out.

10. Boone sees this episode as one which reveals Lucy as the "desiring subject of her own autoerotic quest" ("Depolicing *Villette*" 37), a quest that transgresses and reconstructs the hero's plot of masculine desire in favor of an alternative narrative movement toward female subjectivity. While this analysis addresses forms of female desire that lie outside the scope of my study, I find Boone's argument compelling and cogently formulated.

11. My interpretation of the success of Lucy's relationship with Paul results in a wholly different reading of the novel from that of many other critics. Gilbert and Gubar, for instance, who read the novel as "the most moving and terrifying account of female deprivation ever written," see this relationship as "constantly impeded by the haunting [of the nun] and by their common fears of human contact" and take the ambiguity of *Villette's* conclusion to indicate "Lucy's recognition that it is only in [Paul's] absence that she can . . . exercise her own powers" (*Madwoman* 400, 429, 438). John Maynard, on the other hand, in his detailed and impressive account of sexuality in Brontë's novels, agrees that the "loving fulfillment" Lucy experiences with M. Paul replaces the "repressed destructive sexual energies" of the earlier part of her story (208–9).

3

✧ ✧ ✧

GEORGE ELIOT

Feminist critics have always had trouble with George Eliot, largely because of her seemingly scornful attitude toward the women's movement of her day, but also because of a perceived patriarchal stance in her work. Recently, however, feminists have attempted to reclaim George Eliot as their own, with interesting results. Dorothea Barrett, for instance, disagrees with previous analyses of the "sublime resignation" of Eliot's heroines and with "the tendency amongst modern critics . . . to attribute to [the sexual] a naïve or at best maternal cast" (22) in Eliot's work. Barrett, whose project is "to reclaim the canonical writers, to point out the radicalism that has been obscured by generations of conservative interpretation" (xi), claims that although Eliot "clearly intends" to recommend submissiveness, "the texts themselves" subvert this intention (42), and that her novels display "the belief that a woman's sexual need is actually the means of her oppression, [and] that in order to overcome male domination from without she must first overcome the domination of sexual desire within her" (68).

This is an interesting argument from my point of view, particularly as Barrett bases her contentions to an extent on a psychosexual analysis, claiming that "the rebelliousness and iconoclasm of [Eliot's] work is closely related to its erotic content" (x). Briefly, although her argument is well worked out and persuasive at many points, I have to differ slightly with Barrett's basic contention: my search for a female subject of desire in George Eliot's work revealed (disappointingly) a much lesser degree of "rebelliousness and iconoclasm," at least in the area of gender issues. Eliot's endorsement of feminine submissiveness is inescapable (although not necessarily a weakness; Christine Sutphin, who also wishes to claim Eliot as a feminist, makes a convincing case for the notion of "willed submission" as a particular strength of Eliot's heroines). Also, I was able to discover no such battle on the part of her heroines to "overcome the domination of sexual desire" within themselves. This was precisely the battle of Charlotte Brontë's heroines, as I have shown, but Eliot's female characters seem largely oblivious of the erotic power relations between the sexes. Indeed, they frequently seem oblivious of sexual desire itself, either their own or that of the males in the novels they inhabit (until the moment when the males make it known to them).

How then can we account for the fact that George Eliot's novels comprise a corpus that fairly exudes eroticism? My search for a female subject of desire in this corpus reveals a traditional George Eliot but not necessarily a patriarchal one; her repression of female desire is simply a part of her overall sexual repression, which is extreme in its thoroughness and monumental in its effects. The eroticism of Eliot's novels is not (at least not directly) generated by the interplay of forces within the domination/submission hierarchy. It derives instead from the sheer force of Eliot's effort to avoid acknowledging such a dynamic. Such avoidance, so scrupulously adhered to—expunged even from the tacit contract between narrator and reader—acquires the force of a ruling obsession, suggesting its opposite in a peculiarly insistent way. This observation is hardly new—it forms the basis for much traditional Victorian criticism—but it is worth noting that in George Eliot's work such erotic avoidance attains a sort of perfection that makes her unique in even the most repressive of centuries. George Steiner, in the "Eros and Idiom" chapter of *On Difficulty*, speaks approvingly of Eliot's "energy of undeclared content," her "verbal reticence," "nearness of unwasted resource," "deliberate tact" and "chasteness of discourse," all of which give to the novels their "intensity, [their] matchless energy of adult life" (105–6). We may or may not share Steiner's preference for such sexual reticence, but we can certainly agree that Eliot's avoidance of the erotic is consistent and powerful, giving rise to novels that are —paradoxically— intensely erotic.

Post-Freudian critics have had little difficulty in unraveling such a paradox, although they have not all been so happy with it as Steiner is. (Baruch Hochman, for instance, although he acknowledges that "Victorian fiction billows and heaves with a power of wishing and longing that is rare in fiction anywhere," complains that "the Maggies and the Pips of Victorian fiction are never fully embodied or explored, since the aspects of their being that might threaten prevailing values are systematically evaded," 42.) Clearly, the narrator's strenuous suppression of all erotic acknowledgment creates an enormous pressure in Eliot's novels, a pressure that constantly erupts in various forms of erotic displacement. The energy that is denied expression in the form of sexual desire reappears in the enthusiastic espousal of other desires (which then become eroticized). In most of the potentially erotic encounters between her characters, for instance, Eliot's narrator appeals overtly to religion, to art or to childhood innocence as motivating forces, thus seemingly "laundering" such encounters of erotic effects. What occurs, however, is of course the exact opposite, so that her heroines' spirituality seems inevitably to partake of the orgasmic passion of a St. Theresa, art appears in the light of sexual innuendo and, most frequently of all, childhood innocence—the "safest" form of affection in the Victorian ethos—is transformed into oedipal and incestuous obsessions that seem all the more erotic for their ingenuous disavowals. Thus the image of two children holding hands, Eliot's favorite trope in her adult love scenes, belies its own innocence.

Other displacements occur in Eliot's work as well, such as the displacement into metaphor noted both by Steiner (who points out, for instance, the telling aptness of Celia's view of Casaubon's learning as "a kind of damp which might in due time saturate a neighbouring body," 103) and by Juliet McMaster (who, in her examination of George Eliot's language, "confess[es] to having found sex in almost everything," 24). There is also, perhaps not surprisingly, a displacement of erotic energy into various forms of violence. All of the non-spiritual women in the four novels I shall discuss display murderous desires of some kind: Hetty murders her child; Rosamond (following Laure) figuratively murders Lydgate, as the epilogue makes clear; and Gwendolen feels guilty of Grandcourt's murder. Maggie murders no one (except possibly herself, as Elizabeth Ermarth points out in "Maggie Tulliver's Long Suicide"); but she has definite violent impulses, as we can see in her treatment of her Fetish. George Eliot does not avoid aggression except for sexual aggression, which she avoids almost completely (even Grandcourt's aggression toward Gwendolen is not overtly sexual, as the narrator is careful to point out).

It seems clear that erotic desire constitutes the thorn in George Eliot's flesh. Just why this is so it is impossible to say, apart from the vague biographical speculation that her union with Lewes made her unduly sensitive about such issues, even by the stringent standards of her day. In a way her novels constitute a vast amorphous protest as to their author's "purity." In fact, they had precisely the opposite effect on her contemporary reviewers, of whom Swinburne is a fairly typical (albeit somewhat shrill) example; he calls Maggie's relationship with Stephen "astonishing and revolting, . . . shameful, . . . vile, . . . [an] ugly and lamentable case" (qtd. in Carroll 164).

So where does George Eliot stand in relation to the domination/submission hierarchy? Curiously, in a way she stands—or would like to stand—outside it. Her attempt to ignore it is at once the weakness and the greatness of her art, and deserves fuller critical treatment than it has received so far. The heroines of the four novels I shall discuss, *Adam Bede*, *The Mill on the Floss*, *Middlemarch*, and *Daniel Deronda* (chosen simply because they are the most obviously erotic of Eliot's works), fall into two groups: spiritual or "pure" women (Dinah, Lucy, Dorothea and Mirah) and desiring women

(Hetty, Maggie, Rosamond and Gwendolen). At a glance it would seem that the second group would be good candidates for female subjects of desire but, broadly speaking, this is not so. The potential erotic impulses of all of these desiring heroines apart from Maggie (a more intricate case) are effectively neutralized, deflected and displaced into less volatile desires for either material goods or personal homage. It is true that Maggie's situation is more complicated, as I shall show in the following chapter (she genuinely desires Stephen), but it is also true that she is punished more severely than the other women in this group (and they are all punished). There are interesting complications as well in the case of Dorothea, who seems to desire Will as well as noble deeds (although, as Barrett cogently remarks, "Dorothea is marred from the first by an innocence verging at times on stupidity," 152). It is also interesting to note that only the spiritual women achieve satisfactory marriages; the desiring women remain single or participate in domestic disasters.

It is difficult to avoid the somewhat facile conclusion that in George Eliot's moral universe, erotic desire on the part of the female is a weakness to be punished, while its absence is a virtue to be rewarded. This is not precisely the conventional madonna/whore dichotomy, however. Although the female characters occur in pairs in each novel, and although these pairs divide themselves neatly into a "desiring" versus a "spiritual" woman, the narrator's reluctance to ascribe erotic impulses even to her desiring characters and an inordinate degree of passion in the spiritual characters make these oppositions more complex than we might expect.

Also, these seemingly conventional oppositions become less clearly differentiated as George Eliot's novel-writing career evolves. Over the course of her life, Eliot was drawn closer and closer to the vexed issue of female desire. There is an obvious erotic progression among the four novels, in that the desiring woman, by the end of her career, is firmly at the center of George Eliot's stage. There is a failure at the heart of this progression, however. Eliot moves from overt condemnation of the desiring female in her treatment of Hetty and Rosamond to a much gentler approach in the case of Gwendolen, but she cannot sustain the erotic implications of such a shift. Maggie, the heroine most capable of a genuine erotic impulse, is eliminated by death even though she is not overtly condemned, while Gwendolen—hardly coincidentally—is neurotically repulsed by sex, much like Hardy's Sue Bridehead.

This sustained avoidance of the erotic gives rise to the formation of a curious relationship in Eliot's novels between the narrator and the reader, who in most Victorian novels share a tacit awareness of the sexual nature of the characters' motives and actions. Post-Freudian readers are accustomed to viewing with a tolerant eye the Victorians' ingenious deflections of the erotic impulse into incestuous or lesbian effusions (such as the passionate and often very physical relationships between family members or between female friends), so that the narrator's apparent naïveté toward Maggie's inordinate fondness for Tom, for instance, hardly seems unusual.[1] But Eliot's narrator strains the bounds of such erotic innocence in her resolute disavowal of sexual awareness (her own or her characters') in her delineations of the close spiritual connections between several of her adult male and female characters (Lydgate and Dorothea, for example, or even more notably Daniel and Gwendolen).[2] It is as though the narrator herself partakes—or would like to partake—of her female characters' innocence, subtly inviting the reader to do likewise. This "zone of silence" so greatly admired by Steiner ("She would not search out the last privacy of self," 106) could be considered a flaw in Eliot's work (Hochman, for instance, thinks that "her chief problems stem not from her attempt to depict what she didn't know but rather from her reluctance to carry to the end what she knew all too well," 34).

Steiner and Hochman are both "right": George Eliot's sexual reticence can be seen as both immensely powerful and immensely annoying. What is more interesting, from my point of view, is the question of why such reticence exists in the first place. What is the ideological rationale behind the narrator's insistent protestations of erotic innocence, particularly for her female characters? I think that the key to Eliot's ambivalence on this point, and the key to the strength and failure at the heart of her achievement, is her unquestioning acceptance of the male principle of transcendence. In keeping with the values of her era, she fully endorses the notion of a "lower" (animal) self which needs to be controlled by a "higher" (spiritual) self. Although Barrett notes that by the end of her career she has "overcome the last vestiges of her early Christianity" (159), Eliot never relinquishes—or even questions—the classical opposition of mind and body. Her official narratorial stance, therefore, cannot encompass the erotic as a positive value.

As Marilyn French points out (and as I noted in Chapter One), the Platonic ideal of transcendence is quintessentially patriarchal, in that it is rooted in male fears of the body. It is her valorization of this somatophobic principle, in fact, which makes Eliot's narrator occasionally seem masculine. The ideal of transcendence is also the basis for her notion of renunciation, or "willed submission," insofar as the latter involves the subduing of a character's "lower" nature (her personal vanity, for instance; as I have noted, few of Eliot's characters have any overt erotic desire to subdue). In fact, renunciation becomes more central to George Eliot's narratives as her career progresses: of the four heroines I shall discuss, Dinah has nothing to renounce, Maggie renounces her desire but too late, Dorothea is constantly ready to renounce any personal desire she might experience, and Gwendolen learns the lesson of renunciation painfully over the course of the novel. The ideal woman, like the ideal man, transcends not only the physical but also the merely personal.

The problem, of course, particularly in the case of a writer like Eliot whose art is so powerfully evocative of a corporeal reality, is that the life she depicts in her novels—what French calls "that mass of breathing flesh, sweating pores, darting sensation, uncontrollable being (523)"—conflicts with the principle of transcendence at every turn, or at best exists only in uneasy juxtaposition with it. The strength of her novels in fact springs from this constant tension between cerebral principle and burgeoning life, between the denial of the erotic and the erotic itself. Seen in this light, neither the controlled absence nor the uncontrolled presence of the erotic in George Eliot's novels is such a mystery.

It is in the politics of the gaze that George Eliot's endorsement of male transcendence is most problematic, both for herself and for her female reader. The appreciation of beauty—the valuing of the physical—would seem to be in direct conflict with the principle of transcendence, which specifically devalues the physical. This conundrum is not unique to George Eliot, of course; it is part of the ethical perplexity of the entire century. And Eliot resolves it in the conventional patriarchal way, by relegating the attribute of beauty to the "realm of woman" and by investing it with sublime significations in an attempt to reconcile it with the concept of a "higher" nature. It is women who are appreciated for their beauty in George Eliot's novels, and in fact beauty appears to be a prerequisite in her female characters; she (disappointingly) never creates a plain heroine. In standard patriarchal fashion, the beautiful women characters in George Eliot's novels are offered as objects for the delectation of the (male) gaze: the gaze of the reader, of the narrator and of the male characters in the novel. And the erotic component of this gaze, as in much Victorian fiction, is specifically disclaimed by appeals to classical art (Dorothea is compared to Cleopatra and Ariädne, and Gwendolen is compared to Lamia, Hermione and Diana the Huntress), to religion (Dinah and Dorothea are likened to the Madonna) or simply to an amorphous notion of divine love. Women whose beauty does not signify the latter, in fact (such as Hetty and Rosamond) are severely disapproved of by the narrator. George Eliot's narrator apparently would like, along with Kenneth Clark, to be able to assess a woman's moral worth by her appearance (in his monograph *Feminine Beauty*, Clark tells us that Veronese's females "are beautiful because they are healthy and unselfconscious. We can see that they have never had a mean or malicious thought," 20). The term "unselfconscious," in particular, is significant. Used repeatedly to characterize Eliot's heroines, it connotes both a kind of selfless goodness and a child-like sexual innocence. Such disclaimers, of course, do nothing to strip Eliot's beauties of erotic appeal; as in much Victorian fiction, these protestations actually enhance the characters' eroticism while freeing the reader to enjoy it with a clear conscience. A beautiful woman is automatically at once an aesthetic object and a sexual object, and the look of desire is automatically male.

There is a discernible difference, however, between Eliot's treatment of feminine beauty and that of most male novelists of her day, in that her narrator experiences significant difficulty with the concept. In *Adam Bede*, the most scopophilic of Eliot's novels, it is abundantly clear that she is able to understand the male's appreciation of female beauty from within, as it were; the apology for Adam's mistaken evaluation of Hetty borders on religious ecstasy in its exaltation of the aesthetic delight such beauty inspires. But Eliot goes on to speculate about the validity of this delight, concluding that female beauty does not always connote selfless goodness (and she will reach the same conclusion in *Middlemarch* with regard to Rosamond). Clearly the conferral of value according to appearance does not sit well with her, incompatible as it is with the concept of bodily transcendence and unfair as it is to women who are not blessed with physical beauty. (Her own lack of beauty must have made this unfairness painfully obvious to her, even though she never creates a heroine with a similar lack; a diary entry by John Chapman gives us an inkling of her pain on this score: "I dwelt also on the incomprehensible mystery and witchery of beauty. My words jarred upon her and put an end to her enjoyment. Was it from a consciousness of her own want of beauty? She wept bitterly," Haight 172.) George Eliot's solution, however, is not to question the value of female beauty but to reinforce it by insisting that characters such as Hetty and Rosamond are exceptions, cases of false advertising, as it were, leaving in place the comfortable patriarchal equation of beauty with goodness. The seeing/seen dyad, however uneasily, is left intact in her work.

The look of desire in George Eliot's novels, then, is ineluctably male. Her female characters never look desirously at males, and they are ideally unaware that they themselves are looked at constantly. Nor do her heroines own the language of desire; not surprisingly, they participate in their creator's erotic silence, and the erotic is accordingly displaced, as I have already remarked, into extraordinarily sensual metaphor. Under these circumstances, the enactment of female desire would seem to be out of the question, and this is indeed the case. Any of her female characters' actions that could be remotely interpreted as enacting erotic desire—even passively or inadvertently—is denigrated by Eliot's narrator (as in the case of Hetty or Rosamond) or punished by the events of the novel (as in the case of Maggie or Gwendolen). That these punishments are so severe is perhaps not surprising in light of the inevitable harshness of the ideal of transcendence, which leaves no room for erotic lapses; as Susan Griffin points out, "From the moment the mind decides to deny nature through culture, it becomes committed to an ordeal of cruelty and suffering" (46). Eliot's females are by and large not permitted to make any moves in the direction of the males in the novels; instead they wait, gracefully and preferably without much sexual awareness, for the males to move toward them. This waiting bears no resemblance to that of Charlotte Brontë's heroines (it is neither as protracted nor as painful), and it merges imperceptibly into the general practice of self-renunciation that all of Eliot's heroines learn to adopt.

In terms of the erotic subjectivity of her heroines, George Eliot is clearly reactionary in comparison to Charlotte Brontë, whose (female) narrator acknowledges erotic love as desirable and who allows her plain heroines to achieve it. By not dealing with the erotic head-on, George Eliot forcibly reinscribes male values. And yet it is impossible to dismiss Eliot's novels as hopelessly patriarchal. Although she accepts wholesale some of the most damaging tenets of patriarchy—such as the need for bodily transcendence and the repudiation of the physical (including the sexual) in favor of a "higher" reality—she is deeply concerned with the needs, hopes and passions of women. The central question in all of her novels is that of how women should live, and the novels I shall discuss in this chapter are "about" issues that have a direct bearing on this question: they are novels about beauty (*Adam Bede*), love (*The Mill on the Floss*) and marriage (*Middlemarch* and *Daniel Deronda*). On the surface, her heroines never evolve beyond submission, seemingly adhering to the conventional domination/submission pattern I have been discussing. On closer examination, however, these characters are far from conventional Victorian romantic heroines. They are indubitably desiring subjects, even though their desires are (ostensibly) spiritual rather than erotic, and their submission is not to the males in the novels or to romantic love but to a variety of other external and internal forces. In short, they constitute a gallery of strong, complex and interesting women characters who appear in some of the most erotic novels of the Victorian period.

ADAM BEDE

George Eliot's first novel, *Adam Bede*, can be viewed—significantly—as as novel "about" female beauty. In this respect, it is an enormously interesting novel for feminists, for in it Eliot raises (and settles) the complex and problematic issue of female representation and objectification in ways that affect her entire canon. All of her subsequent novels rest uneasily on the highly ambivalent conclusions about female beauty that she reaches in *Adam Bede*. What these conclusions are I have already outlined; in the following pages I shall examine them in more detail.

At first glance (as it were), the narrator's well-documented scorn for Hetty's vanity would seem to constitute evidence of Eliot's incipient feminism: she seems to despise Hetty for allowing herself to be an object of the male gaze. In the scene in which Hetty dresses up in front of the mirror, for example, the narrator denigrates her for seeing herself through Arthur's eyes: "Hetty looked at herself to-night with quite a different sensation from what she had ever felt before; there was an invisible spectator whose eyes rested on her like morning on the flowers" (195). As modern feminist film critics would put it, Hetty carries her own Panopticon, seeing herself through the appraising eyes of the male. Implicit in the narrator's criticism of Hetty is a potential protest against the seeing/seen dyad in which a male subject judges a female object according to her physical appearance, and a potential encouragement for women to decline to be viewed and judged in this way.

A closer reading, however, negates both of these possibilities in favor of a decidedly non-feminist interpretation: Hetty is scorned, not for assuming so readily her position as viewed object, but for being aware of this position in the first place. Throughout Eliot's work, such awareness on the part of her heroines is consistently labeled "vanity," and it almost always signals a lack of moral feeling. Rosamond Vincy and Gwendolen Harleth are similarly self-conscious and similarly disapproved of by Eliot's narrator; Lucy Deane is a noteworthy exception, as I shall show. George Eliot seems to be saying that love of self such as Hetty displays precludes the possibility of her loving anyone else, and she makes this clear in her many references to Hetty's shallowness and hardness. Hetty has no fondness for small children in general or for Totty in particular, or for the fluffy chicks she herself is likened to, and to Eliot's mind this is damning evidence of her lack of moral worth. "People who love downy peaches are apt not to think of the stone," she says darkly, "and sometimes jar their teeth terribly against it" (198).

Dorothea Barrett makes a convincing argument that Eliot punishes both Adam and (even more severely) Lydgate in order to wreak her revenge on John Chapman and Herbert Spencer, who similarly preferred beautiful women to plain women like herself (146). This seems plausible on one level, but Eliot's underlying ideology is not quite so straightforward. Both Adam and Lydgate are punished, it is true; but the blame for their respective disasters rests in the last instance not with them but with the beautiful women who entrap them. These women characters, Hetty and Rosamond, are faulted on two counts: for being aware of the power of their beauty, and for using that power. What such characters "should" be like is indicated in the narrator's elaborate apology for Adam's "mistake" in loving Hetty.

This apology consists of several bursts of narratorial polemic that are scattered throughout the text. Immediately after the description of Hetty's solitary fashion show in front of the mirror, for instance, the narrator reflects at length: "Ah, what a prize the man gets who wins a sweet bride like Hetty! . . . The dear young, round, soft, flexible thing! Her heart must be just as soft, her temper just as free from angles, her character just as pliant. . . . Those kitten-like glances and movements are just what one wants to make one's hearth a paradise" (197). The venom that fuels this is unmistakable, and the heavy irony underlines the foolishness of the male who would make such an error of judgment. Adam's mistake in this scene, we may note, prefigures the folly of Lydgate, who also thinks to make his "hearth a paradise" in this way. Underlying the venom and the irony, however, is the disappointment of an unmet ideal, the ideal of the beautiful woman whose heart *is* soft, whose temper *is* free from angles, and whose character *is* pliant. The implication might be that all women should have these characteristics, but the narrator goes on to explore the significations of the beautiful woman in particular:

Every man under such circumstances is conscious of being a great physiognomist. Nature, he knows, has a language of her own, which she uses with strict veracity, and he considers himself an adept in the language. Nature has written out his bride's character for him in those exquisite lines of cheek and lip and chin, in those eyelids delicate as petals, in those long lashes curled like the stamen of a flower, in the dark liquid depths of those wonderful eyes. How she will dote on her children! She is almost a child herself, and the little pink round things will hang about her like florets round the central flower. . . .
    It was very much in this way that our friend Adam Bede thought about Hetty. (197–98)

This puts in place another segment of the ideal: the beautiful woman should dote on her children.
    Up to this point, Eliot's narrator stands aside from such errors as Adam's, shaking "his" head with an air of sorrowful superiority over the folly of such idealization. He does not maintain this stance, however; the logical extension of this train of thought would have produced very different novels from the ones George Eliot in fact wrote, novels in which the hero, having learned his hard lessons about the potential vanity and selfishness of beautiful women and his own woeful inadequacy as a "physiognomist," goes on to achieve true happiness with a less-than-beautiful partner. (Charlotte Brontë's *Jane Eyre*, we will recall, enacts this very scenario.) But Eliot's narrator, it seems, is deeply ambivalent about such a logical progression. His tone changes abruptly from heavy irony to thoughtful seriousness as he pursues the matter further:

After all, I believe the wisest of us must be beguiled in this way sometimes. . . . Nature has her language, and she is not unveracious; but we don't know all the intricacies of her syntax just yet, and in a hasty reading we may happen to extract the very opposite of her real meaning. Long dark eyelashes, now: what can be more exquisite? I find it impossible not to expect some depth of soul behind a deep grey eye with a long dark eyelash, in spite of an experience which has shown me that they may go along with deceit, peculation, and stupidity. . . . One begins to suspect at length that there is no direct correlation between eyelashes and morals. (198–99)

Despite the last sentence, it is clear that this narrator—who sounds masculine at this point simply by virtue of his inclusion in the "we" who are doing the looking—remains unconvinced about the invalidity of the beauty/goodness connection. Nature is "not unveracious" in her language of beauty; it is we who make mistakes because of our "hasty reading" of this language.

Adam (and all who make such mistakes) is further exonerated from blame by the phrase "the wisest of us," a phrase that is echoed in a later, still more thoughtful passage in which the narrator speculates that it is "the noblest nature [that] sees the most of this . . . expression in beauty." This lengthy passage begins with the ironic observation, "Of course, I know that, as a rule, sensible men fall in love with the most sensible women of their acquaintance, see through all the pretty deceits of coquettish beauty, never imagine themselves loved when they are not loved, cease loving on all proper occasions, and marry the woman most fitted for them in every respect." Again, however, such tongue-in-cheek musing becomes serious, turning into an extended aside to the reader on the nature of female beauty. The narrator's use of the first person lends weight and credence to the speculations in this aside, and I think it is worth quoting at length:

For my own part, . . . I respect [Adam] none the less: nay, I think the deep love he had for that sweet, rounded, blossom-like, dark-eyed Hetty . . . came out of the very strength of his nature, and not out of any inconsistent weakness. Is it any weakness, pray, to be wrought on by exquisite music—to feel its wondrous harmonies searching the subtlest windings of your soul, the delicate fibres of life where no memory can penetrate, and binding together your whole being past and present in one unspeakable vibration: melting you in one moment with all the tenderness, all the love that has been scattered through the toilsome years, concentrating in one emotion of heroic courage or resignation all the hard-learnt lessons of self-renouncing sympathy, blending your present joy with past sorrow, and your present sorrow with all your past joy? If not, then neither is it a weakness to be so wrought upon by the exquisite curves of a woman's cheek and neck and arms, by the liquid depths of her beseeching eyes, or the sweet childish pout of her lips. For the beauty of a lovely woman is like music: what can one say more? Beauty has an expression beyond and far above the one woman's soul that it clothes, as the words of genius have a wider meaning than the thought that prompted them: it is more than a woman's love that moves us in a woman's eyes—it seems to be a far-off mighty love that has come near to us, and made speech for itself there; the rounded neck, the dimpled arm, move us by something more than their prettiness—by their close kinship with all we have known of tenderness and peace. The noblest nature sees the most of this *impersonal* expression in beauty. . . , and for this reason, the noblest nature is often the most blinded to the character of the one woman's soul that the beauty clothes. Whence, I fear, the tragedy of human life is likely to continue for a long time to come. (399–400)

Several points emerge from this effusion. First of all, it articulates an objectification of the female so complete as to leave no doubt as to the gender of the narrator: what we have here is a woman writer adopting the perspective of the sex that "matters" and thinking, feeling and writing as a man. It can only be a male—or an honorary male—who speculates thus about the effect of female beauty on the observer in such profound and poetic terms, as it is tacitly assumed that the observer is male ("it is more than a woman's love that moves us"). Second, in true Victorian fashion, the sexual response is immediately subsumed in and justified by the aesthetic response (the response of the observer's "higher nature") in order to transcend the physical. In other words, Hetty is simultaneously a sexual and an aesthetic object to Adam, whose keen appreciation of her is laudable in precisely the way that a sensitive connoisseur's appreciation of a piece of music is laudable; only the "noblest natures" are capable of such appreciation. Further, the aesthetic blends imperceptibly with the religious in a combined response that gives rise to the rapture with which the passage is imbued: a beautiful woman reminds us of "a far-off mighty love," of "all we have known of tenderness and peace." And finally, the narrator openly acknowledges—emphasizes, in fact—the "impersonal" nature of such a response. The sight of a beautiful woman evokes responses in the male observer that have nothing to do with her as a person; she is a signifier for a kind of divine or maternal goodness. This is a striking instance of Kaja Silverman's observation that "the structuration of the female subject begins not with her entry into language, . . . but with the organization of her body. That body is charted, zoned and made to bear meaning, a meaning which proceeds entirely from external relationships" ("*Histoire d'O*" 325).

The poetic intensity of the passage as a whole reveals much about George Eliot's approach to the politics of the seeing/seen dyad. Despite the acknowledgment of the potential folly of this approach in the last sentence of the passage, it is clear that she basically endorses the idealization of beautiful women . She is able to understand and appreciate the male gaze from within, identifying not with the female object but with the male subject. Undoubtedly this male identification is at the root of much recent and conflicting speculation as to the gender of George Eliot's narrators, a truly intriguing question to which there is ultimately no satisfactory answer.

We can see, then, that a beautiful woman, in George Eliot's schema, should signify exactly what the male needs her to signify in the domination/submission hierarchy: she should be a suitably reluctant object who at once symbolizes sexuality and a reassuringly "safe" denial of it, and who confers "tenderness and peace" once she finally yields to the male's desire. In fact, a beautiful woman who fails to signify these things (like Hetty and later Rosamond) is culpable, fraudulent, almost a case of false advertising. On her head, rather than on that of the appraising male, rests the responsibility for "the tragedy of human life." Needless to say, such a view is deeply conservative, questioning neither the standard position of the woman in the traditional subject/object configuration nor the configuration itself. George Eliot was to modify considerably her views on female beauty by the end of her career; but she never fully abandoned the patriarchal vision of a beautiful female offering up her divine maternal goodness to an adoring male.

As we might expect, the look of desire is immensely important in the relations between women and men in George Eliot's novels, and particularly in *Adam Bede*, which is undoubtedly the most scopophilic of them. As we also might expect, this look is monopolized almost exclusively by the male characters as well as by the male-identified narrator. We are given endless descriptions of Hetty, and several of Dinah, all from the point of view of an appreciative male observer. The descriptions of Hetty, in fact, constitute a virtual orgy of description, a perfect instance of Laura Mulvey's "fetishistic scopophilia" (which, as we may recall, masters castration threats by investing the woman's body with an excess of aesthetic perfection). As Helena Michie points out, these descriptions, like film close-ups, have "a life and erotic energy of [their] own" (85). This agglomeration of authorial description, as much as the narrator's polemic, betrays Eliot's patriarchal bias. The tone in which these descriptions is rendered is at once enormously condescending and enormously worshipful, a familiar combination in the domination/submission hierarchy. Hetty is constantly trivialized by comparing her to babies of all species (calves, ducklings, kittens, birds, butterflies, puppies, chicks, lambs, humans) and occasionally to fruit and flowers. The narrator's epithets for her, which usually include the qualifiers "little" and "foolish" (as in "little puss," 197, and "foolish child," 316) parallel Arthur's terms of endearment (speaking to her "as if she were a bright-eyed spaniel with a thorn in her foot," he at one sitting calls her "you little frightened bird! little tearful rose! silly pet!" 182). The more general terms "thing" and "creature" are perhaps the most telling, as they obviously suggest both the inanimate and the bestial, even though they are usually paired with laudatory adjectives (as in "dear, young, round, soft, flexible thing," 197, and "pretty round creature," 295). George Eliot's insistence that "all intelligent mammals, even . . . women" would appreciate this kind of innocent beauty is obviously designed to defuse any erotic charge inherent in such descriptions, but it is followed by a curiously violent and disturbing image; she calls such cuteness "a beauty with which you can never be angry, but that you feel ready to crush for inability to comprehend the state of mind into which it throws you" (127). "You" could presumably never be angry with this beauty because of its helplessness and innocence, but on the other hand "it" is paradoxically active and dangerous, throwing the "you" into a state of mind that "it" does not understand.

Side by side with this dismissive condescension is an almost ecstatic acclamation of Hetty's physical beauty. As in many Victorian novels, the first description of her is the most complete and the most significant, setting the stage for what is to follow. As Juliet McMaster points out, the enormously sensual description of Mrs. Poyser's dairy with which Chapter Seven begins is an important part of the description of Hetty which it introduces. The sensuality of the "coolness, . . . purity, . . . fresh fragrance of new-pressed cheese, of firm butter, of wooden vessels perpetually bathed in pure water; . . . soft colouring of red earthenware and creamy surfaces, brown wood and polished tin, grey limestone and rich orange-red rust on the iron weights and hooks and hinges" (127) is a perfect analogue for Hetty's sensuality, just as Hardy's "oozing fatness and warm ferments of the Var Vale" would be for Tess's sensuality nearly four decades later.

And, just as in Hardy's novel, the pleasure we derive from the lush heroine descriptions in *Adam Bede* is slightly uncomfortable for female readers, requiring them to exercise the "double vision" outlined by Jonathan Culler ("Women . . . have read as men. . . . To ask a woman to read as a woman is in fact a double or divided request," 49) and by feminist film critics such as Teresa de Lauretis ("Women spectators are engaged in a twofold . . . identification . . . with the gaze . . . and . . . with the image," 144) and Mary Ann Doane ("The female spectator is . . . imaged by its text as . . . a hermaphrodite," 19). As readers we must participate in the perspective of the male viewer of female beauty, just as George Eliot's narrator does, a fact that underlines the feminist observation that women have traditionally both read and written as men. Our only other option is to identify with the female object of the gaze, which in Hetty's case is extremely difficult to do as a result of the narrator's constant denigration and infantilization of her.

The actual description of Hetty herself is a Victorian set-piece, one of Helena Michie's "cysts" or "ornaments," containing the usual amount of fragmentary detail: "It is of little use for me to tell you that Hetty's cheek was like a rose-petal, that dimples played about her pouting lips, that her large dark eyes hid a soft roguishness under their long lashes, and that her curly hair . . . stole back in dark delicate rings on her forehead, and about her white shell-like ears" (128). The narrator is right; such standard fragments are "of little use" in making us "see" Hetty. The description of her butter-making, as McMaster also points out, is more interesting, partly because of the "borrowed" sensuality it derives from the earlier description of the dairy itself:

They are the prettiest attitudes and movements into which a pretty girl is thrown in making up butter—tossing movements that give a charming curve to the arm, and a sideward inclination of the round white neck; little patting and rolling movements with the palm of the hand, and nice adaptations and finishings which cannot at all be effected without a great play of the pouting mouth and the dark eyes. And then the butter itself seems to communicate a fresh charm—it is so pure, so sweet-scented; it is turned off the mould with such a beautiful firm surface, like marble in a pale yellow light! (129)

The eroticism of this is also partly derived from the participles ("tossing," "charming," "patting," "rolling," "finishing" and "pouting" nicely confuse sensual butter-making actions with sensual heroine description) and from the blurring of the linguistic boundary between Hetty and the butter itself (both are by association "pure" and "sweet-scented" and have "such a beautiful firm surface").

At least part of the culpability of this innocent young thing for the tragedy that follows derives from her awareness of the effect of her beauty on the observer, and on Arthur in particular, which is indicated by her flirtatious glances in his direction. She is not a full-fledged seductress like Rosamond, but even when we first see her she has "a self-possessed, coquettish air, slily conscious that no turn of her head was lost" (127) and looks at Arthur with "a half-shy, half-coquettish glance" (129). This glance, in particular, is Arthur's undoing, which is not surprising in such a visually oriented novel. She does not exactly appropriate the look of desire from its proper male preserve, but she does look at Arthur in ways that suggest surrender and helplessness, automatically calling into play the highly charged domination/submission hierarchy. When they meet for the first time in the woods, Arthur "actually dared not look at this little buttermaker for the first minute or two" (176), and with good reason. When he does look at her ("with a look of coaxing entreaty"), the result is electric: "Hetty lifted her long dewy lashes, and met the eyes that were bent towards her with a sweet, timid, beseeching look," and Arthur is doomed. The narrator takes this opportunity to reflect that "love is such a simple thing when we have only one-and-twenty summers and a sweet girl of seventeen trembles under our glance" (177), reinforcing the male perspective in the scene and underlining the fact that it is Arthur's glance that is active, while Hetty's is merely a response—but a response that should not be made. It causes Arthur to forget the inappropriateness of any relationship between them ("While Arthur gazed into Hetty's dark beseeching eyes, it made no difference to him what sort of English she spoke," 177–78), setting the stage for the disastrous events of the rest of the novel. The female should not only refrain from looking, but she should refrain from looking back.

Arthur is implicitly exonerated in all of their lovemaking scenes by the stock defense of the beguiled male; it is suggested throughout that "he couldn't help it." When Hetty "looked up at him with two great drops rolling down her cheeks," the narrator asks, "What else could he do but speak to her in a soft, soothing tone?," and when she "slowly got courage to lift her eyes to him," we are told, "That look was too much: he must have had eyes of Egyptian granite not to look too lovingly in return" (182). There is irony here, but not much; the truth of such protestations is reinforced by the vivid descriptions of Hetty's irresistibility I noted earlier. Perhaps the most damning aspect of Hetty's passive seduction, in the ideological complexities of the novel, is its disruption of the domination/submission hierarchy—not laudably, as in Charlotte Brontë's novels, but improperly. Partaking in the terrible passive power that Rosamond will later hone to perfection, Hetty's flirting causes the males in the novel to be mastered by their feelings for her and to lose control (domination) in ways that disrupt the entire social structure. Arthur feels "as if his horse had wheeled round from a leap, and dared to dispute his mastery. He was dissatisfied with himself, irritated, mortified" (183), and Adam reflects, "It's a strange thing to think of a man as can lift a chair with his teeth, and walk fifty mile on end trembling and turning hot and cold at only a look from one woman out of all the rest i' the world" (168). The seductive woman, in this view, has much to answer for.

For all the erotic metaphor surrounding her, however, it is important to note that Hetty herself never assumes the position of the subject of desire, not even in her thoughts. The narrator speaks of "the sweet intoxication of young love," but goes on to emphasize that "Hetty's dreams were all of luxuries: to sit in a carpeted parlour and always wear white stockings; to have some large beautiful earrings, . . . to have Nottingham lace round the top of her gown, and something to make her handkerchief smell nice. . . . She thought, if Adam had been rich and could have given her these things, she loved him well enough to marry him" (144). Even after she is involved with Arthur, the narrator makes it clear that she admires the earrings he has given her for their own sake and not for what they represent ("She was not thinking most of the giver when she smiled at the earrings, for now she is taking them out of the box, not to press them to her lips, but to fasten them in her ears," 295). Similarly, the narrator refers to Hetty's feeling for Arthur as "another passion; only a little less strong than her love of finery" (296). Such avowals have the effect of emphasizing Hetty's shallowness (her vanity eclipses every other impulse) and also of disavowing any erotic desire on her part. It is as though George Eliot could not bear to make even Hetty, whom she openly despises, into a scarlet woman; she is supposed to strike the reader as foolish, certainly, but not evil—as she would if she acted out of sexual desire.

The proper conduct for a beautiful woman in *Adam Bede* is exemplified in the character of Dinah, who would never think of flirting. Indeed, she is unconscious of her own beauty, a trait that becomes the hallmark of a morally good woman in George Eliot's later novels: Maggie, Dorothea and Mirah will all follow this pattern. The dichotomy in her women characters that critics have sensed throughout Eliot's canon, in fact, could be said to rest on this distinction. Barrett calls this dichotomy "the vain/soulful paradigm" (34); William Myers refers to George Eliot's polarization of "passion and vanity" (139). However the other term is characterized, "vanity" or the awareness of her own beauty seems to be the defining and damning characteristic of the foolish or morally reprehensible woman in Eliot's work. These categories are quite independent of the categories I outlined earlier, of desiring and non-desiring female characters; Maggie, for instance, is clearly a desiring heroine but not a "vain" one.

In any event, Dinah is described as having a "total absence of self-con-sciousness in her demeanour" and as being "as unconscious of her outward appearance as a little boy" (66). Her preaching, too, is characterized by the term "boyish" ("The simple things she said seemed like novelties, as a melody strikes us with a new feeling when we hear it sung by the pure voice of a boyish chorister," 71), obviously in order to emphasize her lack of erotic desire as well as the child-like candor so admired by Eliot. But the narrator leaves no doubt as to Dinah's physical beauty, outlining it in as much detail (albeit in a more restrained tone) as the first "portrait" of Hetty:

[Dinah's] was a small oval face, of a uniform transparent whiteness, with an egg-like line of cheek and chin, a full but firm mouth, a delicate nostril, and a low perpen-dicular brow, surmounted by a rising arch of parting, between smooth locks of pale reddish hair. . . . The eyebrows, of the same colour as the hair, were perfectly horizontal and firmly pencilled; the eyelashes, though no darker, were long and abundant. . . . It was one of those faces that make one think of white flowers with light touches of colour on their pure petals. (67)

This is stripped of the lushness which saturates the descriptions of Hetty throughout the novel (of which there are many). Instead, it projects a kind of austere delicacy which renders the usual disclaimers of erotic attraction unnecessary; while Hetty's beauty is compared at length to music in the way I have already noted, Dinah's is merely likened briefly to "white flowers" with "pure petals."

Dinah's beauty, however de-eroticized, maintains a place similar to Hetty's in the scopic economy of the novel, in that it makes her a fit object of the male gaze. Her relationship with Adam, categorized as implausible by many critics, is nevertheless erotically prefigured by a scene earlier in the novel in which Adam "sees" her (appraises her aesthetically and sexually) for the first time. Dinah has come to help Lisbeth, and Adam, hearing her on the stairs, thinks it might be Hetty. When he sees Dinah instead,

It was like dreaming of the sunshine, and awakening in the moonlight. . . . Her slim figure, her plain black gown, and her pale serene face, impressed him with all the force that belongs to a reality contrasted with a preoccupying fancy. . . . He . . . looked at her with the concentrated, examining glance which a man gives to an object in which he has suddenly begun to be interested. Dinah, for the first time in her life, felt a painful self-consciousness; there was something in the dark penetrat-ing glance of this strong man so different from the mildness and timidity of his brother Seth. A faint blush came, which deepened as she wondered at it. This blush recalled Adam from his forgetfulness. (161–62)

Here we have what could be described as the quintessential gaze of the male subject directed toward the female object in the nineteenth-century novel, condensed and encapsulated. Adam's "preoccupying fantasy" of

Hetty's image gives way to what can only be a new fantasy, that of "an *object* in which he has suddenly begun to be interested" (emphasis added). His "dark penetrating glance," that of a "strong man" (in contrast to a "mild" and "timid" one), is at once sexual and appraising. It causes Dinah ("for the first time in her life"—the object is pristine) to be aware of both the surveyed and the surveyor in herself; she experiences "a painful self-consciousness" as she receives it. She does not gaze back (she is the object, not the subject, of desire), and not looking is combined with not speaking. Her only response—the stock Victorian response—is to blush, a signally passive, almost wholly involuntary reaction. The syntax of the passage underlines this passivity: it is not Dinah who (actively) blushes, but the blush itself which "came" and "deepened." All she can do is (passively) to "wonder" at it.

Thus Dinah takes her place unobtrusively but firmly in the seeing/seen dyad, which, as we have seen, is such an integral part of the erotic domination/submission hierarchy. Although she has all the hallmarks of a female subject (her career, her intelligence, her independence), in matters of the heart Dinah remains an object, to be viewed, appraised, wooed and won by the male subject of the novel. (It is hardly surprising, in this view, that Adam later explicitly likens Dinah to an object: "She's a rare bit o' workmanship. You don't see such women turned off the wheel every day," 185.) In the love scenes that eventually transpire between her and Adam, Dinah is similarly passive. When Adam finally declares his love for her, "Dinah's lips became pale, like her cheeks, and she trembled violently under the shock of painful joy. Her hands were cold as death between Adam's. She could not draw them away, because he held them fast." Here Dinah enacts the part of the appropriately reluctant object, growing pale, trembling and attempting to pull away from the desiring male subject. When he entreats her to tell him that she loves him, she trembles and cries, and when she answers it is to tell him she cannot be his lover. "The tears were trembling in Dinah's eyes, and they fell before she could answer. But she spoke in a quiet low voice . . . 'We must part' " (551). And when she does speak her desire for Adam (after much persuasion), it is in terms of submission and dependence: "The thought of you had *taken hold of me,* so that my soul had *lost its freedom,* and was *becoming enslaved* to an earthly affection. . . . My heart waits on your words and looks, almost as a little child waits on the help and tenderness of the strong on whom it *depends"* (553, 555, my emphasis). Dinah, like many of George Eliot's strong and spiritual heroines who follow her, disappointingly owns neither the look nor the language of desire, and the enactment of desire accordingly appears to be out of the question for her.

Adam Bede is a novel about beauty, and it is also, by extension, a novel about love. The contrast between Hetty and Dinah is instructive in this context as well. William Myers, making a case for the equation of passion and renunciation in George Eliot's novels, notes a distinction between the lovemaking scenes of Hetty and Arthur on one hand and of Dinah and Adam on the other to illustrate his point. Hetty and Arthur's first encounter provokes the narrator to compare them to "two velvet peaches that touch softly and are at rest; they mingle as easily as two brooklets that ask for nothing but to entwine themselves and ripple with ever-interlacing curves in the leafiest hiding-places" (177). Dinah and Adam, by contrast, are likened to "two little quivering rain-streams, before they mingle into one. . . . Those slight words and looks and touches are part of the soul's language. . . . They happen to be the signs of something unspeakably great and beautiful" (537). Myers points out that "The parallels between the two passages are evidently carefully worked, and one can only conclude that the passion of the altruistic lovers has been deliberately emptied of erotic content" (138).

Myers' point is a good one, and the two passages constitute a good example of how the erotic in George Eliot's novels resides almost exclusively in their figurative language. The Hetty/Arthur passage is saturated with suggestive imagery. The "two velvet peaches" that "touch softly and are at rest" is an enormously tactile image, suggestive only obliquely of the peach juice beneath the velvet surfaces, and the "two brooklets" exhibit markedly lover-like behavior (mingling, entwining, rippling, interlacing, hiding). The two brooks of the Dinah/Adam passage are indeed described much differently, appearing quite meager by contrast. "Little" and "quivering" connote childishness and timidity as opposed to adult fullness, and the image is quickly referred to the realm of the abstract, the cerebral, the transcendental: the "slight words and looks and touches" are valued not for themselves but as "signs of something unspeakably great and beautiful." To modify Homans's terms, the two passages embody a shift from the feminine literal to the masculine symbolic, even though both are couched in metaphor.

These two scenes, in fact, are a perfect example of the tension that informs *Adam Bede*, a tension that is a reflection, as critics have suggested, of Eliot's own deep ambivalence. On the symbolic level, the novel makes a clear statement about the nature of love: it is "hardly distinguishable from religious feeling. . . . At its highest flood [it] rushes beyond its object, and loses itself in the sense of divine mystery" (81). But on the literal level, this message is all but eclipsed, not only by the lush descriptions I have noted, but also by the seeming paucity of the non-erotic alternative. When the two women are together in Hetty's bedroom, for instance, Dinah is compared to "a lovely corpse into which the soul has returned charged with sublimer secrets" (204), which even apart from its necrophilic connotations is a "deadening" image. Likewise, when Hetty wishes, too late, that she "could have had the past undone, and known no other love than her quiet liking for Adam" (413), the reader intuits how lifeless this mundane alternative would seem (as similar regrets by Maggie about Philip seem in *The Mill on the Floss*). There is a discrepancy between what George Eliot tells us and what she shows us about love in *Adam Bede*, just as there is between what she tells and shows us about beauty. Even the narrator's musing about second love ("How is it that the poets have said so many fine things about our first love, so few about our later love? Are their first poems their best? or are not those the best which come from their fuller thought, their larger experience, their deeper-rooted affections?" 547) seems to contradict the avowed preference for loyalty to child-like first attachments.

We can see, then, that *Adam Bede* is an extremely erotic novel, but in an extremely oblique, "Victorian" way. The elevated polemic (of which Dinah and Adam's relationship seems to be a part) is continually eclipsed by the throbbing life of the erotically charged descriptive language. This does not, however, point to a rebellious or iconoclastic novel. The eroticism with which the figurative language is imbued is utterly conventional, as I have shown, conforming exactly to the traditional domination/submission paradigm. Not surprisingly, there is no female subject of desire in these pages: Hetty is an object rather than a subject, and while Dinah is a subject, she is not a subject of desire. (This is a dichotomy that will begin to blur as George Eliot's career progresses: it will become more and more difficult to divide Eliot's women characters neatly into subjects and objects.) Neither character owns the look or the language of desire, and neither seems to feel any erotic desire to enact. In *Adam Bede* we find none of the feminist frustration and exasperation with the sexual status quo that we find in Charlotte Brontë's novels, for example, in which the heroines frequently rail against enforced feminine passivity. Nor does Eliot ever objectify her male characters as Brontë does, seeing and appraising them from the female's point of view. Eliot's female characters in *Adam Bede* exist in a traditional patriarchal world, in which the only erotic desire is male.

THE MILL ON THE FLOSS

The Mill on the Floss is in many ways unique in George Eliot's canon, and several of its distinctive characteristics have a direct bearing on the question of Eliot's feminism. It is the only one of her novels to deal extensively with childhood, for example, and with its all-pervasive influence on adult complexities. Also, it deals directly with male-female oppositions in a way that throws into doubt Eliot's uneasy espousal of the male principle of transcendence, making this a potential turning point in her career. While her other novels emphasize the desirability of a single moral standard for men and women, *The Mill on the Floss* contains an incipient protest against the fact that this standard privileges the patriarchal values of duty and rational responsibility over the more relational values of love and feeling. As it turns out, the protest is stifled and the patriarchy "wins"; but it is an ambivalent victory that barely conceals a great deal of feminist anger, exacerbating rather than resolving Eliot's feminist perplexity with the entire issue. Finally, and perhaps most significantly, there is no sharp dichotomy between the women characters in *The Mill on the Floss* as there is in most of George Eliot's other novels. Maggie and Lucy do not represent a desiring and a spiritual woman, a vain and a selfless woman, or any other set of female oppositions. This enables Maggie to emerge as a desiring woman who is also spiritual, a seemingly ideal candidate as a female subject of desire. Though the latter construct remains largely a possibility rather than an actuality, like the novel's submerged protest against patriarchal values, these truncated possibilities are extremely tantalizing, both for themselves and for the glimpses they afford us of Eliot's ideological struggle. In the following discussion I shall attempt to outline in some detail the feminist ramifications of several aspects of this struggle.

Given the importance and complexity of the issue of female beauty in *Adam Bede*, published only a year earlier, perhaps a logical place to begin my discussion of *The Mill on the Floss* is with the beauty of its two heroines. Maggie and Lucy, like Dinah and Hetty, are both beautiful; but there are striking differences in Eliot's treatment of female beauty between the two novels. First of all, it is immediately apparent that there are many fewer physical descriptions of the heroines in *The Mill on the Floss*. The moments in which the narrator invites the reader to step back and contemplate the details of her characters' appearance, moments of spectacle or iconicity which momentarily halt the flow of the narrative, are conspicuously sparser in the later novel, with the result that the novel itself is much less scopophilic than its predecessor. This marks a genuine advance in Eliot's presentation of female subjects; as I have shown, Hetty (and even Dinah, to some extent) is objectified aesthetically and sexually to the point where any potential subjectivity on her part is out of the question. This is not to say that the gaze is not important in *The Mill on the Floss*—it is, but in an entirely different context, as I shall show.

Nor is the question of female vanity completely laid to rest. As in *Adam Bede* (and in all of Eliot's novels to some degree) a female character's beauty signals a concomitant potential for vanity, unless the character is unconscious of her beauty. Dinah, Dorothea and Mirah fall into the latter category, for instance, while Hetty, Rosamond and Gwendolen—all keenly aware of their appearance and its effect on the observer—are denigrated by the narrator to various extents for their shallowness. *The Mill on the Floss* represents an interesting departure from this pattern, in that neither Maggie nor Lucy is similarly denigrated, despite the fact that they are both aware of their own attractiveness. Maggie is relatively easy for the narrator to exonerate from the charge of vanity, simply because she is relatively unconscious of her beauty until she meets Stephen and by then the habits of a lifetime prevent her from becoming preoccupied with it. On the day of the church bazaar, we are told of her "satisfactory consciousness which had necessarily come from being taken before Lucy's cheval-glass, and made to look at the full length of her tall beauty, crowned by the night of her massy hair" (383). Significantly, she is "taken" before the glass and "made to look" at her reflection, which nicely draws to the reader's attention both her beauty and her natural modesty, without negating her pleasure in the former. "Maggie had smiled at herself then," we are told,

and for the moment had forgotten everything in the sense of her own beauty. If that state of mind could have lasted, her choice would have been to have Stephen Guest at her feet, offering her a life filled with all luxuries, with daily incense of adoration near and distant. . . . But there were things in her stronger than vanity—passion, and affection, and long deep memories of early discipline and effort, of early claims on her love and pity; and the stream of vanity was soon swept along and mingled imperceptibly with that wider current. (383)

Maggie's vanity, then, is only momentary and is easily quelled by her transcendent self, a self which includes passion, we may note; as William Myers points out, "passion" in George Eliot's lexicon is sometimes to be distinguished from "the intoxicating egoism of young love" (139). More specifically, it is often to be distinguished from any sort of mature erotic desire, as I shall show.

Lucy, the less complex of the two attractive women, has a larger share of "vanity" than Maggie and is therefore somewhat more difficult to absolve. Intellectually Maggie's inferior and quite conscious of her own beauty, Lucy is potentially the parallel of Hetty and later of Rosamond. Obviously, though, there is a huge difference between her "place" in the novel and theirs, as she earns none of the extreme narratorial disapprobation that attends both Hetty and Rosamond. Unlike them, she is not judged to be shallow. To see why this is so, it is necessary to examine a somewhat lengthy passage illuminating her awareness of herself as a beautiful object. After Stephen leaves her sitting-room, where the two lovers have been flirting, the narrator says in a confidential aside to the reader,

You will not, I hope, consider it an indication of vanity predominating over more tender impulses, that she just glanced in the chimney-glass as her walk brought her near it. The desire to know that one has not looked an absolute fright during a few hours of conversation, may be construed as lying within the bounds of a laudable benevolent consideration for others. And Lucy had so much of this benevolence in her nature that I am inclined to think her small egoisms were impregnated with it, just as there are people not altogether unknown to you, whose small benevolences have a predominant and somewhat rank odour of egoism. Even now, that she is walking up and down with a little triumphant flutter of her girlish heart at the sense that she is loved by the person of chief consequence in her small world, you may see in her hazel eyes an ever-present sunny benignity, in which the momentary harmless flashes of personal vanity are quite lost; and if she is happy in thinking of her lover, it is because the thought of him mingles readily with all the gentle affections and good-natured offices with which she fills her peaceful days. (324–25)

How different this is from the narrator's severe condemnation of Hetty, even though the "triumphant flutter of her girlish heart that she is loved by the person of chief consequence in her small world" might just as easily describe the latter. Hetty's preening, so severely dealt with, is in Lucy benevolently dismissed, for some reason, as "momentary harmless flashes of personal vanity." What makes Lucy so blameless, and Hetty so culpable, within the confines of each novel? It is not only that Lucy's lover is "suitable" while Hetty's is not—Rosamond will be found just as culpable as Hetty, even though Lydgate is just as "suitable" as Stephen. Rather, it is because of her "ever present sunny benignity," her "gentle affections and good-natured offices" that Lucy's awareness of her own beauty is so gently excused. Unlike Hetty, she is a "true" signifier, a beautiful woman whose beauty signifies what it is supposed to signify, a sort of universal loving-kindness (also unlike Hetty, for instance, "she was fond of feeding dependent creatures, and knew the private tastes of all the animals about the house, delighting in the little rippling sounds of her canaries . . . and in the small nibbling pleasure of . . . 'the more familiar rodents,' " 325). This quality of Lucy's serves to emphasize the moral dilemma in the novel, of course; but the narrator's difficulty in reconciling it with even a touch of "vanity" is evident, as her lengthy apology indicates.

Nevertheless, this blurring in *The Mill on the Floss* of Eliot's customary distinction between the spiritual and the vain woman seems to indicate a wavering in her application of the ideal of transcendence, making room for a more exploratory approach to the question of female desire. For so long as a "good" woman must remain unaware of her own beauty, she must also remain a sexual object, an icon of goodness to be desired and pursued by the male, unaware of (and therefore not in control of) her own sexuality. A vain female character can at least desire to be desired by the male, in obvious conformity to the standard subject/object configuration, while an oblivious one is unable to encompass erotic desire of any kind. Charlotte Brontë, we will recall, went so far as to reverse the seeing/seen dyad, permitting her heroines to experience their own scopophilic desire in relation to the males in her novels. George Eliot does not go this far, but in the character of Maggie she at least acknowledges that the spiritual woman does not have to be completely unaware of her own erotic potential.

Maggie, then, represents George Eliot's closest approximation of a female subject of desire, and as such she is a dangerous character in the Eliot canon, possessing the power to question and disrupt patriarchal values in a way that clearly makes her creator uneasy. Barrett characterizes Eliot's relation to Maggie as "extremely ambivalent," providing "the central tension of the work" (53), and several critics have commented on Maggie's demonism, a further sign of ambivalence.[3] In fact, Maggie is a disturbing creation, a disorderly and disruptive female force whose presence challenges patriarchal tenets—including those championed by Eliot—more directly than any of her other heroines. If Hetty's story intimates a submerged reading of *Adam Bede*, a reading that exists in opposition to the novel's received polemic, in *The Mill on the Floss* this contrary reading has risen to the surface. There is an even more pronounced discrepancy in the later novel between what Eliot's narrator tells us and what she shows us, and these two readings are fairly evenly balanced, giving rise to the truly ambivalent and conflicting interpretations which the novel has always occasioned. On one hand the narrator valorizes the patriarchal ideal of transcendence, which forms an integral part of Eliot's system of values, but on the other hand the character of Maggie, a being who functions according to a system entirely at odds with the law of the fathers, exists as a dramatic refutation of this ideal. The novel's implied reproof (to Tom, and to all such male lawgivers) lies in the fact that it is Maggie's best qualities that prevent her from attaining success in patriarchal terms.

Among Maggie's appealing qualities is one that makes her perhaps the most human and likable of George Eliot's heroines: her emotionality, what the narrator terms her "passion." Dorothea, too, has something the narrator terms "ardour," but in her case it seems to be a spiritual rather than a simply human quality, too ethereal to invite identification. Maggie's passion, on the other hand, is much more prosaic, almost always bound up with her relationships with other people and particularly with her need for affection. That this need is sometimes destructive is indicated early in the novel in the description of her doll, on whom she lavishes "so many warm kisses . . . that the waxen cheeks had a wasted unhealthy appearance" (17). It can even drive her to violence, as we can see in her treatment of her Fetish, into whose head she pounds nails and with which she "soothe[s] herself by alternately grinding and beating the wooden head against the rough brick of the great chimneys" (25). It is interesting, and part of the disruptive matrix of the novel, that Maggie's emotionality springs from her feminine nature and yet manifests itself in ways that are often aggressive and conventionally masculine. Maggie is tender-hearted and vulnerable, needing love in order to survive, yet she is no demure maiden; she is at least as aggressive as any of Charlotte Brontë's heroines, for example. Her tomboy behavior as a child (cutting her hair, running away to join the gypsies, pushing Lucy into the mud) nicely exemplifies this blurring of gender distinctions, as does her tall stature (she is one of what critics have referred to as George Eliot's "monumental" heroines).[4]

Such apparent rebelliousness is by no means unequivocally condoned by Eliot's narrator, much as it endears Maggie to the reader. Almost all of her actions are simultaneously deplored and applauded, and to an equal extent; the narrator is at once sympathetic to and impatient with most of

Maggie's peccadilloes. Even when she is a child, we are told that "Maggie rushed to her deeds with passionate impulse, and then saw not only their consequences, but what would have happened if they had not been done, with all the detail and exaggerated circumstance of an active imagination" (57). Her need for love is the motivating force behind most of her failures, including her final one, and we can see Eliot's perplexity with this fatal feminine flaw: is it to be lauded as a humanizing openness or condemned as a headstrong thoughtlessness? "When Maggie was not angry," we are told, "she was as dependent on kind or cold words as a daisy on the sunshine or the cloud: the need of being loved would always subdue her" (344). This subduing is very different from the "willed submission" of many of Eliot's heroines; Maggie attempts the latter in desperation at several points (assisted by her reading of Thomas à Kempis), but it never really works for her.

Perhaps the narrator's description of her passionate response to music is the best index to Maggie's character: "Her sensibility to the supreme excitement of music was only one form of that passionate sensibility which belonged to her whole nature, and made her faults and virtues all merge in each other—made her affections sometimes an impatient demand, but also prevented her vanity from taking the form of mere feminine coquetry and device, and gave it the poetry of ambition" (352). "Vanity" here refers to Maggie's delight in being loved, rather than her delight in being looked at; although both of these refer to a need to be appreciated or admired, only the delight in being looked at is systematically scorned by Eliot as feminine superficiality. Maggie's need to be loved is seen by Eliot as a selfish need (as opposed to the utterly selfless needs of a Dinah, say, or even a Dorothea) and as such also comes under the general rubric of vanity, but Eliot also recognizes it as somehow legitimate, having "the poetry of ambition." A curious phrase, this last, revealing Eliot's uneasiness with the erotic, and perhaps with the feminine; if Maggie's love needs can be safely tied to the (masculine) attribute of "ambition," they do not need to raise the spectre of female desire. William Myers notes this maneuver with some frustration: "Maggie's relations with Stephen are subtly but consistently de-eroticised, just as Dinah and Adam's were: the apparently erotic response is always interpreted as something else. Thus Stephen's love appeals to Maggie's delight in admiration, in effect to her vanity, while it is specifically passion which enables her to resist him" (138–39).

This dissociation of the erotic from passion, in fact, lies at the heart of George Eliot's dilemma in *The Mill on the Floss* and militates against the genuine feminist thrust of the narrative. A passion denuded of eroticism is necessarily relegated to altruism or to "innocent" child-like bonds of affection, which of course is exactly what occurs in Eliot's ideal universe. Recognizing that a selfless altruism on its own is an inadequate motivation in most human relationships, Eliot refers repeatedly to childhood love as the perfect paradigm for adult love, particularly between male and female characters. Again and again in her novels, two lovers are likened to two children holding hands or playing together. This makes a kind of sense from a phallocentric point of view, in that childhood can be seen as a state in which characters can be legitimately and more or less safely regressed, loving without evoking the profoundly unnerving fear of merging that adult eroticism inevitably engenders in the rigidly differentiated psyche.

We can see that for Eliot, as for so many of her Victorian counterparts (and for the same somatophobic reasons), the erotic incontrovertibly falls into the category of humanity's "lower" nature and as such demands to be transcended. This is precisely why the novel, although it contains overt and specific protests against many sexist practices and attitudes (such as the preferential treatment accorded the male child over the female, the greater worldly power of men and the disparaging judgments made by some of the males in the novel, such as Lawyer Wakem's remark that "we don't ask what a woman does—we ask whom she belongs to," 374, and Tom's castigation of Maggie as being "ten times worse" than Stephen, 427), contains no protest against the terribly sexist domination/submission hierarchy in erotic relations. Quite simply, it is because George Eliot wishes her characters to transcend the realm of the erotic in the first place. As I shall show, this requires some ingenious maneuvers on Eliot's part and causes Maggie to be doomed from the start, as a mature erotic relationship would provide the only truly satisfactory fulfillment of her need to be loved.

It is a need that drives her from Tom to Philip to Stephen, in a progression that would normally result in marriage and possible happiness. This progression is sharply curtailed, however, ostensibly by the moral complications of the narrative but also, I think, by Eliot's inability to envision success for a sensibility that functions so completely outside patriarchal norms as Maggie's does. In the last analysis Eliot is unable to see Maggie's need for love as desirable, much as she understands and sympathizes with it. Maggie herself admits, "I begin to think there can never come much happiness to me from loving: I have always had so much pain mingled with it. I wish I could make myself a world outside it, as men do" (363); and when Stephen is solicitous of Maggie, the narrator tells us, "These things will summon a little of the too-ready, traitorous tenderness into a woman's eyes, compelled as she is in her girlish time to learn her life-lessons in very trivial language. And to Maggie such things . . . found her keen appetite for homage quite fresh" (368). Both of these comments spring from a vivid awareness of inequities in the patriarchal division of power. Maggie's cry of pain echoes the bitter awareness of several of Charlotte Brontë's heroines (Caroline Helstone, for example) that males do not concern themselves with love in the same way that females do, simply because they are busy with other things. The second observation, by the narrator, underlines the patriarchal judgment that these other things are more important than feminine concerns with the merely personal, which are dismissed as "very trivial." It also acknowledges (in the phrase "the too-ready, traitorous tenderness") the enormous disadvantage inherent in the female's dependence on masculine desire (or, as Eliot puts it, her "keen appetite for homage"). Eliot's feminist anger with the predicament of the intelligent woman whose substance is wasted in the feminine role (which also appears in a milder form in *Middlemarch*) is largely contained in such small, sharp asides. Their effect, running counter to the dominant message in the novel, is cumulative and telling.

The inequities in the patriarchal division of power show up nowhere so clearly as in Maggie's relationship with Tom, which in many ways is the key relationship in the novel. Tom has more power than Maggie has, not only in the outside world but in their psychic world as well: as Dorothea Barrett points out, "Tom has all the power in the relationship between them because he loves less" (57). This, of course, is a precise recapitulation of the male's preferred position in the domination/submission hierarchy, and springs from the male need for control over both Self and female Other. In Tom's case this need is made strikingly understandable by the narrator's empathic rendering of his point of view, especially during his various humiliations in the world of men. These failures teach Tom firsthand what it is like to be on the other side of the gender hierarchy: "Under this vigorous treatment Tom became more like a girl than he had ever been in his life before. He had a large share of pride, which had hitherto found itself very comfortable in the world, . . . but now this same pride met with nothing but bruises and crushings. . . . His pride got into an uneasy condition which quite nullified his boyish self-satisfaction, and gave him something of the girl's susceptibility" (124). Such experiences make Tom less rather than more sympathetic to "feminine" values, and harden his resolve to succeed in the male world of power, in which Maggie's aberrations seem like a "planless riddle" (345) to him.

In fact, Tom is the father-figure in *The Mill on the Floss*, representing the law of the fathers in a particularly harsh and rigorous manner. His falsely differentiated male consciousness cannot allow him to feel any sympathy for what he sees as Maggie's foibles, as they represent transgressions of the masculine order (including the gender hierarchy) to which he has committed himself. The real father in the novel, Mr. Tulliver, although he is sympathetic to Maggie, is also committed to this order (and to the literal law) to an extent that ultimately costs him his life. It is interesting that Mr. Tulliver is one of the few good fathers in Eliot's canon: Hetty, Dinah, Dorothea and Gwendolen have no fathers, and Mirah has a bad one. This does not prevent him from doing rather badly by Maggie, however, in that he privileges Tom over her both materially and psychically in a way that makes Maggie dependent on Tom's esteem throughout their lives. Even the good father cannot save his daughter from punishment by the patriarchal order.[5]

Tom represents the father that Maggie can never please yet on whom her psychological well-being depends, and from whom she must free herself if she is to attain healthy adult autonomy: the narrator tells us, "Her brother was the human being of whom she had been most afraid, from her childhood upwards: afraid with that fear which springs in us when we love one who is inexorable, unbending, unmodifiable—with a mind that we can never mould ourselves upon, and yet that we cannot endure to alienate from us" (425). Maggie's is the classic dilemma of the dependent, subordinate female caught in a hopeless interaction with an alienated, falsely differentiated male. She constantly attempts to move toward merging, while Tom constantly repulses her ("It was no use trying to make Tom feel that she was near to him. He always repelled her," 345). As we know, she ultimately fails to free herself and (fatally) succeeds in merging. As Gillian Beer puts it, "Her heart's desire—the return to childhood, erotic reunion with her brother, the knitting up again of the divided self which has been split into the twin forms of male and female each with their separate order: these are desires which it is given to all to feel and none to fulfill. That is why she must die: she has refused Stephen *Guest*, the fleeting displacement of an older desire, as his name suggests" (99).

But on a very deep level, Maggie is not meant to accept Stephen; even apart from the obvious moral dilemma of his engagement to Lucy, I think that Eliot shies away from endorsing a relationship between two characters who share so much erotic attraction. What she attempts instead, as Mary Jacobus points out, is a fleeting return to childhood innocence, a transcendence of the erotic in a wishful merging with the longed-for father figure:

The Mill on the Floss gestures toward a largely unacted error, the elopement with Stephen Guest. . . . Instead of this unrealized fall, we are offered a moment of attempted transcendence in the timeless death embrace which abolishes the history of division between brother and sister. . . . What is striking about the novel's ending is its banishing not simply of division but of sexual difference as the origin of that division. The fantasy is of a world where brother and sister might roam together, "indifferently," as it were, without either conflict or hierarchy. We know that their childhood was not like that at all, and we can scarcely avoid concluding that death is a high price to pay for such imaginary union. (75)

The grievous flaw in Eliot's fantasy lies in its patriarchal bias, which demands transcendence. It is this principle that decrees Maggie must die, death being the only true form of bodily transcendence. Ironically, Eliot's dream of merging could only be fulfilled (and then only partly) by embracing that which she and her contemporaries so feared, the erotic itself. What Maggie could more profitably seek, instead of the father love represented by Tom's approval, is mother love with its comfort, nurturing and understanding, such as that sought—and found—by Charlotte Brontë's heroines in their erotic relationships. The oedipal father love that Maggie craves is a self-destructive impossibility for her, consisting largely of a wish to be like the father (legitimate, powerful) and most of all to be accepted by him in spite of her gender, which she too views as a shortcoming to be forgiven. The tragic ending of *The Mill on the Floss* lends credence to the feminist contention that the core of a healthy erotic relationship, whether heterosexual or homosexual, is a psychic replication of the primary pre-oedipal connection with the mother: unconditional, interdependent and mutually satisfying. Maggie might have profitably sought such a relationship, given her real mother's psychologically inadequate mothering; when Maggie is a child her mother continually urges her to conform to a cramped feminine stereotype, and when she is older we are told that "the mother was getting fond of her tall, brown girl, the only bit of furniture now on which she could bestow her anxiety and pride" (257). Mrs. Tulliver is not exactly a bad mother (when Tom savagely rejects Maggie near the end of the book, for instance, she calls to Maggie, "My child! I'll go with you. You've got a mother," 427); like so many mothers dismissed by so many daughters of the fathers, she is simply weak, trivial and powerless.

This is perhaps another way of approaching the incestuous aspect of the novel, on which critics have commented at length. Dorothea Barrett contends that incest is "related to retentiveness in that it is one manifestation of the desire to retain or conserve original attachments" and therefore sees Maggie's "incestuous love for Tom . . . [as] connected with the wider conservatism of George Eliot's thought" (53). Certainly Maggie's longing for Tom's approval characterizes one of her "original attachments": "To have no cloud between herself and Tom was still a perpetual yearning in her, that had its root deeper than all change," we are told (399). This need for patriarchal approval is set up to be in direct conflict with any of Maggie's attempts to find a love outside it, first with Philip and then with Stephen. The opposition that Eliot thus mobilizes is an impossible one for her heroine, that of erotic love or passion versus duty. Like vanity, erotic love involves a "selfish" or personal desire, and as such stands no chance in this moral conflict, particularly given the positive connotations of "duty" in Eliot's moral universe. Therefore Stephen, who desires Maggie, comes across to the reader as a less worthy character than Tom, whose adherence to "duty" is unimpeachable. (In fact, it may be true to say that George Eliot's most admirable male characters, as well as her most admirable female characters, love selflessly and un-erotically; Adam Bede—with Dinah— and Daniel Deronda come immediately to mind.)

This conflict of personal desire versus duty is one that hounds Maggie in all of her relationships. She is constantly torn, between Tom and Philip, between Philip and Stephen, and finally between Stephen and the rest of the world, including Tom, Philip and Lucy. In the first of these conflicts it is not exactly erotic passion that is pitted against duty, but rather Maggie's love of being loved. Maggie feels pity for Philip rather than desire, but his wish to befriend her appeals to her "innate delight in admiration and love" (264). In Philip, Maggie finds the brother love she has always sought in Tom: warmth, understanding and unconditional support. "What a dear, good brother you would have been, Philip," Maggie tells him. "I think you would have made as much fuss about me, and been so pleased for me to love you, as would have satisfied even me. You would have loved me well enough to bear with me, and forgive me everything. That was what I always longed that Tom should do" (288). And later, when Philip tells her he loves her, Maggie replies, "O, it is quite impossible we can ever be more than friends—brother and sister in secret, as we have been" (295). Philip, with his deformity that disqualifies him as a controlling and powerful male, embodies the feminine sensibilities that Tom has expunged from his relentless masculinity ("Maggie . . . stooped her tall head to kiss the pale face that was full of pleading, timid love—like a woman's," 296). While they make him warm and caring, however, Philip's feminine sensibilities also prevent Maggie from feeling any erotic attraction for him: before she meets Stephen, Maggie believes that "if there were sacrifices in this love, it was all the richer and more satisfying" (296). This is much different than the mother love Lucy Snowe finds in her relationship with Paul Emanuel, for example, which has nothing to do with pity or weakness and calls for no such sacrifices on her part.

It is ironic that Maggie's affection for Philip, which is initially pitted against her duty to obey Tom, actually comes to represent her duty later in the novel. For it is not Philip who represents the real threat to Tom's hold over Maggie, but Stephen. After she has become attracted to Stephen, Philip becomes "a sort of outward conscience" for Maggie, to whom she "might fly . . . for rescue and strength. Her tranquil, tender affection for Philip, with its root deep down in her childhood, and its memories of long quiet talk . . . the fact that in him the appeal was more strongly to her pity and womanly devotedness than to her vanity or other egoistic excitability of her nature, seemed now to make a sort of sacred place, a sanctuary where she could find refuge from an alluring influence which the best part of herself must resist" (360–61). Here Maggie's choice is quite plain: it is between "pity and womanly devotedness" and "vanity or other egoistic excitability." It is also plain which alternative she should choose: pity and devotedness are qualities the appropriately obedient woman (like Lucy) possesses instinctively, while erotic desire (obliquely alluded to in the "other egoistic excitability") is selfish and therefore to be avoided. Later in the novel, Maggie outlines similar alternatives in her refusal to marry Stephen: "Love is natural; but surely pity and faithfulness and memory are natural too" (395). "Duty" is clearly a charged term for Eliot, encompassing pity, devotedness, faithfulness and memory in addition to the patriarchal rules that Tom lives by. It is not surprising that erotic love, like vanity, has no chance against this formidable array of virtues.

In the end, the moral conflict posed by the events of *The Mill on the Floss* remains unresolved, probably reflecting George Eliot's own deep ambivalence about it. On the surface, the narrator seems to endorse the notion of duty, including Tom's misguided version of it (as Mary Jacobus points out, Eliot characterizes Tom as the misguided "man of maxims," the "popular representative of the minds that are guided in their moral judgment solely by general rules, thinking that these will lead them to justice by a ready-made patent method, without the trouble of exerting patience, discrimination, impartiality," 438). The events of the novel, too, obviously illustrate the terrible dangers of yielding to passion; Maggie reflects bitterly that she "had made herself an outlawed soul, with no guide but the wayward choice of her own passion. . . . If she could have changed [yesterday] now for any length of inward silent endurance, she would have bowed beneath that cross with a sense of rest" (413). Given the existence of Stephen's engagement to Lucy, the espousal of duty is indeed the only reasonable choice open to Maggie, and the reader (reluctantly) concedes the victory to the patriarchy. Tom is "right" and Maggie is "wrong." But it is a characteristic patriarchal victory that literally takes everything down with it, and several aspects of the novel privilege the triumph of erotic passion instead. It is these aspects, the submerged contrary readings, that are most germane to my study.

In order to arrive at a clear understanding of Eliot's view of Maggie as a subject of desire, it is necessary to remove the obvious moral imperative in the novel—Lucy and Stephen's engagement—and to ask what Maggie's choice should be without it. Should she still feel bound by her reluctant promise to Philip? Would her feelings for Stephen then be morally acceptable? It is revealing that we cannot predict the answers to such questions with any degree of certainty; the issues then become truly ambivalent. On one hand, many of the same arguments apply: Philip has a claim over Maggie that is prior to Stephen's; he appeals to Maggie's "calmer affections" (418); Tom's motives are good; and the concept of "duty" still applies. On the other hand, it is clear that Maggie feels pity rather than love for Philip; Philip has basically coerced her into promising to love him; Tom is harsh and unreasonable; and Stephen himself is fairly likable. Most importantly, however, the relationship between Maggie and Stephen is clearly one of erotic love, and it is this, I suspect, that would still cause Eliot the most difficulty. For, in spite of her narrator's lengthy and convincing polemic in favor of duty and renunciation, Eliot still manages to create a compelling case for the erotic relationship. As in *Adam Bede*, what Eliot shows us vies with what she tells us, running counter to the overt reading of the novel; the difference is that in *The Mill on the Floss* the two readings are much more equal, giving rise to the unresolved tension that informs the entire narrative.

And what Eliot omits to show us is almost as important as what she shows us. As I have already remarked, *The Mill on the Floss* is not a scopophilic novel; we are not shown many physical portraits of Maggie. The "normal" homosocial interaction in which the (male) narrator and (male) reader share the look of desire (at the female character/object) is therefore contravened, and Maggie thus escapes the most blatant form of female objectification. The look of desire is extremely important in *The Mill on the Floss*, however. Remarkably, it is a shared look, unlike the narratorial looking at the female in *Adam Bede* or at the male in Charlotte Brontë's *Jane Eyre*, for example. It is rather a mutual gazing in which Maggie participates as much as Stephen, enhancing her potential erotic subjectivity more than any other element in the novel.

At first, Maggie avoids looking at Stephen when they are alone together, "for some reason or other" (354). But their growing attraction to each other is signaled in a series of more and more intimate looks, which gradually come to seem necessary for both of them. Predictably, these are initially rendered from Stephen's point of view. When he purposely visits her alone for the first time, we are told, "He only wished he dared look at Maggie, and that she would look at him—let him have one long look into those deep strange eyes of hers, and then he would be satisfied. . . . He thought it was becoming a sort of monomania with him, to want that long look from Maggie; and he was racking his invention continually to find out some means by which he could have it" (356). At this stage the look of desire is something that Stephen wants from Maggie (she "lets him have" it), an imperative of his desire rather than hers. But Stephen does not want to look at Maggie (as an object) so much as he wants her to look back at him (as a separate subject), which she finally does, "just glancing" at him (357). Unwittingly, Maggie displays a reassuring reluctance to Stephen's desire for her to look at him, finally "yielding" to his desire; the domination/submission hierarchy is operative here even if the seeing/seen dyad is not. Stephen is accordingly "delighted with that glance, and get[s] determined to stay for another" (357). Another look is indeed "granted" just before he leaves, and he "look[s] into the half-unwilling, half-fascinated eyes, as a thirsty man looks towards the track of the distant brook" (358). Repeated again and again, this look becomes a correlative for sexual intimacy in *The Mill on the Floss*, as well as a form of sustenance similar to the food and drink metaphors in Charlotte Brontë's novels.

For all that she comes to enjoy it (we read on a later occasion that "nothing could prevent that mutual glance from being delicious to both, as it had been the evening before," 368), Maggie never actually initiates the look of desire, which despite its mutuality continues to be rendered in terms of domination and submission. At one point, in fact, Stephen reflects, "Was it possible to quarrel with a creature who had such eyes—defying and deprecating, contradicting and clinging, imperious and beseeching—full of delicious opposites? To see such a creature subdued by love for one would be a lot worth having" (359). Here Stephen is clearly the dominant male, who views Maggie as an object, a "creature" to be "subdued by love." Similarly, just before the scene in the conservatory, "something strangely powerful there was in the light of Stephen's long gaze for it made Maggie's face turn towards it and look upward at it—slowly, like a flower at the ascending brightness" (387). This commanding male gaze, which "made" Maggie's face turn "upward" toward it in a stock metaphor for adoration and dependency, is in stark contrast to the gaze that was formerly shared by Maggie and Philip, which neatly reverses this metaphor ("The full lustrous face, with the bright black coronet, looked down like that of a divinity well pleased to be worshipped, on the pale-hued, small-featured face that was turned up to it," 287). As we know, the latter gaze is not erotic, at least not from Maggie's point of view; the erotic hierarchy cannot easily be reversed.

As Maggie becomes aware of the dangers inherent in what Eliot describes as "that long grave mutual gaze which has the solemnity belonging to all deep human passion" (387), her struggles to resist it become more and more violent. During Stephen's visit to her at her Aunt Gritty's, for instance, "she opened her eyes full on his for an instant, like a lovely wild animal timid and struggling under caresses, and then turned sharp round" (394). Again, this is a metaphor of domination: Maggie as wild animal struggles against the caresses of her would-be keeper. Finally, however, she stops struggling and gives in to Stephen's "beseeching look which she felt to be following her like a low murmur of love and pain": "She refused it less and less, till at last the evening for them both was sometimes made of a moment's mutual gaze: they thought of it till it came, and when it had come, they thought of nothing else" (403).

Given the power accorded the look of desire in this novel, it is hardly necessary for Eliot to have her characters employ the language of desire to any great extent. Maggie and Stephen speak with their eyes, say much by their silences and communicate through the lovers' language of music. Early in their relationship, before they have acknowledged their attraction to each other, "if Lucy left them together, they never spoke to each other . . . [but] each was oppressively conscious of the other's presence, even to the finger-ends" (354), and when Maggie first takes Stephen's arm, "not a word was spoken. If it had been, each would have been less intensely conscious of the other" (358). When they finally do speak of their love, however, it is Stephen who employs the language of desire while Maggie listens. When they run away, "some low, subdued, languid exclamation of love came from Stephen from time to time. . . . otherwise, they spoke no word" (407), and later, on the Dutch boat, Stephen "murmured forth in fragmentary sen-

tences his happiness—his adoration—his tenderness—his belief that their
life together must be heaven—that her presence with him would give
rapture to every common day—that to satisfy her lightest wish was dearer
to him than all other bliss—that everything was easy for her sake, except
to part with her. . . . Such things . . . to poor Maggie . . . were like nectar held
close to thirsty lips" (411). Maggie is clearly the recipient, rather than the
initiator, of the language of desire.

And, while she undoubtedly feels desire for Stephen, the enactment of
desire is something Maggie actively struggles against (or at best acquiesces
in) rather than promotes. Overall, although she is indubitably a subject—
spirited, intelligent and independent—she can hardly be called a subject of
desire. In her relations with the males in the novel she is consistently
submissive, despite her apparent waywardness. She submits initially and
always to Tom (when he discovers her secret meetings with Philip, for
instance, "she felt it was in vain to attempt anything but submission. Tom
had his terrible clutch on her conscience and her deepest dread," 302),
momentarily to Philip and finally to Stephen. With the latter she readily
assumes her role in the male-female domination/submission hierarchy, at
least until her final refusal to interact with him at all. In fact, Eliot paints a
beguiling picture of this archetypal configuration, one which is almost as
erotic as the connection between Jane Eyre and Rochester. As in Brontë's
rendition, part of the erotic charge comes initially from the transgression of
polite social norms by the spirited heroine; when Maggie first meets
Stephen she intimates by her conversation that she thinks him conceited,
so that "Lucy was rather alarmed: she thought Stephen and Maggie were
not going to like each other" (331). Of course, this touch of aggression
merely adds spice to the male fantasy of domination which, as I have
already noted, quickly comes into play for Stephen.

And Maggie is equally drawn to the female fantasy of submission.
Insofar as her feelings toward Stephen are described for us, they turn out
to be strongly suggestive of infantile fantasies of a wish to be taken care of
by a powerful Other: when he prevents her from slipping as she gets out
of the boat, for example, he says, " 'You have not hurt yourself at all, I
hope?' . . . bending to look in her face with anxiety. It was very charming
to be taken care of in that kind graceful manner by some one taller and
stronger than oneself. Maggie had never felt just in the same way before"
(336). As gender-relations theorists have recognized, the seductive aspect
of this fantasy is its passivity (all Maggie has to do is to "be taken care of"),
and a key element is the real or imagined superiority of the active male
(Stephen is "taller and stronger" than she is). When Stephen asks her to
take his arm for the first time she experiences similar regressive feelings,
this time reported by the narrator: "There is something strangely winning
to most women in that offer of the firm arm: the help is not wanted
physically at that moment, but the sense of help—the presence of strength

that is outside them and yet theirs—meets a continual want of the imagi-nation. Either on that ground or some other, Maggie took the arm" (358). What Eliot is describing here is clearly a rescue fantasy, which again appeals to Maggie's wish to be looked after by a powerful Other.

More specifically, the female in the domination/submission configura-tion does not have to take responsibility for her own desire. According to Jessica Benjamin, "The fantasy of submission in ideal love is that of being released into abandon by another who remains in control" ("Desire" 97). This is certainly what occurs when Maggie runs away with Stephen:

And they went. Maggie felt that she was being led down the garden among the roses, being helped with firm tender care into the boat, having the cushion and cloak arranged for her feet, and her parasol opened for her . . . .—all by this stronger presence that seemed to bear her along without any act of her own will, like the added self which comes with the sudden exalting influence of a strong tonic—and she felt nothing else. Memory was excluded. (407)

This is a perfect description of being "released into abandon"; Maggie is borne along "without any act of her own will," totally immersed in the present sensation ("memory was excluded"). And it seems like merging to her: Stephen, the "stronger presence," seems like an intoxicating "added self." This sense of merging is reiterated when Stephen asks her to get up so that he can put her cloak over her shoulders: "Maggie obeyed: there was an unspeakable charm in being told what to do, and having everything decided for her. . . . Maggie was hardly conscious of having said or done anything decisive. All yielding . . . is the partial sleep of thought; it is *the submergence of our own personality by another*" (410, my italics). It is perhaps disconcerting to note that Maggie's response in such instances parallels almost exactly Rosalind Coward's description of every heroine's response in every Harlequin Romance, "the projection of active desires by yourself onto another person, who then becomes responsible for that desire" (194). Quite simply, Maggie is absolved from the necessity of acting on her own desire by the urgency of Stephen's desire. She recovers from the temptation to yield to this fantasy, as we know; but the fantasy itself is presented with uncanny accuracy.

In the more detailed episodes, too, Maggie is reactive (to Stephen's desire) rather than active, playing to perfection the part of the reluctantly responsive object. In the scene in the conservatory, for instance, where Maggie and Stephen go to escape from the party, Maggie

blushed deeply, turned away her head, and drew her arm from Stephen's, going up to some flowers to smell them. . . .

Maggie bent her arm a little upwards towards the large half-opened rose. . . . Who has not felt the beauty of a woman's arm?—the unspeakable suggestions of tenderness that lie in the dimpled elbow, and all the varied gently-lessening curves down to the delicate wrist, with its tiniest, almost imperceptible nicks in the firm softness. A woman's arm touched the soul of a great sculptor two thousand years ago, so that he wrought an image of it for the Parthenon which moves us still as it clasps lovingly the time-worn marble of a headless trunk. Maggie's was such an arm as that—and it had the warm tints of life.

A mad impulse seized on Stephen; he darted towards the arm, and showered kisses on it, clasping the wrist.

But the next moment Maggie snatched it from him, and glared at him like a wounded war-goddess, quivering with rage and humiliation. . . .

He came and stood humbly before her. But Maggie's bitter rage was unspent. (388–89)

This episode, reminiscent of the many detailed descriptions of Hetty in *Adam Bede*, is easily the most scopophilic scene in *The Mill on the Floss*. Maggie's blush, her association with the also-beautiful rose ("half-opened") and the lovingly detailed description of her arm from Stephen's point of view are familiar components of the standard nineteenth-century love scene. The passage also incorporates the standard apology for Stephen and for all such viewers of feminine (ch)arms: Maggie's arm is irresistible and he "can't help" acting on his desire to kiss it. The declamatory generalization ("Who has not felt the beauty of a woman's arm?") on reflection applies primarily to male viewers of female beauty, and the arm's exquisitely rendered details identify it as a sexual object. (As Juliet McMaster points out, George Eliot is an "arm woman," 23.) The arm is simultaneously constituted as an aesthetic object, however, using a familiar Victorian technique of displacement: its "unspeakable suggestions of tenderness" are at once elevated to the transcendent status of art by the invocation of Greek sculpture. And finally, Maggie as an object of desire waxes suitably resistant, unwittingly enhancing her beauty even more (she looks "like a wounded war-goddess").

Overall, the "war" that Maggie and Stephen wage turns out to be the standard sparring between an active male subject and a passive female object. Not surprisingly, their relationship is generally described in the language of conflict, of conquering and submission. When she first sees Stephen at her Aunt Gritty's, "Maggie felt a beating at head and heart—horrible as the sudden leaping to life of a *savage enemy* who had feigned death" (391); Stephen "look[s] eagerly at her face for the least sign of *compliance*" (394); Maggie reflects that "this strange, sweet, *subduing* influence . . . should not *conquer* her," while Stephen is impelled to "deepen the *hold he had on her*" (403); the narrator speaks of Maggie's "fatal *yielding*" (409); Stephen has a "hovering dread of some *resistance* in Maggie's nature that he would be unable to *overcome*" (414, my emphasis throughout). Such battle terminology, subtly evocative of the fantasies of domination and submission, adds imperceptibly to the eroticism of the whole.

We can conclude, then, that although Eliot constitutes Maggie as a true subject in other ways, in the final analysis she retreats from constituting her as a subject of desire. As a subject who functions by principles antithetical to the patriarchal order, she is regarded by the males in the novel (including Lawyer Wakem, who, like Tom, is an unbending representative of patriarchal law and order) as "rather dangerous and unmanageable" (376). Eliot too, somewhat reluctantly, sees Maggie's need for love as dangerous because of its potential transgression of the patriarchal principle of transcendence, which the novel (again somewhat reluctantly) ultimately endorses. This need causes Maggie to lose control, albeit temporarily, and to submit to the wrong male in the novel at the wrong time. Christine Sutphin thinks that "Maggie commits the greatest wrong in her own and Eliot's eyes, when she is passive, when she abdicates responsibility, when she is most traditionally feminine" (344). But Eliot certainly endorses a traditional version of femininity in erotic relations, even though she may not endorse passivity; ideally, Maggie would voluntarily renounce her desire for Stephen before being "carried away" by it, thus attaining a state of willed submission to patriarchal law (which she finally attains anyway, but too late).

In many ways, however, Eliot's second major novel marks a great deal of progress in her delineation of male/female relations. While Maggie is finally made to eschew erotic subjectivity, she is by no means objectified to the same extent as most heroines of the nineteenth-century novel. She is beautiful without becoming an object of the male gaze, either for the reader or for the males in the novel, largely because of Eliot's courageous creation of a mutual look of desire. Also, and somewhat remarkably in Eliot's canon, she is permitted to be aware of her own beauty without being castigated for her vanity, which represents an advance in Eliot's willingness to descend from the realm of male transcendence and to give the erotic its due. *The Mill on the Floss* is arguably Eliot's most erotic novel, and Maggie is the closest she ever comes to creating a female subject of desire. Nor will Eliot ever again come so close to actively criticizing the world of patriarchal principle. The subversive contrary reading in *The Mill on the Floss* is extremely powerful, enhancing the novel's feminism in ways that extend beyond the confines of the narrative and comprising a violent if somewhat muffled protest against gender inequities. This reading constitutes some of our best evidence that George Eliot herself, highly successful in the world of the fathers and a true Victorian in her determination to transcend the physical, was nevertheless deeply ambivalent in her acceptance of that world.

MIDDLEMARCH

A decade after the publication of *Adam Bede* and *The Mill on the Floss*, George Eliot was to return to the exploration of male-female relationships in her two final novels, *Middlemarch* and *Daniel Deronda*. Her political novels, written in the intervening ten years, contain interesting love stories but are mainly focused on questions of power in the external world. This focus profoundly affects her final two novels, however, in that they are also novels about power, the power inherent in the inner world of personal relations. Interestingly, neither of these final novels can be said to be an erotic novel in the way that *Adam Bede* or *The Mill on the Floss* is. They do not deal with beauty like the former or with love like the latter; instead they deal mainly with marriage, a more prosaic relation in which personal power structures are more starkly revealed, unadorned by the glow of romance. This is not to say that there is an absence of fantasy on the part of the characters in *Middlemarch* and *Daniel Deronda*. But their fantasies are quickly exposed as delusionary and stripped of their seductive appeal, and are not shared by the narrator or by the reader. Instead, Eliot attempts to examine what is really going on in the construction of such fantasies, and in so doing she unearths valuable insights into the power politics of the domination/submission hierarchy. On the whole, Eliot is much more comfortable with this aspect of eroticism than with the more romantic aspects, simply because it involves morality rather than sexuality, transcendence rather than physicality, and thus leaves her Victorian somatophobia undisturbed. For this reason alone, she is able to conduct her examination of such relationships with greater honesty and clarity than she did in her earlier novels.

Middlemarch, in particular, seems to be a novel about manners and morals rather than erotic relationships. But the psychological nuances of domination and submission are the main focus of all of the important relationships in the novel, including the non-erotic connections between Bulstrode and Raffles and between Will and Casaubon. Also, there is a plethora of relationships to come under the narrator's scrutiny: Dorothea and Casaubaon, Dorothea and Will, and Rosamond and Lydgate obviously form the most important attachments, but the attachments between Rosamond and Will, Dorothea and Lydgate, Mary and Fred, Mary and Farebrother, and Celia and Sir James are also significant, if only for reasons or comparison. In some ways Eliot's thinking about male-female relationships in *Middlemarch* simply represents a solidifying of many of the attitudes and proclivities she displayed earlier in *Adam Bede* and *The Mill on the Floss*; but the searching examination of marriage—with results that are not always laudatory—is in itself an important feminist undertaking. By extension, *Middlemarch* and later *Daniel Deronda* both ask how an intelligent woman should live, a momentous nineteenth-century question.

The two intelligent women examined at length in *Middlemarch* are in some ways a reversion to the vain-soulful paradigm that Eliot first implemented in *Adam Bede*. Dorothea and Rosamond are urban, more sophisticated—and, significantly, more powerful—versions of Dinah and Hetty. Like the two earlier heroines, they embody a split between a character who is meant to engage the reader's approval and one who is not, and the one who is not uses her beauty to captivate a desiring male while the "good" heroine remains largely unconscious of her own beauty. And, as in the earlier novel, neither heroine seems to experience erotic desire except obliquely. It is as though Eliot experienced Maggie's quest for love in *The Mill on the Floss* as much too dangerous and perplexing and turned away from it completely in her later work, reverting to the less ambiguous dichotomy of her first novel. "Love" is not the main motivation for either Dorothea or Rosamond, as the former (like Dinah) seeks spiritual goals and the latter (like Hetty) seeks admiration and material gain. These two positions are examined much more carefully and with more acuity than they were in *Adam Bede*, however, with interesting results.

To begin once more with the notion of beauty (always an instructive starting place in a discussion of Eliot's novels), it is immediately apparent that *Middlemarch* is a much less scopophilic novel than *Adam Bede*. Although Rosamond plays a part analogous to that of Hetty, there is a vast difference in the ways these parts are handled by the narrators of the two novels. Somewhat surprisingly, considering the power and significance of her beauty, we are given very few physical descriptions of Rosamond. The first of these, and the most extended, is perhaps the most characteristic. Rosamond and Mary Garth are talking together in Mary's room, and Rosamond

took off her hat, adjusted her veil, and applied little touches of her finger-tips to her hair—hair of infantine fairness, neither flaxen nor yellow. Mary Garth seemed all the plainer standing at an angle between the two nymphs—the one in the glass, and the one out of it, who looked at each other with eyes of heavenly blue, deep enough to hold the most exquisite meanings an ingenious beholder could put into them, and deep enough to hide the meanings of the owner if these should happen to be less exquisite. Only a few children in Middlemarch looked blond by the side of Rosamond, and the slim figure displayed by her riding-habit had delicate undulations. . . . Mary Garth, on the contrary, had the aspect of an ordinary sinner. (109)

This is very different from the lush physical descriptions of Hetty and from the standard "stills" of the heroine in most Victorian novels. The "hair of infantine fairness" and the "eyes of heavenly blue" are typical disembodied Victorian portrait details, as is the "slim figure" with its "delicate undulations"; but the overall impression is one of distaste, as the narrator hints at the hidden, "less exquisite" meanings in Rosamond's blue eyes. The narcissism of Rosamond's self-regard is nicely underlined by the image of the "two nymphs who looked at each other." The contrast with Mary Garth is obviously deliberate, although the narrator is careful to point out that "it would not be true to declare, in satisfactory antithesis, that [Mary] had all the virtues," since "plainness has its peculiar temptations and vices quite as much as beauty; it is apt either to feign amiability, or . . . to show all the repulsiveness of discontent." Eliot is clearly just as preoccupied and perplexed by the issue of female beauty in *Middlemarch* as she was in *Adam Bede*; certainly it does not seem simplified or resolved for her. It does seem less volatile, however. The controlled narratorial self-consciousness of the "satisfactory antithesis" in the preceding passage, for instance, is in striking contrast to the apparent ambivalence of the narrator in *Adam Bede*, whose descriptions of Hetty, so sensual and appealing, constantly seem to take on an erotic life of their own and to undermine the novel's polemic. The look of desire in the earlier novel, we may recall, is contained within the "normal" homosocial dynamic of a female object being regarded and appraised, aesthetically and sexually, by a male-identified narrator and a male-identified reader, so that part of the pleasure in reading *Adam Bede* consists of a pleasure in looking.

In *Middlemarch* the narrator's approach to the beautiful female character is quite different. Rosamond is also regarded and appraised, but the appraisal in this case is moral rather than aesthetic or sexual. Her beauty is stressed, but in the abstract rather than the concrete. We are told that she is "sweet to look at as a half-opened blush-rose, and adorned with accomplishments for the refined amusement of man" (263), for instance, which evokes none of the sensuality with which Hetty was invested in even the briefest of the narrator's descriptions of her. Being told that a character is "sweet to look at" is obviously not the same as being shown that sweetness. Even when she is described from Lydgate's point of view, Rosamond is endowed with none of Hetty's adorable sensual charm: "Lydgate was . . . thinking how lovely this creature was, her garment seeming to be made out of the faintest blue sky, herself so immaculately blond, as if the petals of some gigantic flower had just opened and disclosed her; and yet with this infantine blondness showing so much ready, self-possessed grace" (156). The flatness of such descriptions derives largely from the habitual dispassionate stance of the narrator, who unlike the narrator of *Adam Bede* is never moved by the beauty she is describing. Like Hetty, Rosamond is frequently likened to soft, cuddly animals, for instance; but the effect of such metaphors in the later novel is far from Hetty's ravishing appeal. For instance, we read that Rosamond "put up her hand to touch her wondrous hair-plaits—an habitual gesture with her as pretty as any movements of a kitten's paw." The charm of this (not particularly striking to begin with) is immediately dissipated by the wry narratorial observation, "Not that Rosamond was in the least like a kitten: she was a sylph caught young and educated at Mrs. Lemon's" (157).

This is not to say that there is a complete absence of sensuality in *Middlemarch*. As in many of Eliot's novels, however, it resides largely in the novel's figurative language: Casaubaon's "shallow rill" (62) and the "souls in their young nudity [who] are tumbled out among incongruities" (188–89) on Dorothea's disastrous honeymoon, for example, have been amply commented on by George Steiner and numerous other critics. For my purposes, it is interesting that some of the most erotic of these sensual metaphors are metaphors of domination and submission: when she becomes engaged to Casaubon, Dorothea thinks of "throwing herself, metaphorically speaking, at Mr. Casaubon's feet, and kissing his unfashionable shoe-ties" (51); during her marriage we are told that "she had ardour enough for what was near, to have kissed Mr. Casaubon's coat-sleeve, or to have caressed his shoe-latchet, if he would have made any . . . sign of acceptance" (192); when she speaks to Will, he "did not know what to say, since it would not be useful for him to embrace her slippers, and tell her that he would die for her" (216). Aside from making the facetious observation that in *Middlemarch* George Eliot appears to be a "foot woman" as opposed to an "arm woman," we can note that the kisses, caresses and embraces in these images take place in the context of one of the most submissive gestures a character can perform, a gesture that is also indubitably linked to the character's sexuality in each instance. Power relations are eroticized in *Middlemarch*, as they will be in *Daniel Deronda*, representing a much less romantic concept of "love" than that which existed in Eliot's earlier novels.

Steiner has also commented on the overtones of evil in Eliot's portrait of Rosamond, located primarily in her graceful serpentine neck. It is true that Eliot's condemnation of the vain woman has sharpened considerably since her castigation of Hetty in *Adam Bede*; indeed, Rosamond can be said to be portrayed as one of the most morally degenerate characters in Eliot's entire corpus. Hetty simply wishes to be admired for her beauty, and the narrator regards her as merely shallow and foolish, leaving room for Dorothea Barrett's possible alternative view of her as "a blameless eighteen year-old girl who is crucified for the sins of others" (46), and Lucy, as we have seen, is readily excused for her small "flashes of personal vanity" by the narrator of *The Mill on the Floss*. About Rosamond there is no such ambiguity, and certainly no such tolerance; she is created to evoke fear and loathing, and the narrator of *Middlemarch* condemns her much more roundly than she does Bulstrode, for example. It is not that Rosamond's point of view is omitted—on the contrary, we are given ample direct access to her thought processes. While Hetty is objectified externally by the gaze of the narrator, the male characters and the reader of *Adam Bede*, Rosamond is objectified internally by her own image of herself. She is intensely conscious of herself as a beautiful object in a way that makes Hetty's (and later Lucy's) preening literally look like child's play: " 'Miss Vincy is a musician?' said Lydgate, following her with his eyes. (Every nerve and muscle in Rosamond was adjusted to the consciousness that she was being looked at)." Rosamond has none at all of the child-like innocence so prized by Eliot, and thus none of the concomitant candor and genuineness. Her objectification of herself extends to her inner life, and she has little consciousness of herself except as an object: the narrator tells us that Rosamond "was by nature an actress of parts that entered into her *physique*: she even acted her own character, and so well, that she did not know it to be precisely her own" (114). Rosamond has "become" the reigning beauty stereotype of her day, the young lady of the nineteenth-century conduct books, with chilling results.

It is not this self-objectification in itself, however, that triggers the narrator's severe condemnation of Rosamond. Rather, it is the use she makes of her beauty in the entrapment of Lydgate, which is infinitely more calculated than Hetty's shy pleasure in Arthur's admiration, for instance. Hetty dreams childishly of a pair of earrings; Rosamond's fantasies encompass an elaborately conceived materialistic scenario. After her first encounter with Lydgate, the narrator remarks that "Rosamond . . . was of remarkably detailed and realistic imagination when the foundation had been once presupposed; and before [she and Fred] had ridden a mile she was far on in the costume and introductions of her wedded life, having determined on her house in Middlemarch, and foreseen the visits she would pay to her husband's high-bred relatives" (115). And before she and Lydgate become engaged, we are told that "she seemed to be sailing with a fair wind just whither she would go, and her thoughts were much occupied with a handsome house in Lowick Gate which she hoped would by-and-by be vacant. . . . She imagined the drawing-room in her favourite house with various styles of furniture" (261). Rosamond's materialism, unlike Hetty's, appears to be quite genuine and not simply devised as a convenient screen enabling the narrator to gloss over her heroine's erotic feelings. Rosamond enjoys Lydgate's regard, but the narrator makes it clear that she has very few feelings for Lydgate himself apart from proprietary ones: "Here was Mr. Lydgate suddenly corresponding to her ideal, being altogether foreign to Middlemarch, carrying a certain air of distinction congruous with good family, and possessing connections which offered vistas of that middle-class heaven, rank; a man of talent, also, whom it would be especially delightful to enslave" (115).

Here we have the key to George Eliot's disapprobation of Rosamond's character: it is her wish to dominate, to "enslave," rather than her materialism that Eliot finds so reprehensible. Rosamond has none of the divine or maternal goodness that Eliot's ideal women display; even more than Hetty, she is a false signifier, a beautiful woman who is neither loving nor submissive. She is frequently characterized by such terms as "obstinacy" and "quiet steady disobedience," in contrast to Dorothea's wifely submission and "deep-souled womanhood." Even after she is married, Rosamond has fantasies of "mak[ing] conquests and enslav[ing] men": "How delightful to make captives from the throne of marriage with a husband as crown-prince by your side—himself in fact a subject—while the captives look up for ever hopeless" (429). Such fantasies are reminiscent in a childlike way of Emma Bovary's, even though the narrator comments that "at that time young ladies in the country . . . read little French literature later than

Racine" (429). Like Flaubert's heroine, Rosamond derives her ideas about "falling in love" from stereotypical notions of romance. After she and Lydgate have spent an evening in flirtation, we are told that "Rosamond had registered every look and word, and estimated them as the opening incidents of a preconceived romance—incidents which gather value from the foreseen development and climax. In Rosamond's romance it was not necessary to imagine much about the inward life of a hero, or of his serious business in the world" (163). Ironically, this is precisely how Lydgate would wish his future wife to think of him: "He held it one of the prettiest attitudes of the feminine mind to adore a man's pre-eminence without too precise a knowledge of what it consisted in" (262).

In the disaster that follows, accordingly, both Rosamond and Lydgate are culpable: she of entrapping him, and he of letting her. The disaster itself, and what Eliot really seems to be commenting on, is a perfect enactment of the "normal" erotic relationship between a strong male subject and a beautiful female object. Rosamond is the most culpable partner in this scenario, as she is paradoxically the most "active": "That they were some time to be engaged had long been an idea in her mind; . . . Lydgate had the counter-idea of remaining unengaged; but this was a mere negative. . . . Rosamond's idea . . . had a shaping activity and looked through watchful blue eyes, whereas Lydgate's lay blind and unconcerned as a jelly-fish which gets melted without knowing it" (266). The melted jelly-fish image prefigures the damage that their relationship will ultimately do to Lydgate, as well as the scene in which he is captured, the engagement scene.

Rosamond remains the perfect passive object in this scene. She is completely silent, and when Lydgate kisses her tears away, she "move[s] backward a little in timid happiness" (295). But her power in this and in all of the other scenes between her and Lydgate is undeniable; it is the incredible passive power of the object controlling the subject. In her discussion of popular romances Rosalind Coward comments that "[submission] fantasies are very obviously about a certain transfer of power, from the man to the woman. . . . In romantic fiction, the hero is made dependent only 'fleetingly'. . . . But this momentary impotence allows the woman to acquire power. . . . And the concluding marriage is the symbol of a woman achieving power" (195–96). The usual way in which this "momentary impotence" occurs, as we have already seen, is through some accident or illness that befalls the hero (Rochester and Jane Eyre enacted at least two scenes of this nature). Lydgate's momentary loss of power is brought about much less straightforwardly, through the apparent helplessness of the "weaker" member of the erotic hierarchy: he is "completely mastered by the outrush of tenderness at the sudden belief that this sweet young creature depended on him for her joy" (295). Later in the novel, when the couple is in financial difficulties, this mastery of the stronger by the weaker is described in appalling detail:

She spoke and wept with that gentleness which makes such words and tears omnipotent over a loving-hearted man. Lydgate . . . pressed her delicate head against his cheek with his powerful tender hand. He only caressed her; he did not say anything; for what was there to say? . . . When he left her to go out again, he told himself that it was ten times harder for her than for him: he had a life away from home, and constant appeals to his activity on behalf of others. He wished to excuse everything in her if he could—but it was inevitable that in that excusing mood he should think of her as if she were an animal of another and feebler species. Nevertheless she had mastered him. (655–56)

Elsewhere, too, the differences between men and women are likened to the differences between animals of different species. During their courtship Lydgate sees these differences as charming: he says flirtatiously to Rosamond, "I am sure you could teach me a thousand things—as an exquisite bird could teach a bear if there were any common language between them. Happily, there is a common language between women and men, and so the bears can get taught" (157). After they are married, however, there appears to be no such common language and such dissimilarities lose their charm; Lydgate reflects, "It seemed that she had no more identified herself with him than if they had been creatures of different species and opposing interests" (583). It is a nice irony, and a trenchant comment on the domination/submission configuration, that all of the characteristics Lydgate and Rosamond initially admire in each other are found to be correspondingly distasteful to them during their marriage. The strength of their initial attraction to each other, based on their enactment of the roles of powerful male subject and charmingly compliant female object, becomes an index to the bitterness of their subsequent struggle against each other. The horrible contest between them is portrayed through metaphor as well as through their terrible quarrels, and the metaphors are ones of extraordinary but believable violence. Lydgate's tone of voice is "equivalent to the clutch of his strong hand on Rosamond's delicate arm" (639); he "wanted to smash and grind some object on which he could at least produce an impression" (648); his resolution begins "to relax under her torpedo contact" (648); he "sat down, and got up again restlessly, grasping hard the objects deep down in his pockets" (652); his "need of accommodating himself to her nature . . . held him as with pincers" (655).

The issue between Rosamond and Lydgate is, quite simply, power. The language in which Lydgate ponders the failure of their marriage is laced with phrases such as "the terrible tenacity of this mild creature" (571); "an amazed sense of his powerlessness over Rosamond" (571); "this new form of feminine impassibility revealing itself in the sylph-like frame" (578); and "Rosamond's quiet elusive obstinacy, which would not allow any assertion of power to be final" (648). He is "astounded" to discover that "affection did not make her compliant" (572); that "his will was not a whit stronger than hers" (639); that "the tender devotedness and docile adoration of the ideal wife must be renounced" (639); that "as to saying that he was master, it was not the fact" (648); and that "it would assuredly have been a vain boast in him to say that he was her master" (655). It is difficult to imagine a more ubiquitous use of the term "master" except in a context such as Charlotte Brontë's *Jane Eyre*, where it is used in a much different sense. In portraying so vividly the failure of Rosamond and Lydgate's marriage, it would appear that Eliot is voicing a protest against the gender hierarchy that sets up such unrealistic expectations of domination and control in one member of the partnership. This is not the case, however. Lydgate's is the sympathetic point of view, and there is no suggestion that his expectations are unrealistic or inappropriate; it is Rosamond who is at fault for not meeting them. In other words, the implied ideal is still the domination/submission configuration, which presupposes precisely the kind of womanly compliance, docility and obedience that Lydgate envisions when he first considers marrying Rosamond. In apportioning blame for their marital disaster, Eliot clearly intends the lion's share to fall to Rosamond rather than to Lydgate. Even more than in *Adam Bede*, the beautiful woman who uses her beauty to attract men and then fails to fulfill transcendent patriarchal notions of feminine goodness is seen as an impostor.

Lydgate, too, is blamed much more severely than Adam was for allowing himself to be deceived by the beautiful woman's charms. In fact, the same metaphor for female beauty that was used to excuse Adam's mistake ("The beauty of a lovely woman is like music: what can one say more?") is now used ironically to demonstrate the folly of Lydgate's notions. Soon after he meets Rosamond, he thinks, "That is what a woman ought to be: she ought to produce the effect of exquisite music" (92); and later we are told that "Lydgate felt sure that if ever he married, his wife would have that feminine radiance, that distinctive womanhood which must be classed with flowers and music, that sort of beauty which by its very nature was virtuous, being moulded only for pure and delicate joys" (161). Lydgate is castigated for his misperceptions because he should have known better: he is hardly a rustic like Adam, and he has had the experience of Laure to teach him that beautiful women are capable of destroying their partners. Eliot's view of such errors in *Middlemarch* is considerably less forgiving than in her earlier novels, and she revels in the alacrity with which Lydgate rushes to his doom: "That madness which had once beset him about Laure was not, he thought, likely to recur in relation to any other woman. Certainly, if falling in love had been at all in question, it would have been quite safe with a creature like this Miss Vincy, who had just the kind of intelligence one would desire in a woman—polished, refined, docile, lending itself to finish in all the delicacies of life, and enshrined in a body which expressed this with a force of demonstration that excluded the need for other evidence" (161). Nor does Eliot ever relent. After he has married Rosamond, Lydgate "must walk as he could, carrying that burthen pitifully" (789); she is his basil plant, "a plant which . . . flourished wonderfully on a murdered man's brains" (821).

As in *Adam Bede*, the language of beauty is not to be trusted. Rosamond's appearance patently does not "exclude the need for other evidence" of the "safety" of falling in love with her; on the contrary, she is the most dangerous of women in the patriarchal gallery, the embodiment of male castration anxieties. Her submission to the dominant male is only apparent, and Lydgate's romantic view of "the exquisite wedded affection such as would be bestowed by an accomplished creature . . . who was instructed to the true womanly limit and not a hair's-breadth beyond—docile, therefore, and ready to carry out behests which came from beyond that limit" (344) is sadly mistaken. On one hand Eliot appears to be lodging a feminist protest against a society that objectifies women and judges them by their appearance and petty accomplishments (Lydgate is punished as a representative of this society), but the underlying message is quite contrary to this, a valorization of the domination/submission hierarchy in which a beautiful woman willingly submits to the beneficent mastery of a good man. And, as Dorothea's character illustrates, such womanly submission is desirable even when the man is not particularly beneficent or good, as Casaubon is not.

Throughout the novel, Dorothea's and Rosamond's approaches to marriage are set in counterpoint, filtered through the consciousness of Lydgate. When he is mentally extolling Rosamond's virtues early in their relationship, he reflects in passing that "to his taste . . . here was the point on which Miss Brooke would be found wanting, notwithstanding her undeniable beauty. She did not look at things from the proper feminine angle. The society of such women was about as relaxing as going from your work to teach the second form, instead of reclining in a paradise with sweet laughs for bird-notes, and blue eyes for a heaven" (93). As we know, the error of Lydgate's reasoning as to the "proper feminine angle" of looking at things is forcibly brought home to him over the course of the novel, and Dorothea becomes his (and the reader's) ideal from which Rosamond falls so far short. Dorothea is one of George Eliot's "monumental" heroines, intelligent, spirited and sensitive, a sort of worldly Dinah Morris. She is the precise opposite of Lydgate's initial concept of perfect womanhood, this concept consisting of "an accomplished creature who venerated his high musings and momentous labours and would never interfere with them" (344). Eliot's ideal woman ardently wishes to share her husband's "high musings and momentous labours," and so on this level Dorothea embodies Eliot's feminist contempt for the womanly ideal of her century, "that combination of correct sentiments, music, dancing, drawing, elegant note-writing, private album for extracted verse, and perfect blond loveliness, which made the irresistible woman for the doomed man of that date" (262).

On another level, however, Dorothea projects an image of womanhood that is anything but feminist. (These are the sorts of contradictions, we may note, that make it difficult for George Eliot's critics to assess her relation to the feminist enterprise.) In the area of erotic relations, Dorothea conforms perfectly to the patriarchal ideal of the sublimely submissive partner; the phrase "to devote herself" is used in connection with her as often as "to enslave" is used in connection with Rosamond. She initially attempts to devote herself to someone totally unsuitable in the person of Casaubon, as we know, and to give her her due, Eliot at least creates a negative portrayal of one version of the domination/submission hierarchy, the typical Victorian alliance between an older man and a woman young enough to be his daughter. Just as she pokes fun at Dorothea's exaggerated religiosity ("She felt that she enjoyed [riding] in a pagan sensuous way, and always looked forward to renouncing it," 10), Eliot is quick to point out her heroine's naïveté about marriage: "Dorothea . . . retained very childlike ideas about marriage. She felt sure that she would have accepted the judicious Hooker, if she had been born in time. . . . The really delightful marriage must be that where your husband was a sort of father" (10). Dianne Sadoff has commented at length on the oedipal search of Eliot's heroines for "a sort of father," contending that the informing metaphor in her novels is the Freudian "scene of seduction" and that Eliot's "narrative structure seeks to undercut [the father-figure's] authoritative word and so to usurp it textually as the discourse of a male narrator, the authority of a male author" (3). We will recall a similar search for father-love on the part of Maggie in *The Mill on the Floss*, a search that fails dismally, as Dorothea's does, and a similar undercutting of patriarchal authority. In *Middlemarch* this undercutting is much more straightforward, and accordingly less powerful, than in *The Mill on the Floss*, in that Dorothea is quickly disabused of her belief in such father-love, Casaubon conveniently dies, and the narrator portrays their liaison as folly from the beginning, a scenario that evinces none of the agonized ambivalence of Maggie's conflict.

Dorothea's response to her disillusionment, however, is dismayingly in tune with the "male discourse" of the novel. What she becomes, in fact, is an exemplar of the "tender devotedness and docile adoration" (639) segment of Lydgate's ideal wife fantasy (a segment of which Eliot clearly approves, unlike the segment in which "the ideal wife must somehow worship [his profession] as sublime, though not in the least knowing why," 572). It is to Dorothea's sublime submission to Casaubon that Lydgate explicitly compares Rosamond's wifely disobedience, making himself the more bitter in the process: "He said inwardly, . . . 'It is the way with all women.' But this power of generalizing . . . was immediately thwarted by Lydgate's memory of wondering impressions from the behaviour of another woman—from Dorothea's looks and tones of emotion about her husband . . .—from her passionate cry to be taught what would best comfort that man for whose sake it ͻᴗemed as if she must quell every impulse in her except the yearnings of faithfulness and compassion" (578–79). Dorothea's penchant for submission in her erotic relationships is somewhat difficult to pinpoint as reactionary, simply because it is mingled with her other high-minded and noble characteristics, such as her unawareness of her own beauty (by now a familiar indicator of goodness in Eliot's heroines) and her lack of the materialism that characterizes trivial natures such as Hetty's and Rosamond's (her "notions of marriage," we read, "included neither the niceties of the *trousseau*, the pattern of plate, nor even the honours and sweet joys of the blooming matron," 27).

Nevertheless, such submission is one of Dorothea's salient features, even in her relationship with Will. Christine Sutphin contends that "in this novel Eliot's feminism moves a step forward because she questions her earlier ideal of the husband as mentor. . . . Dorothea learns to see herself as a moral equal in marriage, rather than as a dutiful subordinate" (353, 360), and this is true insofar as Dorothea turns away from a lover whom she initially regards as her superior toward one who is more her equal. But in the psychological nuances of their erotic interaction, Will remains Dorothea's superior as surely as Casaubon ever did, as we can see in the scenes that occur between them. Will worships his chosen love object in the manner of any desiring male subject ("Dorothea, he said to himself, was for ever enthroned in his soul: no other woman could sit higher than her footstool," 460–61), and when they finally confess their feelings for each other it is he who initiates the exchange ("She did not move, and he came towards her," 796) while she enacts the part of the reassuringly reluctant object ("He took her hand and raised it to his lips. . . . Dorothea, withdrawing it in a confusion that distressed her, looked and moved away," 798) who finally submits passively and tenderly to his overtures ("Will . . . laid his hand on hers, which turned itself upward to be clasped," 799). In the latter instance, in fact, Dorothea's hand seems to act independently of her volition, graphically illustrating the "unconscious" nature of her desire for Will. Quite incredibly, Dorothea remains oblivious not only to Will's desire for her but also to her own desire for him until she imagines a connection between him and Rosamond, lending credence to Sadoff's oedipal, triangular, Freudian analysis. And tellingly, Eliot reverts to her "two innocent children" motif in describing an early exchange between Will and Dorothea: "They were looking at each other like two fond children who were talking confidentially of birds"(383).

Once again, Eliot does not allow her heroine, a fully developed subject in other aspects of her life, any appreciable degree of erotic subjectivity. This discrepancy is especially noticeable in a character like Dorothea who is otherwise so self-aware and self-motivated, and critics have been quick to point it out: Elizabeth Ermarth remarks that "Dorothea's secret from herself is that she has personal desires" (*George Eliot* 112); Christine Sutphin says that "in her relationship with Will, she often seems like the traditional passive heroine, afraid to acknowledge or reveal her love" (352); and Baruch Hochman complains that "though George Eliot conveys the exultation that Dorothea feels when Will responds so vividly to her, this exultation is never given a convincingly concrete erotic tinge" (34). Certainly Dorothea does seem to desire Will, but there is an air of something strangely missing in their relationship, a dislocation in the erotic matrix of the novel, that is caused (as critics have also noted) by the relationship that never comes about between Dorothea and Lydgate. This unrealized connection is important by virtue of the fact, running like a persistent undercurrent in the novel, that it is Lydgate rather than Will who has the necessary combination of intellectual, moral and emotional power to be a fitting male Other for Dorothea to submit to. As it is, Lydgate and Dorothea develop a Platonic affection for each other in the context of a "safe" relationship that exists outside their sexual connections to other people. In this context, and in response to "the searching tenderness of her woman's tones," Lydgate is able to unburden himself in a way that is impossible in his adversarial relationship with Rosamond: "He gave himself up, for the first time in his life, to the exquisite sense of leaning entirely on a generous sympathy, without any check of proud reserve. And he told her everything" (752).

A precursor of the relationship between Gwendolen and Deronda, the friendship between Dorothea and Lydgate is a tantalizing device on Eliot's part, a vehicle allowing closeness between a male and a female character without the threat of active eroticism to mar its transcendent purity. Although the "friendship" aspect of this relationship is stressed (Lydgate thinks, "She seems to have what I never saw in any woman before—a fountain of friendship towards men—a man can make a friend of her"), it is undoubtedly erotic. The "searching tenderness" of Dorothea's "woman's tones" makes this clear, as does Lydgate's further speculation as to whether "she could have any . . . sort of passion for a man" (758). Also, he worships her in exactly the same way that Will does, or that any lover would, seeing in her the divine maternal goodness that female beauty ideally signifies: "He thought, 'This young creature has a heart large enough for the Virgin Mary . . . as if she wanted nothing for herself but a chair to sit in from which she can look down with those clear eyes at the poor mortals who pray to her' " (758). Even in a Platonic friendship, the domination/submission hierarchy comes into play, with the male friend occupying the position of the desiring subject, and the female friend (who has no erotic desires of her own) enacting the worshipped and desired object. Such a friendship has its own built-in component of renunciation, we may note, and undoubtedly appeals to Eliot in this way as well.

We can conclude, then, that in *Middlemarch* Eliot retreats from the attempt to explore female desire that she initiated in *The Mill on the Floss* a decade earlier. Dorothea is created to encompass much less erotic subjectivity than Maggie, even though she is generally a more powerful and competent character, and Rosamond simply manipulates the male's desire, her own being relegated to the realm of vanity rather than eroticism. There is no suggestion that either of these female characters could legitimately employ either the look or the language of desire, and enactment (apart from Rosamond's passive maneuvers) is accordingly out of the question. Even the mutual gazing that creates so much of the erotic ambience in *The Mill on the Floss* is ironically dismissed by the narrator of *Middlemarch*, when it occurs between Rosamond and Lydgate, as "that peculiar meeting [of eyes] which is never arrived at by effort, but seems like a sudden divine clearance of haze" (114). Not much erotic looking or speaking takes place in the course of the novel, in fact, but when it does, the male characters invariably initiate it: Casaubon and Will speak and Dorothea listens, Lydgate and Will look and Rosamond is looked at, and even the stolid Mary Garth is actively pursued by Fred and Mr. Farebrother. And all of these relationships, we may note, take place in a system of interlocking homosocial triangles in which the female object is vied for in some sense by two male subjects. The active male subject/passive female object configuration is thus confirmed and reconfirmed in the structure of the novel itself, pointing to an entrenchment of Eliot's earlier views on the role of women in erotic relations. Basically, the ideal woman is still the ideal object, beautiful, submissive and erotically passive.

There are an honesty and a cogency in Eliot's discussion of erotic power structures in *Middlemarch*, however, that do much to redeem her reluctance to explore the possibilities of female desire. Lydgate's and Rosamond's story rings true in every respect, and it takes little extrapolation to locate the source of their marital disaster in the domination/submission roles that they play to perfection. Eliot clearly finds this concept of romance odious, even though she has nothing concrete to advocate in its place and even though she intimates that its inadequacies in this particular case are directly related to Rosamond's failure to submit unreservedly to Lydgate's wishes and judgment. It seems fair to conclude that Eliot remains troubled about erotic relationships in general, an assessment that is confirmed in her last and in some ways her most exploratory novel, *Daniel Deronda*.

DANIEL DERONDA

George Eliot's final novel is, in many ways, her most intriguing. In *Daniel Deronda* we can see the culmination, the logical conclusion, of many of Eliot's approaches to the problematic issue of how men and women should relate to each other and what constitutes a desirable love relationship. The novel's main character, Gwendolen Harleth, is among the most fascinating of nineteenth-century heroines and a radical departure from Eliot's earlier fictional females. The tale itself is an astonishing exploration of domination and submission, including a pre-Freudian analysis of two of the more pathological "minor keys" of sexuality, sadism and frigidity. Nor does this analysis pose any of the expected problems of decorum for Eliot; because it is pre-Freudian, in fact, she can examine freely such sexually aberrant aspects of male-female interactions without openly acknowledging their eroticism. Thus Gwendolen and Grandcourt can play out their intense power struggle, and Gwendolen and Deronda can become priest and confessor to each other, without any mention of the erotic component of such relationships. The result—a tribute to George Eliot's delicate and internalized grasp of Victorian authorial proprieties—is at once a faithful adherence to the ideal of transcendence and, paradoxically, an extremely (albeit obliquely) erotic novel. George Steiner's analysis of Eliot's "zone of silence," the "energy of undeclared content" (105) of her work, is nowhere more applicable.

Gwendolen as a subject of desire is accordingly an interesting proposition. She is obviously very different from Eliot's previous heroines, in that she has none of their innate spiritual goodness. Eliot's familiar dichotomy between the vain and the spiritual woman persists in *Daniel Deronda* in the characters of Gwendolen and Mirah (persists with a vengeance, in fact), but in this case it is the vain woman who is the undisputed heroine of the novel. Gwendolen is more akin to Rosamond Vincy than to any other of Eliot's female characters, but there is no similarity in their treatments at the hands of Eliot's narrator or in their places in the novels they inhabit. Rosamond is the bad example in *Middlemarch*, the foil for Eliot's creation of the womanly ideal in the person of Dorothea, and she is treated with all of the contempt Eliot feels for the type of vain and trivial femininity she represents. She is not a subject, even in her own consciousness, but neither is she the perfectly submissive object she purports to be. Gwendolen is also a vain, power-conscious, willful character; unlike Rosamond, however, she is the true subject of Eliot's novel and is treated with what Dorothea Barrett terms "narratorial gentleness" (159). Barrett sees Gwendolen as "a breakthrough in George Eliot's treatment of women, and a breakthrough in the treatment of women in fiction. . . . In *Daniel Deronda*, George Eliot can finally sympathize with a heroine who . . . is not earnestly and implausibly altruistic but humanly self-seeking and limited. . . . George Eliot at last flouts the establishment values that insisted that the only admirable woman was a selfless woman, a submissive woman, a woman without avowed sexual appetites and aversions" (155, 158).

It is certainly true that Gwendolen represents a new departure for Eliot insofar as she is "humanly self-seeking and limited." The narrator of *Daniel Deronda* shows an amazing tolerance for these moral and spiritual shortcomings, excusing them generally on the basis of Gwendolen's upbringing ("To be protected and petted, and to have her susceptibilities consulted in every detail, had gone along with her food and clothing as matters of course in her life," 253). Barrett's inclusion of "avowed sexual appetites and aversions" in Eliot's revolutionary creation of Gwendolen's character is more problematic, however. The aversions are there, most definitely; but the appetites, as I shall show, are signally missing, and for the reasons we have observed in connection with the elision of the erotic from Eliot's previous novels: even at the end of her career, the Victorian ideal of bodily transcendence remained of beleaguered importance to her. Accordingly Gwendolen, like Maggie Tulliver, remains something of a missed opportunity for Eliot, a character whose capacity for erotic desire is never fulfilled and who instead "triumphs" only by renouncing such desire. And while Maggie's "victory" is at least ambiguous, Gwendolen's, seemingly, is not; the renunciation of all personal desire, as the epigraph stresses, is portrayed as the most valuable lesson she can learn ("Let thy chief terror be of thine own soul: / There, 'mid the throng of hurrying desires / That trample o'er the dead to seize their spoil, / Lurks vengeance"). The result, as in *Middlemarch*, is a novel that falls just short of the feminist statement it seems inclined to make. But, also like *Middlemarch*, it encompasses a brilliant analysis of the domination/submission relation as it reveals itself in a power struggle within marriage, and this in itself makes *Daniel Deronda* a novel of absorbing interest to the feminist critic.

I shall begin my analysis once again with the question of female beauty, which is no less important to *Daniel Deronda* than it is to Eliot's other novels. The entire first paragraph of the book, in fact, consists of a highly scopophilic device, a series of questions about Gwendolen's beauty occurring to an as-yet unspecified observer: "Was she beautiful or not beautiful? and what was the secret of form or expression which gave the dynamic quality to her glance? Was the good or the evil genius dominant in those beams? Probably the evil; else why was the effect that of unrest rather than of undisturbed charm? Why was the wish to look again felt as coercion and not as a longing in which the whole being consents?" (3). Such a direct opening, so unlike the meandering beginnings of many of George Eliot's other novels, poses at once the central dilemma of the novel (Gwendolen's moral status), through the point of view of a character who will be intimately involved in that dilemma. That the observer is male is a given, presupposed by the assumption of the right to appraise, the combination of attraction and repulsion that the look occasions (the "wish to look again" is "felt as coercion") and the very fact of looking itself. This is not quite the look of desire, but it is certainly a concise and vivid encapsulation of the familiar scopophilic dynamic in which the narrator, the reader and a male character engage in looking at the novel's central female character and appraising her aesthetically (and in this case morally). The appraisal is not explicitly sexual, but the erotic is inevitably implicated in such masculine gazing, which is continued throughout the first chapter of the book.

The gaze is troubling to both Gwendolen and Deronda, prefiguring the difficulties their connection will eventually cause each of them. He experiences her attraction for him as "coercion," and she experiences her consciousness of his look as "something like a pressure which begins to be torturing" (6), although this consciousness, like his, is ambivalent ("It was at least better that he should have kept his attention fixed on her than that he should have disregarded her," 7). We are also given the sexual appraisal of Gwendolen by the onlookers at the gambling casino, a device which enhances the erotic ambience of the scene as a whole and reinscribes the dynamics of the seeing/seen dyad as society's customary form of female appraisal. She is described by one group as "a sort of serpent," a temptress for whom "a man might risk hanging," and someone else notices that she has a beautiful complexion, a "delicate nose with [a] gradual little upward curve" and a pretty mouth with lips that "curl backwards so finely," occasioning a further comment by someone called Mackworth that it is the "sort of mouth . . . [that] looks so self-complacent, as if it knew its own beauty. . . . I like a mouth that trembles more" (8). The undertone of violence in many of these observations (the serpent, the hanging, the trembling mouth) foreshadows the sadism which will permeate Gwendolen's story, as does her own commentary as the chapter closes: "I am bored to death. If I am to leave off play I must break my arm or my collar-bone. I must make something happen" (9).

The question of whether or not Gwendolen is beautiful, like the question of her moral status, is never quite resolved (and the former functions as a sort of analogue for the latter). Deronda's initial impression of her as having "a face which might possibly be looked at without admiration, but could hardly be passed with indifference" (5) remains true of Gwendolen herself throughout the novel. To the external observer she appears beautiful but dangerous; she is even more overtly compared to a serpent than Rosamond was, and the narrator remarks on "the undefinable stinging quality—as it were a trace of demon ancestry—which made some beholders hesitate in their admiration of Gwendolen" (60). Even her uncle thinks of her as a "young witch—who . . . was more mischievous than could be desired" (69). Such demonic allusions would seem to indicate a morally suspect character, at the very least. Gwendolen is also vain, delighting in admiration as much as Hetty Sorrel, even to the point of kissing her own reflection in the looking glass. The narrator, however, somewhat surprisingly, treats such vanity as "an allowable indulgence" (12), remarking, "She had a *naïve* delight in her fortunate self, which any but the harshest saintliness will have some indulgence for in a girl who had every day seen a pleasant reflection of that self in her friends' flattery as well as in the looking-glass" (14).

This is not precisely the indulgent narrator of *The Mill on the Floss* who so willingly excuses Lucy's "harmless flashes of personal vanity" on the grounds of her "ever-present sunny benignity"; but neither is it the unforgiving narrator of *Adam Bede* who indeed seems the embodiment of "the harshest saintliness" in the condemnation of Hetty's self-admiration. *Daniel Deronda's* narrator hovers somewhere between these two views of feminine vanity, undoubtedly indicating Eliot's continuing perplexity as to the connection between female beauty and female goodness, a much-debated issue throughout her career. Her creation of Hetty and later of Rosamond—both of whom are beautiful but far from "good"—would seem to argue against such a connection, except that the novel's polemic in each case assures the reader that these individual women characters are the exception rather than the rule. Eliot is still clearly unwilling to relinquish completely the notion of a "language of beauty" that is a reliable indicator of internal goodness (although the narrator of *Daniel Deronda* is dismissive of the naïve exponent of this view, Rex, "a youthful lover . . . [to whom] it seems that the fundamental identity of the good, the true, and the beautiful, is already extant and manifest in the object of his love," 60). This problem is resolved in her final novel, however, by the simple expedient of leaving the issue of Gwendolen's beauty in doubt: significantly, the novel's opening question, "Was she beautiful or not beautiful?" is never answered.

There are not many physical descriptions of Gwendolen, then, as her beauty is not her most striking quality, and on the whole *Daniel Deronda* is not a particularly scopophilic novel. But Gwendolen is an unquestionably vain character, and, like Rosamond, is quite willing to play the part of the beautiful object in order to exploit the power it gives her over her audience, particularly her male audience. When she wins the archery competition, for example, we are told that "the perfect movement of her fine form was certainly a pleasant thing to behold. . . . She was the central object of that pretty picture, and everyone present must gaze at her. That was enough: she herself was determined to see nobody in particular. . . . Mr. Grandcourt was seeing her to the utmost advantage, and was probably giving her an admiration unmixed with criticism. She did not expect to admire *him*, but that was not necessary to her peace of mind" (96). Here Gwendolen is presented as a "thing," an "object" of a "picture," all familiar terms of feminine objectification. We are also given her consciousness of the effect this picture produces on Grandcourt, together with her awareness that such admiration "naturally" flows in only one direction, from the male to the female. That this gives her a certain power Gwendolen is well aware, but as a later passage in the novel indicates, she is also aware that such power is not entirely within her control. She is waiting for Klesmer to come and hear her play the piano, and

Catching the reflection of her movements in the glass panel, she was diverted to the contemplation of the image there and walked towards it. . . . She might have tempted an artist to try . . . the Roman trick of a statue in black, white, and tawny marble. Seeing her image slowly advancing, she thought, "I *am* beautiful"—not exultingly, but with grave decision. Being beautiful was after all the condition on which she most needed external testimony. If any one objected to the turn of her nose or the form of her neck and chin, she had not the sense that she could presently show her power of attainment in these branches of feminine perfection. (233)

In this passage we can see once again Eliot's discomfort with the issue of female beauty. Gwendolen's image is referred to as an "it" and likened to an art object, evoking the notion of aesthetic appraisal that applies to both women and works of art; and the thought that logically follows is a sobering one to the object concerned, the thought that she herself is basically powerless over the impression she makes on the viewer. The irony of the "power of attainment in these branches of feminine perfection" underlines the female's very real lack of control over this attribute to which so much significance is attached. And when Klesmer arrives, it also becomes apparent to Gwendolen that this significance itself is not to be relied on, as Klesmer has "the air of a monster impenetrable by beauty" (238). Such speculations would be beyond the capability of Eliot's other vain heroines, Hetty and Rosamond, who simply use the power their beauty gives them without any thought of its constraints, in the manner of conventional objects of desire. Gwendolen, more intelligent than either of these earlier versions of vanity, is a true subject, using her status as a beautiful object with full awareness of both its power and its weakness. Eliot has clearly made giant leaps in her ability to tolerate and understand the vain woman's vanity since her castigation of Rosamond in *Middlemarch* five years earlier. (According to Gillian Beer, "In Gwendolen, George Eliot makes restitution to those earlier figures such as Hetty and Rosamond excluded from her full sympathy because they could never succeed in fully sympathising with others," 219.)

Not surprisingly, given the marked importance of the gaze from the beginning of the novel, the courtship between Gwendolen and Grandcourt is conducted partly through the exchange of significant looks. At first, these mainly consist of Grandcourt looking at Gwendolen. After they are first introduced, "what is called conversation had begun, the first and constant element in it being that Grandcourt looked at Gwendolen persistently with a slightly exploring gaze, but without change of expression, while she only occasionally looked at him with a flash of observation a little softened by coquetry" (98); and at the archery ball Gwendolen "noticed that he did sometimes quietly and gradually change his position according to hers, so that he could see her whenever she was dancing" (104). Gwendolen is initially content to be the object of Grandcourt's gaze ("If he did not admire her—so much the worse for him," 104), but at one point, at least, she actively gazes back: "Gwendolen suddenly turned her head and looked full at Grandcourt, whose eyes she had felt to be upon her throughout their conversation. She was wondering what the effect of looking at him would be on herself rather than on him." This is a bold and unusual move for the heroine of a Victorian novel, and a measure of Gwendolen's subjectivity. It appears to have little relevance to her erotic subjectivity, being enacted out of curiosity rather than desire, but it is an indication of Eliot's willingness to go beyond the bounds of feminine decorum in her final novel.

It is also a move that confirms Grandcourt's power rather than Gwendolen's, as the "effect of looking at him" turns out to be mesmerizing: "It flashed through her thought that a sort of lotos-eater's stupor had begun in him and was taking possession of her" (120). When she flirtatiously deflects his compliments (in a further futile attempt to control the developing situation between them), "Grandcourt met her laughing eyes with a slow, steady look right into them, which seemed like vision in the abstract" (132). Later, too, when he is pressing her for an answer to his proposal, Grandcourt overpowers her with his gaze: "She . . . looked straight at Grandcourt, whose long, narrow, inpenetrable [sic] eyes met hers, and mysteriously arrested them" (279). Similarly, when she finally accepts him, he stands "looking straight into her eyes, without other movement" (280), and after they are married, Grandcourt continues to control Gwendolen by means of the gaze ("Grandcourt had a delusive mode of observing whatever had an interest for him, which could be surpassed by no sleepy-eyed animal on the watch for prey," 384). And as the battle is joined between them, their looks become correspondingly antagonistic, a fact noted by Deronda: "It was the first time Deronda had seen them speak to each other since their arrival, and he thought their exchange of looks as cold and official as if it had been a ceremony to keep up a charter" (385–86). This is very different from the first searching looks Deronda himself bestows on Gwendolen, and also from the first look he shares with Mirah. The latter look is similarly significant, and an important indicator of the couple's future relationship: "Looking around with a frightened glance, [Mirah] met Deronda's face. It was but a couple of moments, but that seems a long while for two people to look straight at each other. Her look was something like that of a fawn or other gentle animal before it turns to run away: no blush, no special alarm, but only some timidity which yet could not hinder her from a long look before she turned" (171). Unlike Gwendolen, Mirah is an unambiguously appropriate object of the male gaze, being likened to a "fawn or other gentle animal" as opposed to a serpent. The activity of looking in *Daniel Deronda* is central to the key male-female relationships in the novel, whatever their degree of eroticism.

And Gwendolen, the most looked at of the novel's characters, is an extremely interesting heroine. Vain, beautiful, spoiled, daring and willful, yet sympathetically portrayed from the point of view of an intelligent heroine, she would seem to be a perfect instance of a female subject of desire in the nineteenth-century novel. The problem is that she feels no erotic desire; in an enormously interesting sidestep of the entire issue Eliot makes her heroine frigid. It is a sidestep that Hardy will repeat in the final decade of the century with his final heroine, Sue Bridehead, for slightly different reasons which I shall discuss in the next chapter. Eliot's reason for Gwendolen's frigidity is straightforward: it enables her to explore her character's psyche without appearing to condone (or even to acknowledge) female sexuality in any way. And such a move is psychologically plausible, given Gwendolen's careful creation as a spoiled child in whom the "feminine" qualities of tenderness and compassion seem to be lacking, a forerunner too of Ibsen's Hedda Gabler: in the opening scene of the novel we are told explicitly that "she had gone to the roulette-table not because of passion, but in search of it" (13). Tellingly, Gwendolen has none of the typical Victorian heroine's romantic fantasies about marriage, which she regards as a "vexatious necessity," nor about love ("The question of love on her own part had occupied her scarcely at all in relation to Grandcourt. The desirability of marriage for her had always seemed due to other feelings than love," 253). Furthermore, the narrator tells us directly that "she objected, with a sort of physical repulsion, to being directly made love to. With all her imaginative delight in being adored, there was a certain fierceness of maidenhood in her" (63). The latter remark is occasioned by the amorous advances of Rex, whose primary function in the novel is to draw the reader's attention to this idiosyncrasy ("a sort of physical repulsion") of Gwendolen's. In response to Rex's attentions, "the life of passion had begun negatively in her" and "she felt passionately averse to this volunteered love" (73).

Her revulsion is made entirely believable, partly through the use of metaphors of physical sensitivity ("The perception that poor Rex wanted to be tender made her curl up and harden like a sea-anemone at the touch of a finger," 73), partly through direct authorial comment ("Mrs Vulcany once remarked that Miss Harleth was too fond of the gentlemen; but we know that she was not in the least fond of them—she was only fond of their homage," 102; "She was subject to physical antipathies," 107) and partly through her own admissions (she tells her mother, "I shall never love anybody. I can't love people. I hate them.... I can't bear any one to be very near me but you," 74). It is ironic, and vaguely sinister, that later in the novel she is attracted to Grandcourt partly because of his care not to approach her physically. When they first become engaged, for instance, "she thought his manners as a lover more agreeable than any she had seen described. She had no alarm lest he meant to kiss her.... Really, she thought, he was likely to be the least disagreeable of husbands" (282). The suggestion of the kiss and her reaction to it ("alarm") is insidiously implanted by the statement of its contrary, and it is clear that the experienced and cynical Grandcourt is a much greater cause for sexual uneasiness than the naïve and inoffensive Rex, even though the former is careful not to show it.

In a series of similar small incidents leading up to their marriage (and then abruptly ceasing), Eliot subtly implies the physical and sexual domination that Grandcourt undoubtedly engages in after his prey is safely captured, leaving the reader to conjecture the terror of such domination for a woman like Gwendolen. In one of these characteristic incidents, Gwendolen appears to apprehend the danger that lies ahead:

Grandcourt's behaviour as a lover had hardly at all passed the limit of an amorous homage which was inobtrusive as a wafted odour of roses, and spent all its effect in a gratified vanity. One day, indeed, he had kissed not her cheek but her neck a little below her ear; and Gwendolen, taken by surprise, had started up with a marked agitation which made him rise too and say, "I beg your pardon—did I annoy you?" "Oh, it was nothing," said Gwendolen, rather afraid of herself, "only I cannot bear—to be kissed under my ear." She sat down again with a little playful laugh, but all the while she felt her heart beating with a vague fear: she was no longer at liberty to flout him as she had flouted poor Rex. (299–300)

Here Grandcourt's behavior "as a lover" is implicitly contrasted with his future behavior as a husband, which may well include kisses (and other caresses) on Gwendolen's neck (and on other parts of her body). Gwendolen is "afraid of herself" because her natural inclination is to "flout" Grandcourt, thus incurring his disapproval; the hesitation after "I cannot bear" is telling (what she really cannot bear is to be touched at all). The "vague fear" with which her heart beats has, as the reader realizes, ample cause.

In another, similar incident we are given Grandcourt's view of the situation as well as Gwendolen's. The latter has just made a facetious comment, and the issue of kissing comes up again:

"Then I am not to ask for one kiss," said Grandcourt, contented to pay a large price for this new kind of love-making, which introduced marriage by the finest contrast.

"Not one!" said Gwendolen, getting saucy, and nodding at him defiantly.

He lifted her little left hand to his lips and then released it respectfully. Clearly it was faint praise to say of him that he was not disgusting: he was almost charming; and she felt at this moment that it was not likely she could ever have loved another man better than this one. His reticence gave her some inexplicable, delightful consciousness. (301)

Gwendolen's naïveté here is chilling, as it is obvious that Grandcourt's "reticence" is a false reassurance, merely the "large price" he is willing to pay for his marriage, which will be "introduced . . . by the finest contrast." Grandcourt clearly finds this contrast titillating, whereas Gwendolen, ignorant of its very existence, merely classifies his behavior as "not disgusting" on the basis of his agreeing not to kiss her lips but only her hand. It is by such subtle touches that Eliot creates the impression of sexual horrors in their relationship, even though no such horrors are ever mentioned or even alluded to after their marriage. Gwendolen is simply unaware of the sexual component of domination, and continues to be unaware of it until escape is impossible. When Grandcourt announces his "business trip" to Gadsmere, for instance, Gwendolen's "concentration in other feelings had really hindered her from taking notice that her hand was being held" (300); and even on their wedding day, "when her husband said, 'Here we are home!' and for the first time kissed her on the lips, she hardly knew of it: it was no more than the passive acceptance of a greeting in the midst of an absorbing show" (329). We can infer that Gwendolen will accept Grandcourt's conjugal demands "passively," because she has no choice; but we can also be sure that she will loathe them.

In its way, Eliot's depiction of the relationship between Gwendolen and Grandcourt is the quintessential tale of domination and submission between the sexes, every bit as brutal as the *Story of O* but without the sexual element. It is the perfect depiction of a sadistic marriage from a Victorian point of view, and a monument to Eliot's perfect mastery of the idiom of reticence, gaps and silences that constituted the novelist's erotic lexicon in her era. As we have seen, Gwendolen naïvely supposes that marriage will give her more complete control over Grandcourt; she thinks, "What could not a woman do when she was married, if she knew how to assert herself?" causing the narrator to remark, "Here was all constructive imagination. Gwendolen had about as accurate a conception of marriage—that is to say, of the mutual influences, demands, duties of man and woman in a state of matrimony—as she had of magnetic currents and the law of storms" (275). And again, when Gwendolen is "thinking of [Grandcourt] . . . as a man over whom she was going to have indefinite power," the narrator comments, "Poor Gwendolen had no awe of unmanageable forces in the state of matrimony, but regarded it as altogether a matter of management, in which she would know how to act" (288–89). The hints of "storms" and "unmanageable forces" figuratively reinforce the psychological and sexual cruelty of which Grandcourt is capable and of which Gwendolen is so unaware. Ironically, she is in fact attracted to Grandcourt because of his supercilious reserve and lack of tenderness, telling her mother, "He is very proud. But so am I. We shall match each other. I should hate a man who went down on his knees, and came fawning on me. He really is not disgusting" (287).

The word "disgust"—a significant word because of its sublimated allusion to the physical—is often used in connection with Gwendolen's musings about Grandcourt, sometimes in blatantly contradictory ways. The assertion "He is not disgusting" constitutes her highest praise of him; but shortly before she expresses this sentiment to her mother, we are told that "Gwendolen had found no objection to Grandcourt's way of being enamoured before she had had that glimpse of his past. . . . His advances to *her* were deliberate, and she felt a retrospective disgust for them. Perhaps other men's lives were of the same kind—full of secrets which made the ignorant suppositions of the woman they wanted to marry a farce at which they were laughing in their sleeves" (276). The latter statement displays a precocious cynicism on the part of Eliot's heroine, making her a far more interesting character than Rosamond, for example, whose illusions of female power are never dispelled by any negative display of male force. Gwendolen is also more perceptive than the sheltered Rosamond about the attractions of extra-marital affairs after she is married:

As for fascinated gentlemen—adorers who might hover round her with languishment, and diversify married life with the romantic stir of mystery, passion, and danger which her French reading had given her some girlish notion of—they presented themselves to her imagination with the fatal circumstance that, instead of fascinating her in return, they were clad in her own weariness and disgust. The admiring male, rashly adjusting the expression of his features and the turn of his conversation to her supposed tastes, had always been an absurd object to her, and at present seemed rather detestable. (400)

Gwendolen's disgust is a sexual disgust, and takes its place as one of her weapons in the battle she is destined to play out in her marriage to Grandcourt: at one point, "curiously enough she rejected a handkerchief on which her maid had by mistake put the wrong scent—a scent that Grandcourt had once objected to. Gwendolen would not have liked to be an object of disgust to this husband whom she hated: she liked all disgust to be on her side" (560).

And all of the disgust is indeed on her side, but with no effect whatever on Grandcourt (who has all of the power on his side). Before they are married, Gwendolen's distaste for him merely adds to the challenge of capturing her: "His strongest wish was to be completely master of this creature—this piquant combination of maidenliness and mischief: that she knew things which had made her start away from him, spurred him to triumph" (279); and after they are married, she is sure that "he had had a peculiar triumph in conquering her dumb repugnance.... Her imagination exaggerated every tyrannical impulse he was capable of" (560). However much she exaggerates, she will not be far from Grandcourt's capacity for tyranny, which is considerable; Eliot's picture of a sadistic personality is appallingly accurate. Basically, Grandcourt's only mode of interaction with other beings (including Lush, Mrs Glasher and his dogs, as well as Gwendolen) is one of control, and if the control is against the other's will, so much the better. Before he marries Gwendolen we are given access to his thoughts, and

It was characteristic that he got none of his satisfaction from the belief that Gwendolen was in love with him.... On the contrary, he believed that this girl was rather exceptional in the fact that, in spite of his assiduous attention to her, she was not in love with him.... She had been brought to accept him in spite of everything.... on the whole, Grandcourt got more pleasure out of this notion than he could have done out of winning a girl of whom he was sure that she had a strong inclination for him personally.... In any case she would have to submit; and he enjoyed thinking of her as his future wife, whose pride and spirit were suited to command every one but himself. He had no taste for a woman who was all tenderness to him, full of petitioning solicitude and willing obedience. He meant to be master of a woman who would have liked to master him, and who perhaps would have been capable of mastering another man. (293–94)

Here Grandcourt's motives for wanting to marry Gwendolen are made painfully explicit from the point of view of the dominant member of the sexual hierarchy. Stripped of any pretense of love, the power structure inherent in the erotic paradigm emerges in stark clarity, and Grandcourt exults in his sheer mastery of "a woman who would have liked to master him, and who perhaps would have been capable of mastering another man." Grandcourt is a psychologically alienated and isolated male, and his capture of Gwendolen is a clear instance of the traditional patriarchal competition for and ownership of women, the important element being its symbolic elevation of the winner's status over that of other males. Thus, when he notices the developing relationship between Gwendolen and Deronda,

He would have denied that he was jealous; because jealousy would have implied some doubt of his own power to hinder what he had determined against. That his wife should have more inclination to another man's society than to his own would not pain him: what he required was that she should be as fully aware as she would have been of a locked hand-cuff, that her inclination was helpless to decide anything in contradiction with his resolve. . . . Few perhaps may follow him in his contentment that his wife should be in a temper which would dispose her to fly out if she dared . . . [except] those who prefer command to love. (543–44)

His relationship with Mrs Glasher, too, is one of sadistic control, even though "the disposition to exercise power either by cowing or disappointing others or exciting in them a rage which they dared not express—a disposition which was active in him as other propensities became languid—had always been in abeyance before Lydia" because of "the power she had had over him" (315). Grandcourt, like Rosamond, is one of the few characters in George Eliot's canon toward whom she expresses no sympathy whatever, although Rosamond's attempts to control other people seem innocuous in comparison to those of Grandcourt. The latter's active pleasure in tormenting the helpless is evil, while Rosamond's marital resistances are simply misguided and irresponsible.

That Grandcourt's pleasure in mastery is also erotic there is no doubt, as he feels and expresses the most desire for Gwendolen when he most senses her resistance. When she objects to his going to Gadsmere, he "enfold[s] her hand" and "thought that he knew the reason of what he inwardly called this bit of temper, and she was particularly fascinating to him at this moment" (300); and when he sends Lush to speak to her about his will,

" 'She is in a desperate rage,' thought he. But the rage was silent, and therefore not disagreeable to him. It followed that he turned her chin and kissed her" (556). In the face of such experienced and finely tuned sadism, Gwendolen's thoughts of controlling Grandcourt seem ludicrous, consisting of what Eliot refers to as a "piteous equality in the need to dominate" (279). And "piteous" is the right word, as the metaphorical undercurrents of the novel make clear. As critics have noted, the horse metaphor (a common symbol of mastery) that both Gwendolen and Grandcourt use in their thoughts of each other places the advantage entirely with the latter. Gwendolen exults in her power over Grandcourt when he is courting her and she refuses him ("The thought that he was coming to be refused was inspiriting: she had the white reins in her hands again; . . . she was going to exercise her power," 277), but she is naïvely and cruelly mistaken. It soon becomes apparent to her that "it was as if she had consented to mount a chariot where another held the reins" (301). Grandcourt's mental imagery is more cruel and more specific, and captures perfectly the humiliation inherent in Gwendolen's submission to him: "She had been . . . brought to kneel down like a horse under training for the arena" (293). Similarly, when he forces her to wear his diamonds, "Grandcourt inwardly observed that she answered to the rein" (398).

Another disturbing and recurrent image that signifies the seriousness of their struggle (like Rosamond's and Lydgate's, it is a fight to the death) is the image of strangling. On her wedding day, Gwendolen has the sense "that the cord which united her with this lover and which she had hitherto held by the hand, was now being flung over her neck" (326), a perfect metaphor for the reversal of control that occurs when she becomes Grandcourt's wife and a subtle allusion to the pervasive horse imagery. Later, when she tries to refuse to wear the diamonds, the impersonal cord has become Grandcourt's hand, an indirect reference to the physical, the sexual, the unspeakable aspect of their relationship now that they are married: "That white hand of his which was touching his whisker was capable, she fancied, of clinging round her neck and threatening to throttle her" (397). The whisker, too, nicely implies the physical intimacy Gwendolen must now endure, a good example of Eliot's deft and concise sexual shorthand. The strangling image comes to represent all of Gwendolen's fears in the relationship, and she becomes obsessed with it ("She was as frightened at a quarrel as if she had foreseen that it would end with throttling fingers on her neck. . . ," 525–26; "The thought of his dying would not subsist: it turned as with a dream-change into the terror that she should die with his throttling fingers on her neck avenging that thought," 564). In this way the potential violence of the connection between Gwendolen and Grandcourt is constantly brought to the reader's attention. Other metaphors, too, reinforce the sadistic aspects of Grandcourt's gloating male domination and Gwendolen's agonized female submission: "Already, in seven short weeks, . . . her husband had gained a mastery which she could no more resist than she could have resisted the benumbing effect from the touch of a torpedo. . . . She had found a will like that of a crab or a boa-constrictor which goes on pinching or crushing without alarm at thunder" (394); Grandcourt is "conscious of using pincers on that white creature" (547); and "The walls had begun to be an imprisonment, and while there was breath in this man he would have the mastery over her. His words had the power of thumbscrews and the cold touch of the rack" (634).

Thus the erotic in *Daniel Deronda* is dangerous, a violent contest between the genders with no hope of an equitable solution. And women fare the worst in this contest, as we can see not only from Gwendolen's experience but also from that of Mrs Glasher, who is described as "a lost vessel after whom nobody would send out an expedition of search," while "Grandcourt was seen in harbour with his colours flying, registered as seaworthy as ever" (312). The question of love does not enter into it; as we have seen, Gwendolen feels unable to love anyone and Grandcourt is too selfish. Loving or tender feelings would be a distinct handicap in such a battle, as Lydgate discovers in *Middlemarch* and as Deronda's mother believes. The latter's sentiments, in fact, which Gwendolen herself might have expressed, are an explicit protest against the woman's role of submission in the erotic hierarchy: "I am not a loving woman. . . . It is a talent to love—I lacked it. Others have loved me—and I have acted their love. I know very well what love makes of men and women—it is subjection. It takes another for a larger self, enclosing this one" (620). This is an accurate and concise description of the "normal" erotic dynamic in which it is the male who actively desires while the passive female responds to his desire ("Others have loved me—and I have acted their love") and merges her identity in his ("takes another for a larger self"). Gwendolen, too, believes that "to be enamoured was the part of the man, on whom the advances depended" (276).

The blame for the Grandcourts' marital fiasco is equally apportioned, even though it is Gwendolen rather than Grandcourt who is the victim in the overall scenario. They are both blamed for wanting to control the other, Grandcourt because his love of domination is excessive and Gwendolen because of the tacit ideological expectation that a loving woman should not want to dominate at all. Essentially, their marriage is a fictional enactment of what happens when a vain woman like Gwendolen captures a man like Grandcourt instead of a man like Lydgate—when she meets her match, in other words. Lydgate, like Grandcourt, also expects obedience as a matter of course (and there is no suggestion that this expectation is amiss) but is willing to use his male power in order to care for a woman rather than to master her. Likewise (and curiously, since she has the narrator's sympathy), Gwendolen is a more extreme version of Rosamond, in that she makes no pretense of the docility that the latter plays so convincingly. Overall, the battle for control in *Daniel Deronda* is much more straightforward than it is in *Middlemarch*. Eliot's ideological position in the later novel is not so clear, however. Not only does she privilege the point of view of the non-submissive woman, but her exploration of the psychological intricacies of domination and submission results in a ghastly portrait of two people locked together in an embrace of mutual destruction, seemingly indicating a disenchantment with the whole concept of erotic domination. It is strikingly clear that Gwendolen should not, in fact, submit to her husband. On the other hand, the implied ideal in the book—the relationship between Deronda and Mirah—enacts a conventional pattern of male strength and female weakness, an active man rescuing and then pursuing a passive and initially helpless woman; and there is some suggestion that this is the kind of relationship Gwendolen herself could have attained if she had been as sweet and submissive as Mirah.

But Gwendolen has much to learn about the art of submission (she is envious of Mirah's ability to submit to duty, "having an ill-defined consciousness that her own submission was something very different," 517), and the relationship she eventually attains with Deronda is far from conventional. Several critics (Gillian Beer, for example) tend to see this relationship as revolutionary, an exploration by Eliot of "the capacities of human beings to work outside assigned sex roles" (227). I think it is quite the opposite, another characteristic "sidestep" of the erotic by Eliot and a confirmation of the desirability of transcendence in human relationships. Prefigured in the friendship between Dorothea and Lydgate, the connection between Gwendolen and Deronda is another, more fully developed attempt to portray love between the sexes without evoking the erotic. And Eliot partly succeeds in this attempt, mainly by virtue of the devices of Gwendolen's frigidity, which I have already mentioned, and a corresponding quality in Deronda, a sort of androgynous asceticism.

This is a difficult attribute to particularize, and Eliot uses painstaking care in defining it for the reader. Outwardly, it partly resides in his gaze, with which the novel begins and which has such a profound effect on Gwendolen. Later in the book, this look is described as "his usual directness of gaze—a large-eyed gravity, innocent of any intention. His eyes had a peculiarity which has drawn many men into trouble: they were of a dark yet mild intensity, which seemed to express a special interest in every one on whom he fixed them, and might easily help to bring on him those claims which ardently sympathetic people are often creating in the minds of those who need help" (304). This look, which often "penetrates" Gwendolen during the course of the novel, has a particularly moving effect on women, as Sir Hugo's teasing comment to Deronda reveals: "You are always looking tenderly at the women, and talking to them in a Jesuitical way. You are a dangerous young fellow—a kind of Lovelace who will make the Clarissas run after you instead of your running after them" (332–33). This superficially facetious comment nicely encapsulates the contraries embedded in Deronda's demeanor: he is at once without sexual appeal ("Jesuitical") and saturated with it ("a kind of Lovelace"). Nor is this a difficult juxtaposition to understand: as romance writers in any century have always known, the blend of the attractive and the unattainable constitutes the most erotic combination there is, an irresistible challenge to deep and regressive tendencies in the human psyche. Combined with Deronda's "tenderness," such priestly aloofness is bound to evoke the oedipal breaking down of forbidden barriers in his encounters with women. This is an extremely compelling version, we may note, of the fantasy of erotic submission, in which the female longs to be "released into abandon by another who remains in control" (Benjamin, "Desire" 97). Deronda's spirituality is ample evidence of such control, and it is small wonder that Sir Hugo jests about women running after him.

Inwardly, Deronda is also this mixture of opposing impulses, the subtle distinctions of which Eliot takes some trouble to trace. He is instinctively altruistic: "Persons attracted him in proportion to the possibility of his defending them, rescuing them, telling upon their lives with some sort of redeeming influence." On the other hand,

in the movement which had led him to redeem Gwendolen's necklace for her, . . . there was . . . something due to the fascination of her womanhood. He was very open to that sort of charm. . . ; yet . . . he would be more likely than many less passionate men to love a woman without telling her of it. . . . It seemed to foreshadow that capability of reticence in Deronda that his imagination was much occupied with two women, to neither of whom would he have held it possible that he should ever make love. (297–98)

Deronda is obviously far from impervious to sexual attraction (he is "open to that sort of charm" and more "passionate" than many men), but his priest-like altruism creates in him a type of "reticence" that causes him to refrain from acting on it. The exercise of such restraint yields an erotic charm, not only for the women who are attracted to Deronda, we get the impression, but also for Deronda himself; it is the subtle eroticism of denial, of repression, of renunciation. This is obviously not the effect Eliot intended in the construction of her hero, which makes it all the more troubling, a subversive undercurrent in the novel as a whole.

Both inwardly and outwardly, then, George Eliot creates Deronda as a sort of priest-figure, an image that is explicitly reinforced in his relationship with Gwendolen. He becomes "part of her conscience, as one woman whose nature is an object of reverential belief may become a new conscience to a man" (386, another allusion to his androgynous aspect), and we are told that "without the aid of sacred ceremony or costume, her feelings had turned this man, only a few years older than herself, into a priest" (401). Deronda's look, as well, so disturbing to Gwendolen at the gambling table, is transformed into a religious encounter as their relationship develops: at Sir Hugo's party, "for what was an appreciable space of time to both, though the observation of others could not have measured it, they looked at each other—she seeming to take the deep rest of confession, he with an answering depth of sympathy that neutralized other feelings" (383). The "other feelings" are not exactly neutralized, however; they are merely repressed, and accordingly surface at every mention of the supposedly Platonic interaction between Deronda and Gwendolen, despite the narrator's diligent efforts (like this one) to stress its "neutrality."

Such efforts, which increase as the novel progresses, merely serve to emphasize the unrealized potential for erotic interaction between the two characters. The erotic is invoked in this way again and again: we are told, "There was not the faintest touch of coquetry in the attitude of her mind towards him" (386); "She was curiously free from alarm lest he should think her openness wanting in dignity" (418); "The idea of herself separated from her husband, gave Deronda a changed, perturbing, painful place in her consciousness: . . . she felt some tingling bashfulness at the remembrance of her behaviour towards him" (561); "She was not in the least blind to the construction that all witnesses might put on her giving signs of dependence on Deronda, and her seeking him more than he sought her" (710). The incident in which Gwendolen covers her "white pillar of a neck" (566) before seeing Deronda is a particularly telling instance of such negative reinforcement of the idea of a possible sexual liaison between the two characters ("Now that it was too late she was shaken by the possibility that he might think her invitation unbecoming," 565). The figurative language, too, in which these encounters are often described is steeped in erotic suggestion: Deronda realizes that "Gwendolen's soul clung to his with a passionate need" (712); "it was not her thought, that he loved her and would cling to her. . . : it was her spiritual breath" (716); "considerations such as would have filled the minds of indifferent spectators could not occur to her, any more than if flames had been mounting around her, and she had flung herself into his opened arms and clung about his neck that he might carry her into safety" (717). In this way the idea of the possibility of a sexual liaison between Gwendolen and Deronda is constantly reiterated, so that their "friendship" emerges as by far the most erotic relationship in the entire novel.

That this erotic effect is inadvertent does not make it any less powerful. Gwendolen, like the other women Deronda encounters, is erotically attracted to him, and for the same reasons. Priest-like, he exhorts her to submit (to her marriage, to circumstances), but what she achieves instead is a desire to submit, lover-like, to him. His "power over her" is mentioned frequently, and the metaphorical reference to his rescue of her from the "flames . . . mounting around her" is obviously a romantic fantasy of the rescue of the weaker by the stronger in perfect conformity with the domination/submission paradigm. Elsewhere this paradigm is evoked even more clearly: when she confesses her "crime" to Deronda we are told, "She had a vague need of getting nearer to that compassion which seemed to be regarding her from a halo of superiority, and the need turned into an impulse to humble herself more. She was ready to throw herself on her knees before him" (647).

The thick cluster of child images—always an indication of Eliot's desire to transcend the realm of the erotic—surrounding the conclusion of their relationship is a further clue as to its intensely erotic nature. The climax of their erotic attraction to each other is marked by Eliot's familiar device of two children holding hands: after Gwendolen's confession of guilt about Grandcourt's death, Deronda "took one of her hands, and clasped it as if they were going to walk together like two children: it was the only way in which he could answer, 'I will not forsake you' " (643). After this point, these images tend to cast Gwendolen as the helpless child and Deronda as the soothing adult: "She cried as the child cries whose little feet have fallen backward—cried to be taken by the hand, lest she should lose herself. The cry pierced Deronda" (718); "He could only seek words of soothing and encouragement; and . . . she gradually revived under them, with that pathetic look of renewed childlike interest which we see in eyes where the lashes are still beaded with tears" (742). The tenderest moment between them, in fact, is captured in one of these child images. Deronda has just told Gwendolen that he is going to marry Mirah, and "sobs rose, and great tears fell fast. Deronda would not let her hands go—held them still with one of his, and himself pressed her handkerchief against her eyes. She submitted like a half-soothed child" (749–50). This is clearly erotic—far more erotic than anything that occurs between Deronda and Mirah, for instance—and a tantalizing intimation of the mother-love that Gwendolen might have found in a relationship with Deronda. The latter's androgynous quality supports this interpretation, as does his own mother's lack of nurturing, which has in turn stimulated the caregiver in him ("All the woman lacking in her was present in him," 615). This confirmation of the female's need for mother-love in a male-female relationship is a new departure for Eliot; as we have seen, mother-love is something her heroines generally give to males rather than seek for themselves. Nor are many of her heroes capable of dispensing it (Lydgate is another, being a doctor and "used to being gentle with the weak and suffering," 295, an attribute which unfortunately helps to put him at the mercy of Rosamond's "weakness").

This vision of a nurturing love is abruptly curtailed, however, in what seems to me to be an entirely characteristic retreat of Eliot from the exploration of erotic fulfillment in favor of a valorization of the principle of transcendence, in much the same way that she retreats in *The Mill on the Floss* and *Middlemarch*. Both of these earlier novels contain the potential for satisfying love relationships (between Maggie and Stephen and between

Dorothea and Lydgate), but both contain a built-in necessity for the renunciation of this potential. In *Daniel Deronda* there is no such necessity, but the
renunciation occurs anyway, in one of the most paradoxically erotic farewell scenes in the history of the English novel. It is agonizing for Deronda
as well as for Gwendolen: "Deronda's anguish was intolerable. He could
not help himself. He seized her outstretched hands and held them together
and kneeled at her feet. She was the victim of his happiness. . . . His eyes
too were larger with tears. She wrested one of her hands from his, and
returned his action, pressing his tears away." Finally, "she bent forward to
kiss his cheek, and he kissed hers. Then they looked at each other for an
instant with clasped hands, and he turned away" (749–50). This scene—
which might be called Eliot's ideal love scene—is a virtual orgy of renunciation, a last scintillating attempt by Eliot to reconcile her awareness of
human passion with her need to transcend it. Her solution—the exclusion
of the erotic from a male-female love relationship—only partly succeeds.
The attempt at exclusion is itself erotic, in that all of the interactions in this
relationship have the added piquancy of the forbidden, and furthermore it
affords Eliot a false sense of security in allowing her characters to touch
each other physically within the bounds of their "Platonic" love. As we can
see from the preceding examples, such touching far exceeds any that occurs
in most of the love scenes in Eliot's earlier novels.

Daniel Deronda, then, is an extremely interesting novel, in which Eliot
reverses several of her earlier attitudes toward erotic relationships and
confirms others. The vain woman is no longer automatically condemned
as morally unworthy, but submission is still seen as her proper role. Erotic
desire, even that of the male, is presented with Eliot's characteristic ambivalence, so that Gwendolen's erotic subjectivity seems not to be an issue. Not
caring what people think and unconstrained by love for a lawgiving father
or brother, Gwendolen would seem to be a much better candidate as a
subject of desire than Maggie, for instance (whose potential is considerable). But her emotional frigidity leads her to seek power rather than love,
and when she does find love it is in an avowedly non-erotic context. We
can infer that Gwendolen feels erotic desire for Deronda from the few
broken hints that Eliot gives us about Gwendolen's state of mind in their
encounters ("Her imagination had not been turned to a future union with
Deronda by any other than the spiritual tie which had been continually
strengthening; but also it had not been turned towards a future separation
from him. Lovemaking and marriage—how could they now be the imagery
in which poor Gwendolen's deepest attachment could spontaneously
clothe itself?" 717) and from her violent reaction to the announcement of
his intention to marry Mirah. But her desire is never directly acknowledged,
even by the narrator, so that none of her conduct toward Deronda can really
be viewed as the enactment of desire. The novel's enormous erotic energy
is channeled into the "safety valve" of erotic renunciation.

George Eliot remains a conundrum for feminists because her wish for female equality is selective rather than inclusive. Certain aspects of the reigning patriarchal stereotype of pure and passive womanhood are abhorrent to her, such as the powerlessness of women to act in the world (Gwendolen's complaint that "we women can't go in search of adventures. . . . We must stay where we grow, or where the gardeners like to transplant us. We are brought up like the flowers, to look as pretty as we can, and be dull without complaining," 120, might be the complaint of Maggie or Dorothea as well). In the area of sexual relationships, however, Eliot endorses the stereotype of the docile and submissive female whose participation in the erotic is confined to passivity. The man acts and the woman reacts; Eliot's female characters are not even permitted to perceive the desire of the male characters in her novels until it is pointed out to them. Certainly they are never permitted to initiate the look or the language of desire, even in the most intimate of male-female encounters. Nor do they want to: when Catherine Arrowpoint is forced to confess her love for Klesmer, "to her the effort was something like the leap of a woman from the deck into the lifeboat" (226). Submission and renunciation remain part of the womanly ideal throughout Eliot's career, even though her heroines become progressively more spirited and independent. The horrors of the domination/submission hierarchy are openly acknowledged in her last two novels, yet her heroines (with the possible exception of Dorothea) still long to submit to superior males. Unlike Charlotte Brontë's heroines, George Eliot's female characters do not chafe against the unfairness of the beauty ideal or rail against the unwritten sanctions that prevent them from expressing erotic desire. Nor do they seek the comfort and mother-love that Brontë's heroines ultimately find with the males in her novels. Eliot's females are beautiful, and they are pursued; their task is to choose wisely among their admirers.

In short, Eliot's valorization of the patriarchal principle of transcendence—which devalues the sexuality that "woman" has been made to represent—causes her likewise to endorse the patriarchal solution of banishing female desire from the womanly ideal. The good woman stimulates male desire (through her beauty) and then responds to it, evincing none of her own. In every other area Eliot's female characters long for autonomy, a fact that underlines her Victorian discomfort in the area of erotic relations. A true product of her age and a brilliant novelist, George Eliot is a complex and contradictory daughter of the fathers. Based on a fine balance among powerful and unstated oppositions, her novels are a rich source of speculation for the feminist critic.

NOTES

1. That such relationships existed in reality there is no doubt, as we can infer from Eliot's own history and from accounts such as the following of Ellen Wee-

ton's distress at her childhood separation from her brother (who was later very unkind to her): "When, at the age of fourteen, my brother was [apprenticed to a lawyer in Preston], what an affliction it was to me! I thought it was like interring him; for I was entirely bereft of the companion of my girlish days; the promotor of mirth and frolic; the stimulator of my studies. For some weeks after he was gone, I visited each place where he used to be seen, with the most melancholy ideas. . . . Many an hour have I sat alone in the room we called his, thinking over the transactions, the pleasing pastimes of days that were gone. I revered and loved my mother, but I loved my brother a great deal better. I used to console myself with the idea that when he was established in business, I should, as we had from almost infancy promised each other, again live with him." Ellen Weeton, *Miss Weeton: Journal of a Governess, 1807–1811*, ed. Edward Hall (Oxford: Oxford University Press, 1936), qtd. in Murray 104.

2. For convenience, throughout this chapter I refer to Eliot's narrator (except for the contrived male narrator of *Adam Bede*) as "she" and collapse the distinction between "George Eliot" and "Marian Evans," even though I am aware that this simplifies several complex issues.

3. See Auerbach, "The Power of Hunger," for example.

4. See Barrett, 25–27, for example.

5. For a detailed discussion of Tom as the "figurative father" in the novel, see Sadoff, *Monsters* 84–85.

4

✧ ✧ ✧

THOMAS HARDY

> The heroines of Hardy's early novels are presented primarily as objects of erotic interest not only for the narrators and for the male characters . . . but also for the implied reader/voyeur. . . . What they think or feel seems not to matter; the focus of attention is on the feelings they arouse in a variety of men. (Wright 34)

To what extent is Thomas Hardy a feminist novelist? The question of Hardy and the representation of women has perturbed literary critics since the turn of the century. Just as mainstream critics remain unsure about Hardy's formal virtuosity (citing him with equal conviction as both a great literary artist and a crass technical bungler), feminist critics seem undecided whether to accept Hardy with distaste or to reject him with reluctance. Like Hardy himself, many remain ambivalent; Katharine Rogers reaches the fairly typical conclusion that "these novels show the tenacity of sexist assumptions even in so humane and enlightened a man as Hardy" (257). He is noted both for his revolutionary protests against social conventions that restrict women's freedom—Sue's repugnance for being "licensed to be loved on the premises" comes to mind—and for the blatantly sexist remarks that are scattered throughout his oeuvre like some kind of sexist graffiti. Not surprisingly, however, the root of Hardy's feminism (or lack of it) is to be found elsewhere than in such superficial evidence.

As a late Victorian creator of erotic novels that deal frankly with women's issues, Hardy bears comparison with most feminist writers of his day. Moreover, his novels are populated with strong, interesting female characters, most of whom would appear to be much more "modern" than any of the fictional creations of either Brontë or Eliot. Also, the Grundyesque constraints of the Victorian era had relaxed slightly by the time

Hardy's career ended, so that his final novels, at least, might be expected to evince a new openness in erotic relations compared to those of earlier Victorian writers. I have chosen to analyze the erotic ideology embedded in his four best-known novels, which also happen to be his most erotic: *Far from the Madding Crowd*, *The Return of the Native*, *Tess of the d'Urbervilles* and *Jude the Obscure*. The heroines of these novels—Bathsheba Everdene, Eustacia Vye, Tess Durbeyfield and Sue Bridehead—are at least as "monumental" as any of George Eliot's female characters and arguably more famous than any of Charlotte Brontë's. Their subjectivity would seem to be beyond question, simply because Hardy's readers have the sense of "knowing" them so well. Accordingly, these Hardy heroines should potentially encompass the greatest erotic subjectivity of any of the fictional personalities in this study.

That they do not, in fact, display such subjectivity is an excellent example of Myra Jehlen's point that "a work may be . . . quite wrong and even wrongheaded about life and politics and still an extremely successful rendering of its contrary vision" (72). Hardy's "contrary vision" is very successful indeed, making it extremely difficult for even the most rigorous feminist critics to elucidate the cause of their discomfort with his novels. Some critics, in fact, disavow any such discomfort, casting Hardy as the champion and indignant defender of his own strong women characters. The latter interpretation holds true for certain aspects of Hardy's narratives, such as their surface polemic and possibly their narrative grammar (a term used by Laura Mulvey which I shall discuss presently), but overall such studies tend to overlook the glaring fact that both the narrator and the implied reader in all of Hardy's novels are invariably male, and sexist as well.

The unspoken camaraderie of the closed and confidential conversation taking place between (male) narrator and (male) reader, the insistence with which Hardy's novels invite male partisanship on the part of the reader, is not to be underestimated. Mainstream critics who have come under feminist fire for their assumption of the implied reader's masculinity are, in a sense, simply complying with the invitation Hardy's texts typically extend, even to female readers, to read them (in Culler's phrase) "as a man."[1] Hardy's critics continue to circumnavigate with difficulty his phallocentric reader-narrator dynamic, often maintaining a somewhat uneasy neutrality toward it. But as feminist criticism has taught us new ways of reading, it has become increasingly unworkable to ignore questions of gender in Hardy's work, particularly in light of recent feminist observations about the politics of the gaze. Such observations have made it virtually impossible to discuss the look in the realist novel without acknowledging its powerful sexist ramifications, ramifications which in Hardy's case color his entire oeuvre in ways that profoundly affect our understanding and appreciation of it.

So what about Hardy's feminist reader? If he or she resists reading "as a man," what happens to the experience of reading these novels? First of all, it is clear that in order to arrive at a satisfactory analysis of Hardy's erotic ideology, such a reader must resist the seduction of his realism—with its lulling sense of a transparently obvious verisimilitude—and the pleasure it affords. Of course, this is the same sacrifice of pleasure that any ideological examination of realism entails, as Laura Mulvey points out when she sets out "to make way for a total negation of the ease and plenitude of the narrative fiction film" and to "destroy the satisfaction, pleasure, and privilege of the 'invisible guest' " (16, 26). As I pointed out in Chapter One, many theorists wish to destroy this pleasure—which is inevitably attached to successful examples of the realist genre—because they see realism itself, and particularly the traditional representation of women, as irredeemably sexist, participating in voyeuristic or fetishistic viewing mechanisms.

The dynamics of looking that Mulvey describes is particularly applicable to a novelist like Hardy because of what Judith Bryant Wittenberg refers to as his "spectatorial narrator" (152). By a considerable margin, Hardy is the most scopophilic of the novelists in my study, and not coincidentally he is also one of the most characteristic exponents of the realist genre in an era of high realism (the Victorian novel corresponding in this respect to Hollywood cinema). The pleasure derived from reading a Hardy novel comes primarily from its air of solid "reality" and not from any formal technique; indeed, critics frequently comment on the infelicities of Hardy's rather amateurish style, forgiving these on the basis of his much-vaunted "sincerity" and his abilities as a storyteller. Like the audience of a realist film, the reader of a Hardy novel is encouraged to escape into the narrative, suspending all disbelief and all critical sense in favor of an avid interest in the characters and their world. Feminist critics have noted, however, that this world seems real, is recognizable, partly because it parallels the patriarchal world we know, especially in its tacit assumptions about gender. In particular, the narrator and implied reader of Hardy's texts share a gaze that is ineluctably male, as I shall show, and looking is their predominant activity. It is an extremely intimate activity, as the "vision" Hardy shares in this way is intensely personal, giving rise to the plethora of criticism extolling the reader's sense of "knowing" Hardy through his novels.

What makes Hardy's vision so personal, I would submit, is the eroticism that informs it, so that the relation that constantly applies is a literary recapitulation of the dynamic that occurs in representational visual art, for instance, between a male artist and his viewer. Art critic Sarah Kent describes this dynamic as "a complex interaction . . . focused on the nudity of the female model. Intimacy is created through sexual rivalry—perhaps a sublimated form of homosexuality—in which the model appears to be the subject of the conversation when she is, in fact, only a form of currency in a male centered exchange" ("Looking Back" 59–60). Hardy's females are not literally nude, but they are similarly perceived in a cozy conspiracy of looking between the overtly male narrator and the projected male reader. The look the latter two entities share is compounded of curiosity, longing, affection, fear, contempt and adoration; in short, it is the look of desire of a falsely differentiated, ambivalent male. (It is also the look of the pornographer; as Helena Michie points out [112], Jocelyn Pierston's infatuation with women who are "copies" of each other in *The Well-Beloved* is the quintessential example of a "safe" distancing between male viewer and female object.) Moreover, such looking in Hardy's novels is typically unmediated by the male characters (who in many Victorian novels function as filters for the male look of desire), so that the desire the reader thus becomes privy to seems to be Hardy's own. And, as is the case in all such male gazing, the female object of the gaze is denied any real subjectivity.[2]

This may seem an absurd assertion, given the distinctive personalities of such characters as Bathsheba, Eustacia, Tess and Sue. A closer examination, however, reveals the subjectivity of these characters to be largely illusory, and the seeming absurdity to be a function of Hardy's persuasive realism. His female characters are seen almost exclusively from the outside, in terms of physical description, action and dialogue, a fact that has no doubt contributed to his reputation as a "balladeer" among novelists. These characters are physically present in an immediate and very sensual way, which tends to obscure the fact that their point of view is explored only superficially. Such enormously significant elisions of female consciousness are a result of the omnipresent male gaze, which I shall examine in detail in the following pages, in combination with a subtler stylistic tendency, namely Hardy's consistent avoidance of the device of free indirect speech, a favored technique among nineteenth-century novelists. Even at crucial turns of the plot—points normally conducive to character revelation using this device—the reader is admitted only sketchily to the inner lives of his heroines. Writing before the conception of the stream-of-consciousness novel, authors of realist novels tended to rely heavily on a "blend" of voices—a character's and the narrator's—in order to convey their characters' mental processes. This blend (labeled free indirect speech by stylistic critics) basically consists of the reporting of a character's thoughts in the narrator's voice, marked linguistically by the idiom, semantics and emotive punctuation of direct speech.[3] Hardy tends to eschew this device in favor of precise and detailed descriptions of his female characters' physical qualities, an entirely different mode of "knowing" them. Ironically, the resulting richness of detail in Hardy's descriptions of women has helped to earn him the reputation of a novelist who portrays female characters with great sensitivity. Feminist critics, however, have noted that these portrayals focus primarily on externals; Rosalind Miles points out that "Hardy really is a lover of women in the fullest physical sense. . . . His females are drawn from very close up; there is an almost myopic insistence upon the grain of their skin, and texture of hair. Sound, scent, mouth, cheeks, downy plumpness—no detail of their physical presence is allowed to escape our senses" (31). This detailed portraiture is myopic in more than just a physical sense, serving to distract the reader's attention from what would otherwise seem a glaring omission of female consciousness in the form of free indirect speech.

That male consciousness is *not* elided in this way is a telling comment on Hardy's patriarchal bias; Jude, for instance, muses at length during Sue's wedding to Phillotson in the following way:

> By the time they were half way on with the service he wished from his heart that he had not undertaken the business of giving her away. How could Sue have had the temerity to ask him to do it—a cruelty possibly to herself as well as to him? Women were different from men in such matters. Was it that they were, instead of more sensitive, as reputed, more callous, and less romantic; or were they more heroic? Or was Sue simply so perverse that she wilfully gave herself and him pain for the odd and mournful luxury of practising long-suffering in her own person, and of being touched with tender pity for him at having made him practise it? He could perceive that her face was nervously set. (181–82)

Except for the first and last sentences, this passage consists entirely of Jude's free indirect speech—endorsed, in this case, by the male narrator. The perplexed questions, the mournful chagrin, are a skillful rendition of Jude's mental processes at this crucial turn of events. Sue's perceptions, by contrast, are hardly ever rendered in this mode, even when she is alone and pensive (as she is when she buys the statuary, for example). The reader, like Jude, is left to interpret her thoughts from her actions and her dialogue, a fact that undoubtedly has much to do with the mystery that has always surrounded her character in the copious amounts of criticism it has occasioned.

We can see, then, that Hardy seems at once excessively close to and excessively distanced from his female characters, creating an authorial proximity that seems too close physically and too remote in other ways. His unwillingness or inability to explore the consciousness of his heroines has led to much critical bafflement as readers try to deal with the nebulous personalities Hardy thus presents them with. Tellingly, his creations include no Lucy Snowe, Maggie Tulliver or Dorothea Brooke with whom the female reader can readily identify; as Rosalind Miles points out, "Hardy women *seem* different from one another—Bathsheba is mistress, Fanny is maid, Tess is rounded while Sue is slight—but on closer examination they all prove to originate from one prototype" (28). And the prototype, unfortunately, is invidiously sexist, a mysterious, unpredictable and alien entity called Woman, who is capable of ruining men's lives (Miles remarks that Hardy "saw women as dangerous simply in being, to themselves as well as to men," 27). The authorial perspective we can sense in Hardy's novels, in fact, is simply the conventional perspective of a heavily defended, psychically isolated male toward the castrated, castrating female Other—which is why Laura Mulvey's analysis of the conventional (male) audience of the realist film fits Hardy so well. The angle of vision is from outside the female (hence we are not given her perspective) and obsessed with the female (hence we are given minutely detailed, fetishistic portraits of her). The look that is thus brought into play—the male look of desire, of curiosity, of control—is especially evident in unobtrusive shifts of narrative focus, which inevitably culminate in what Judith Bryant Wittenberg calls the "voyeuristic moment" ("the moment in which the seeing subject and the seen object intersect in a diegetic node that both explicitly and implicitly suggests the way in which the world is constituted in and through the scopic drive," 151).

The gaze, then, is of supreme importance in Hardy's novels. They are "cinematic" in every sense, as critics have noted in the dozens of books and articles on vision and perspective in Hardy's work, and they readily translate into film. In Hardy's case the fictional "eye" could easily be a camera, and the questions of whose eye it is and what it sees are easily answered: the eye is Hardy's own (he himself observed that "a writer . . . looks upon the world with his personal eyes," Orel 152), and what it mainly sees is women. It is no accident that there is so much spying, particularly in the early novels (Gabriel Oak's and the reddleman's activities are obvious instances), or that the characters spied on are female. There is no male spy as such in *Tess of the d'Urbervilles* simply because the voyeur in that novel is Hardy himself in the guise of the male narrator. The vision of his heroines that is thus constructed is at once intensely erotic and intensely personal, evoking a strong sense of "knowing" these women, as I mentioned earlier; but the character we really get to know, and to know very intimately, is Hardy. Tess, in particular, elicits this intimate response, so that Rosalind Miles calls her "the apotheosis of Hardy's sensuous realisation of woman-hood . . . he is lover-like in his attention to her. . . . As a lover he becomes too involved with his fictional creations; so that we feel that the blood that courses through the veins of his heroines is drawn straight from his own heart" (31–32). On the other hand, Katharine Rogers realizes that "even *Tess of the d'Urbervilles*, the Hardy novel most sympathetic to women . . . does not evoke the same empathy with her that one feels with Hardy's male heroes" (249). This seeming discrepancy is easily explained on the basis of the scopic economy that is consistently operational in Hardy's novels, in which male consciousness is explored subjectively (through free indirect speech, for example) while female consciousness is elided in favor of the obsessive objectification of women by means of the male gaze.

Having said all that, it may seem futile to examine Hardy's work for evidence of erotic female subjectivity, and it is certainly true that his female characters generally possess much less subjectivity than most traditional criticism credits them with. But Hardy does not create passive heroines (there is no Caroline Helstone among them, for example), nor does he shy away from exploring erotic relations. In his frankness about sexual issues he is by far the most modern and least Victorian of the authors in my study, chafing against the restrictive literary conventions of his day and holding no such brief for Victorian transcendence as George Eliot does, for example. Love is no romantic panacea in Hardy's novels; it can go flat and stale, and in typical twentieth-century fashion it can botch people's lives. Women fit into this scenario uneasily, sometimes wreaking the havoc, sometimes having it wrought upon them. But they are often active participants in the erotic paradigm, despite their objectification at the level of semiotic analysis. Accordingly, it would be no surprise to discover that they look, speak and enact their desire. Also, the scopophilic aspect of Hardy's novels fluctuates over the course of his career, culminating in *Tess of the d'Urbervilles*, so that in his last novel, *Jude the Obscure*, it is considerably diminished.

In addition, we need to remember that Hardy's scopic economy is only one (albeit an important) aspect of his narrative achievement. If we examine his novels from the point of view of Laura Mulvey's "narrative grammar," for instance, they appear in a wholly different light. For although the gaze in Hardy's novels is relentlessly male, the narratives themselves invariably place a female character at the center of the action in precisely the way that Mulvey describes in the "woman-orientated strand" of melodrama in classical cinema. According to Mulvey, the placement of a woman at the center of these stories produces a new kind of narrative discourse, shifting the emphasis from exterior to interior drama. The woman typically has to choose between "two conflicting desires" which "correspond closely with Freud's . . . oscillation between 'passive' femininity and regressive 'masculinity,' " represented by the law-abiding hero (who represents her passive, feminine, socially acceptable self) and the exciting villain (who represents her active, masculine, regressive self). Ultimately, neither of these choices is adequate, because the dilemma itself is formulated in male-oriented terms. In other words, there is no place for such a heroine either in the hero's masculine symbolic or in the villain's phallic, regressive rebellion against it (35). Hardy's novels, interestingly, can also be viewed in this way, as the narrative grammar of many of them follows exactly this pattern, with a central heroine (Bathsheba, Eustacia, Tess, Sue) caught between two potential partners, neither of whom is entirely satisfactory. And, like Mulvey's melodramas, such texts can be viewed as implicit protests against the cultural marginalization of the feminine, opening up an empathic narrative position with which the female reader/spectator can comfortably and pleasurably align herself. (On the other hand, however, the two-suitor plot can also function as a patriarchal "lesson" for the wayward heroine, in which she learns to renounce her first, "unsuitable" lover for a more stable, responsible one whose virtues she would do well to emulate; see Kennard 10–11).

Hardy's critics, therefore, will undoubtedly continue both to applaud his feminism and to deplore his sexism, sensing simultaneously in his novels their narrative grammar, which apparently empathizes so deeply with the plight of the culturally marginalized female, and their scopic economy, in which male consciousness is explored subjectively while female consciousness is quietly and systematically elided. The tension between these two aspects of Hardy's representation of women, in fact, makes his work one of the richest and most complex sources of feminist commentary in the realist novel. It is no wonder that Hardy's novels tend to perplex and fascinate his feminist readers, yielding a peculiarly ambivalent kind of pleasure. In their representation of women, they function both as indignant condemnations of the ideological misdeeds of patriarchy, and—ironically, paradoxically—as formidable examples of such misdeeds themselves.

Hardy, then, presents an interesting challenge for the feminist critic. His offensive sexist remarks are only superficial indicators of the more complex literary dynamic which must be analyzed in order to arrive at an accurate assessment of his erotic ideology. It is this ideology that I shall examine in this chapter, as well as particular instances of the scopic economy I have described. Intellectually, Hardy himself would no doubt have argued vigorously in favor of women's erotic subjectivity; emotionally, however, he was handicapped by the perceptions of the classically ambivalent male whose castration anxieties are disturbingly close to the surface. The novels that result from this volatile combination are interesting indeed, containing "more than meets the eye" in terms of both their sexism and their feminism.

FAR FROM THE MADDING CROWD

In some ways Hardy's fourth novel is his most overtly sexist work, making it difficult for the female reader, with the best will in the world, to read it without some degree of irritation. The only ideological position open to her is the one described by Jonathan Culler in "Reading as a Woman": "Women can read, and have read, as men" (49). Hardy's narrator in *Far from the Madding Crowd* persistently addresses his reader as a co-conspirator in a male alliance against the desirable but exasperating female Other, in a series of sexist asides ranging in offensiveness from "that sympathetic manipulation of roots and leaves which is so conspicuous in a woman's gardening" (when Bathsheba replants the flowers on Fanny's grave, 346) to "the imitative instinct which animates women" (when Bathsheba prays after seeing Gabriel pray, 324). These unfortunate comments usually take the form of generalizations, and they are usually aimed at some feminine "foible" or weakness. We are told that Bathsheba is "that novelty among women—one who finished a thought before beginning the sentence which was to convey it" (26); that Bathsheba "had too much womanliness to use her understanding to the best advantage" (198); that Liddy cries "not from any particular necessity, but from an artistic sense of making herself in keeping with the remainder of the picture, which seems to influence women" (208–9); and that "Bathsheba's feeling was always to some extent dependent upon her whim, as is the case with many other women" (402). In such instances the narrator tolerantly shakes his head from a position of male superiority at the endearing shortcomings of the "weaker" sex; occasionally, however, these asides betray real bitterness, usually in connection with women's lack of fairness in love relationships. Of Bathsheba's reaction to Boldwood's distress, for example, we are told that "the situation was not without a fearful joy" for her because "the facility with which even the most timid women sometimes acquire a relish for the dreadful when that is amalgamated with a little triumph, is marvellous" (168); and of Gabriel's affection the narrator remarks, "Women are never tired of bewailing man's fickleness in love, but they only seem to snub his constancy" (169).

The characters, too, are made to voice and think derogatory sentiments about women: Matthew Moon remarks that "maids rather like your man of sin" (234); Liddy says, "What rum things we women be" (376); Troy experiences "an unexpected revelation of all women being alike at heart" (when he realizes that Bathsheba is jealous of Fanny, 311); and Bathsheba herself, when faced with Boldwood's remonstrances, "in spite of her mettle, began to feel unmistakable signs that she was inherently the weaker vessel" (214). Gabriel, as well, whose point of view is perhaps the most reliable in the book, ponders on "the contradictoriness of that feminine heart which had caused [Bathsheba] to speak more warmly to him [now] than she ever had done whilst unmarried" (264), and he also delivers one of the most dismissive judgments in the novel: "You should be thankful to me for biding. How would the farm go on with nobody to mind it but a woman?" (203). In short, the female reader is not simply written out of the picture in *Far from the Madding Crowd*; she is specifically excluded by a deluge of disparaging commentary that saturates the entire novel. That she has managed to accommodate this so well for so long is simply a result of her rigorous training in the process Culler describes ("Reading as a woman is not necessarily what occurs when a woman reads"). Even so, it is difficult to imagine a female reader comfortably concurring in comments such as the narrator's casual observation in the first chapter, for instance, that Bathsheba did not thank Gabriel for paying her toll fee because "in gaining her passage he had lost her her point, and we know how women take a favour of that kind" (11). The "we" here (which pertains throughout the following chapters) is the patriarchal "we" who are inherently superior to women, embodied in the male duo of narrator and reader who good-naturedly agree on such matters.

The dynamic that is thus established—the familiar homosocial alliance between male artist and male audience that pertains in film and the visual arts as well as in literature—is echoed in the scopic structure of the novel.

This structure is established in the first chapter, "Description of Farmer Oak—An Incident," in which the "incident" consists of Gabriel looking at Bathsheba as she looks at herself in the mirror. The gaze follows its predictable trajectory, from the male to the female, whose own gaze is self-reflexive and relatively powerless.[4] The scene presents the reader with a highly charged event which contains all the elements of voyeurism. Gabriel watches without being watched (he has "casually glance[d] over the hedge"), Bathsheba is furtive about her action ("She turned her head to learn if the waggoner were coming. . . . She blushed at herself, and seeing her reflection blush, blushed the more"), and the titillating effect of the action itself is all but made explicit: "The change from the customary spot and necessary occasion of such an act—from the dressing hour in a bedroom to a time of travelling out of doors—lent to the idle deed a novelty it did not intrinsically possess." "Novelty" here is obviously a Victorian euphemism for "eroticism," as the "dressing hour in a bedroom" suggests. Also, it is noteworthy that Bathsheba's beauty is not particularly stressed in this scene; she is merely described as "a woman, young and attractive," a "handsome girl" (9–10).

This is obviously not what Laura Mulvey would term a fetishistic scene, a cinematic close-up that "freeze[s] the flow of action in [a] moment of erotic contemplation" and invests the female object with an excess of physical perfection so that she becomes "reassuring rather than dangerous." Rather, it is a clear instance of voyeurism, which according to Mulvey is associated with narrative, with action rather than portraiture (in this chapter, in fact, it *is* the action) and with sadism. The voyeur "catches" someone in a forbidden act, and "pleasure lies in ascertaining guilt (immediately associated with castration), asserting control, and subjecting the guilty person through punishment or forgiveness" (19–22). Bathsheba's guilt is established at the outset, as the narrator casually makes the condemnatory remark that will cling to her throughout the novel: "Woman's prescriptive infirmity had stalked into the sunlight." It is the female character who is judged to be guilty (and guilty on the basis of her castrated sex—she is demonstrating *woman's* prescriptive infirmity), even though it is the male observer who is conducting himself in a way that could be seen as morally questionable. The narrator's judgment is then deftly transferred to this male observer in a passage of righteous conjecture: "A cynical inference was irresistible by Gabriel Oak as he regarded the scene, generous though he fain would have been. There was no necessity whatever for her looking in the glass. She did not adjust her hat, or pat her hair. . . . She simply observed herself as a fair product of Nature in the feminine kind." The root of his disapprobation is then indicated in the following speculation: "her thoughts seeming to glide into far-off though likely dramas in which men would play a part—vistas of probable triumphs—the smiles being of a phase suggesting that hearts were imagined as lost and won" (10–11). The language of domination ("triumphs," "lost and won") underlines the accuracy of Mulvey's Freudian point about castration anxiety as basic to both fetishism and voyeurism, even though the former exalts the female object and the latter diminishes her. The female's guilt and the male's condemnation of it in fact form the material of Hardy's narrative in *Far from the Madding Crowd*, as Gabriel ultimately rescues Bathsheba (asserts control, exercises forgiveness) from the results of her "infirmity," her disastrous relationships with Troy and Boldwood. And accordingly, Mulvey's description of the sadistic aspects of individual instances of voyeurism might well apply to the entire novel: "Sadism demands a story, depends on making something happen, forcing a change in another person, a battle of will and strength, victory/defeat, all occurring in a linear time with a beginning and an end" (22). The change is in Bathsheba, and the victory is Gabriel's.

The first chapter of *Far from the Madding Crowd* thus sets the tone for the rest of the narrative. The seeing/seen relation is firmly established along gender lines, subtly asserting male superiority in spite of Bathsheba's seemingly dominant position (she is Gabriel's social superior, and she looks down on him from atop the wagon). This first voyeuristic "incident" is quickly followed by two more, one in which Gabriel watches Bathsheba as she feeds the cows and one in which he watches her as she does gymnastics on horseback. In these episodes, as in the first one, Gabriel is in the position of a spy, seeing without being seen, this time intentionally rather than accidentally. In the cowshed scene, we are told that he "stepped up behind, where, leaning down upon the roof and putting his eye close to a hole, he could see into the interior clearly," a perfect voyeuristic vantage point. Once again the focus of attention is not so much the female object's beauty ("He could form no decided opinion upon her looks, her position being almost beneath his eye"), but rather an action she performs: "By one of those whimsical coincidences in which Nature, like a busy mother, seems to spare a moment from her unremitting labours to turn and make her children smile, the girl now dropped the cloak, and forth tumbled ropes of black hair over a red jacket" (18–20). As in the first incident, the eroticism of this is unmistakable. The regression suggested by the mother image applies to the (male) reader as well as to Gabriel, and the action itself, tantamount to a woman undressing, causes them both to "smile" with satisfied voyeuristic curiosity. The horseback riding scene is similarly gratifying to the curious male observer, who in this case "peep[s] through the loophole" of his hut to watch for Bathsheba. Once again he is not disappointed, as she performs an action she would only perform if she thought she were unobserved ("Satisfying herself that nobody was in sight, she seated herself in the manner demanded by the saddle, though hardly expected of the woman"), and once again the action calls attention to the observed female's sexuality.

In the latter instance Gabriel makes the mistake of letting Bathsheba know that he has observed her performance, whereupon he experiences his own guilt for the first time ("A perception caused him to withdraw his own eyes from hers as suddenly as if he had been caught in a theft"). The narrator makes it clear, however, that it is his telling, rather than his looking, that is amiss: "His want of tact had deeply offended her—not by seeing what he could not help, but by letting her know that he had seen it." "What he could not help" is debatable, as Gabriel easily could have stationed himself to watch for Bathsheba out in the open instead of behind the walls of his hut. In any case, it is the female object whose guilt is uppermost in such scenes, as Mulvey points out; and it is interesting that the narrator then makes the following comment: "Without law there is no sin, and without eyes there is no indecorum; and she appeared to feel that Gabriel's espial had made her an indecorous woman without her own connivance" (21–25). This is not exactly a report of Bathsheba's point of view—it is only a description of how she "appeared to feel"—but it does show some awareness of the female character's feelings in such cases. The mention of "sin" is particularly telling, and the concept of *Gabriel's* espial making *her* an indecorous woman is a perfect encapsulation of the voyeur's control and disparagement of his chosen object. It is the observed woman who is guilty, even though it is the observing male who does the looking. (No such guilt attends the male character when he is secretly observed by the female, as Gabriel is later in the novel when Bathsheba sees him praying, for example.) Such voyeuristic male spying is characteristic of Hardy's early novels—the reddleman's activities are another example of it—and it establishes even more firmly than its sexist asides the patriarchal bias of *Far from the Madding Crowd*.

Charlotte Brontë, writing much earlier and very differently from Hardy, also uses the device of spying, we may recall, and it is worth noting the difference in the way she uses it. In *Shirley*, for instance, the lovesick Caroline Helstone spies on her beloved Robert Moore from a stile under a thorn tree, from which point she can see Robert's light in the counting-house window: "If, while she gazed, a shadow bent between the light and lattice, her heart leaped—that eclipse was Robert: she had seen him" (187). This is hardly voyeuristic in the sense Mulvey describes, or indeed in any sense at all. There is no sharing of a forbidden point of view with the reader, there is no observed action—what she actually sees is an "eclipse," an absence—and if there is any guilt in the scene it is attributable to Caroline herself, who appears furtive and pathetic. The components of the seeing/seen dyad, as I have noted previously, are not readily interchangeable. There is spying as well in *Villette*, but most of it has to do with obtaining information rather than with eroticism. Even when the looking is connected to a love relationship, the voyeuristic element seems to be missing. Paul Emanuel's secret observation of Lucy as she weeps in the refectory, for instance, is related in the following way: "As I looked up a cap-tassel, a brow, two eyes filled a pane of that window; the fixed gaze of those two eyes hit right against my own glance: they were watching me. I had not till that moment known that tears were on my cheek, but I felt them now" (289–90). The difference between this and Hardy's spying incidents is highly significant. The episode is related from the point of view of the observed female character, the reader's attention is drawn immediately to the aggressive aspect of the activity of looking (Paul Emanuel's eyes "hit right against" Lucy's), and while Lucy becomes self-conscious it is not because of her sexuality but because of her emotion: she realizes that she is weeping. There is no question in this scene of the male spy ascertaining the sexual "guilt" of the spied-upon female, even though she is engaged in a private act, because the point of view is firmly anchored in the female's consciousness. Nor would there be any such guilt in Hardy's spying scenes if this were the case. In the absence of a shared male perspective among the narrator, the reader and a secretly observing male character, Bathsheba's actions of looking in the mirror, horseback riding and removing her cloak— intrinsically fairly mundane—would lose their voyeuristic potential entirely. Brontë's novel, in fact, goes on to specify the guilt of the voyeur: of his spying into the garden, Lucy tells Paul Emanuel, "This coming and going by stealth degrades your own dignity. . . . Every glance you cast from that lattice is a wrong done to the best part of your own nature" (459).

Not all of the male gazing in *Far from the Madding Crowd* is voyeuristic, of course. The narrator also appraises Bathsheba's beauty in conventional Victorian "portraits," Mulvey's fetishistic close-ups, in which the woman's visual presence draws attention to itself and works against the diegesis, temporarily halting the story in moments of erotic spectacle. When Gabriel meets Bathsheba to return her hat, for example, he studies her appearance for the first time:

The adjustment of the farmer's hazy conceptions of her charms to the portrait of herself she now presented him with was less a diminution than a difference. . . . All features of consequence were severe and regular. It may have been observed by persons who go about the shires with eyes for beauty that in English women a classically formed face is seldom found to be united with a figure of the same pattern. . . . Here criticism checked itself as out of place, and looked at her proportions with a long consciousness of pleasure. From the contours of her figure in its upper part, she must have had a beautiful neck and shoulders, but since her infancy nobody had ever seen them. (22–23)

Here we have an amazingly frank and unself-conscious acknowledgment of the power dynamics of the seeing/seen configuration in Hardy's work. The point of view is unabashedly male, that of an observer who sits back and judges while the female "presents him" with a "portrait of herself." This observer is initially Gabriel, but soon expands to include "persons who go about the shires with eyes for beauty." This self-appointed judge of female beauty openly reveals his aesthetic appraisal to include a sexual appraisal, as he regards Bathsheba's figure (her "proportions") "with a long consciousness of pleasure." The pleasure is obviously erotic, as his mental undressing of her indicates, and the reader is tacitly invited to participate in it.

The male looks and judges, and the female is looked at and judged: Hardy's narrator is not unaware of the scrutinized object's discomfiture in such an exchange, but confidently categorizes it as "natural":

That the girl's thoughts hovered about her face and form as soon as she caught Oak's eyes conning the same page was natural, and almost certain. . . . Rays of male vision seem to have a tickling effect upon virgin faces in rural districts; she brushed hers with her hand, as if Gabriel had been irritating its pink surface by actual touch, and the free air of her previous movements was reduced at the same time to a chastened phase of itself. (23)

A woman's appearance, it is implied, is tantamount to a "page" that is open for anyone to read, and the "touch" metaphor makes the sexual implications of such looking explicit: it virtually amounts to a physical violation (the "virgin" faces are "tickled" and "irritated" by the "rays of male vision," and the "free air" of their owner's movements is thereby "chastened"). The light-hearted tone in which this observation is made, as much as the declaration of its naturalness, indicates the narrator's complacent satisfaction with this distribution of scopic power.

The single instance of a reversal of this power structure, in which the observed female has power and control over the observing male, is portrayed as singularly unnatural: Boldwood is finally revealed to be mentally unbalanced, largely because of this "weakness." It is significant that initially he is the only male character who does not observe Bathsheba (he fails to give her "the official glance of admiration which cost nothing at all. . . . It was faintly depressing that the most dignified and valuable man in the parish should withhold his eyes," 100–101). When he does finally scrutinize her ("as something foreign to his element, and but dimly understood") as a result of receiving the valentine, she appears to him as a collage of fragmented female parts: "He saw her black hair, her correct facial curves and profile, and the roundness of her chin and throat. He saw then the side of her eyelids, eyes, and lashes, and the shape of her ear. Next he noticed her figure, her skirt, and the very soles of her shoes." Nor can Boldwood assemble these parts into a coherent whole in order to make sense of them: "Boldwood, it must be remembered . . . had never before inspected a woman with the very center and force of his glance; they had struck upon all his senses at wide angles." This belated attention from Boldwood, unlike the other male glances in the novel, is solicited by Bathsheba herself and therefore welcomed, at least initially, as evidence of her powers of attraction: "All this time Bathsheba was conscious of having broken into that dignified stronghold at last. His eyes, she knew, were following her everywhere. This was a triumph" (122–23). The control in this exchange, as the battle imagery of the shattered stronghold indicates, rests with Bathsheba; but the "triumph" she thus obtains is soon replaced with dismay as Boldwood begins to exercise his inexorable will against hers. The female object of the male gaze never achieves power for long.

The other appreciative male look in *Far from the Madding Crowd* is that of Sergeant Troy, who uses his prerogative of male appraisal (in conjunction with "woman's prescriptive infirmity") to gain control over Bathsheba. His look, which is frankly sexual, is "too strong to be received pointblank with her own" (171), and "Bathsheba surveyed him curiously from the feet upward as high as she liked to venture her glance, which was not quite so high as his eyes" (141). The look of desire is rigorously gendered; Bathsheba never looks, nor does she look back, at the males in the novel (she fires Gabriel, for instance, with "her eyes flashing at his, though never meeting them," 141). It is significant that Troy wins Bathsheba by flattery, a direct appeal to her wish to be considered beautiful. Hardy's message about the folly of female vanity in *Far from the Madding Crowd* is almost as strong as George Eliot's in *Adam Bede*, in fact. Both novelists recognize the extreme importance of female beauty in any interchange between the sexes; George Eliot, we will recall, saw such beauty as an impersonal aesthetic quality that ideally pointed beyond itself to transcendent values of divine goodness and maternal love. Hardy employs no such transcendent reference system, cheerfully classifying Bathsheba's beauty as "belonging rather to the demonian than to the angelic school" (143). Also, Eliot's definition of "vanity" seems much broader than Hardy's. Her "vain" female characters—Hetty, Maggie, Rosamond and Gwendolen—ultimately seek love and admiration, whereas Bathsheba seems to crave flattery for its own sake. It is Troy's telling her point-blank that she is beautiful, over and over again, that causes her to fall in love with him, and "it was a fatal omission of Boldwood's that he had never once told her she was beautiful" (175). In Hardy's novel the female is duped through her own susceptibility to flattery, while in Eliot's novels (particularly *Adam Bede* and *Middlemarch*) it tends to be the male who is duped by the female's angelic appearance.

The look of desire in *Far from the Madding Crowd*, then, belongs to the males—to the narrator, his reader and a male character (usually Gabriel), a complicit trio who right from the very first "incident" described in Chapter One share a sometimes appreciative, sometimes judgmental, always appraising view of the novel's heroine. This gazed-upon heroine is sometimes performing an action and sometimes at rest; the result is a highly "cinematic" novel containing both episodes and close-ups characteristic of the viewing paradigm Mulvey and other feminist film critics describe, in which the male-identified viewer watches and judges the female film character.

Such looking leaves little room for a female look of desire, and Bathsheba, predictably, remains the object rather than the subject of the look throughout the novel.

The language of desire is not so straightforward, partaking as it does of the slippery nature of language in general, which Hardy's narrator refers to in the "Sheep-Shearing" chapter: "There is a loquacity that tells nothing, which was Bathsheba's; and there is a silence which says much: that was Gabriel's" (153). Bathsheba's frustration with male language in particular as a means of expressing herself (she tells Boldwood, "It is difficult for a woman to define her feelings in language, which is chiefly made by men to express theirs," 364) would appear to indicate Hardy's awareness of the inadequacy of patriarchal discourse for women's purposes, particularly in the area of "feelings." The novel's implied solution to this problem, however—not that women should find a new language of desire, but that they should be careful whom they listen to—is far from feminist. Bathsheba, in fact, inadvertently misuses the male language of desire—when she inscribes the words "MARRY ME" on the seal of the valentine—with dire consequences. Her lack of experience with this man-made language also enables Troy to seduce her with it, and it is a "weapon" with which he is particularly adept. "If you can only fight half as winningly as you can talk, you are able to make a pleasure of a bayonet wound!" (184) she tells him, and later we are told that his "voice . . . was beginning to have a strange power in agitating her" (189). "Power" is exactly the right description for the effect of Troy's speech on Bathsheba, who over the course of the novel becomes not simply the object of the language of male desire but also its victim. The male speaks, and the female listens—at her own risk. And finally, as critics have noted, the language of desire is also inscribed in the narrator's use of metaphor in *Far from the Madding Crowd*—in the blush of the sheared sheep, for instance, or in the aftermath of the swordplay scene—prefiguring the lush sexual idiom of *Tess of the d'Urbervilles*, another Hardy novel that will privilege male language as well as male desire.

The enactment of desire, too, is portrayed in *Far from the Madding Crowd* as a male preserve that females encroach upon at the risk of their own and society's disapprobation. Bathsheba indicates her awareness of this societal code early in the novel, when Gabriel assumes she will marry him because she has run after him to tell him she has no sweetheart. She indignantly retorts, "Why, if I'd wanted you I shouldn't have run after you like this; 'twould have been the *forwardest* thing!" (34). Likewise, she chastises herself for the action of sending the valentine ("It was a wanton thing which no woman with any self-respect should have done," 133), and Gabriel chastises her for her subsequent conduct toward Boldwood (calling it "unworthy of any thoughtful and meek and comely woman," 140). At the end of the novel, the same strictures against the enactment of female desire still apply; when, in a deliberate reversal of the situation in the first chapter,

Bathsheba again "runs after" Gabriel, this time to tell him she *will* marry him, she ruefully remarks, "It seems exactly as if I had come courting you—how dreadful" (409). Of course, the reader understands that it is not dreadful at all, that it is in fact entirely appropriate at this juncture—not because such unfeminine conduct is now acceptable, but because the woman has learned her lesson. She who has been pursued for so long must now do the pursuing, not in the spirit of freedom and enlarged possibilities of a new-found subjectivity, but as a form of punishment for failing to choose the "correct" male desire to respond to in the first place.

But Bathsheba does feel desire, even though she is not permitted to look or to speak it during most of the novel, and, remarkably, she enacts this desire directly in her midnight ride to join Troy in Bath. She also lives to tell about it and to love again, as Thomasin will in *The Return of the Native*, a distinct advance over Maggie's aborted enactment in *The Mill on the Floss*, for instance. This episode can hardly be adduced as evidence of Hardy's enlightenment or of Bathsheba's subjectivity, however. For one thing, the latter's desire, on close examination, seems reactive and submissive in the traditional feminine way; what she really desires is for Troy to desire her (we are told that she "loved him no less in thinking he might soon cease to love her—indeed, considerably more," 226). For another, the enactment itself brings about its own punishment in the form of Bathsheba's marital misery. If anything, the novel as a whole could be said to militate against the notion of female erotic subjectivity, in that the female it portrays turns out to be quite mistaken in her choice of a male desire to respond to, and compounds her error by acting on this desire in an inappropriate way. She is accordingly punished by the events of the novel, which "tame" her in exactly the way she insists she needs when Gabriel first asks her to marry him ("It wouldn't do, Mr. Oak. I want somebody to tame me . . . and you would never be able to, I know," 36).

The language of taming, of conquering and domination, is frequently used to characterize love relationships in *Far from the Madding Crowd*, in fact, indicating Hardy's firm adherence at this stage of his career to the classic domination/submission pattern of male-female relationships. Such language is mostly used in connection with Bathsheba (who is conquered by her love of Troy) and with Boldwood (who is conquered by his love of Bathsheba). Bathsheba "capitulates" to Troy's flattery (182), her laughter being "the removal of yet another stake from the palisade of cold manners which had kept him off" (190), and she seems "as one who, facing a reviving wind, finds it blow so strongly that it stops the breath" (196). Love causes Boldwood, too, to "live outside his defenses for the first time, and with a fearful sense of exposure" (127). There is a curious parallel, in fact, between these two characters, in that Hardy describes both of them as strong personalities who are undone by the destructive power of love. We read that "Bathsheba loved Troy in the way that only self-reliant women love when they abandon their self-reliance. When a strong woman recklessly throws away her strength she is worse than a weak woman who has never had any strength to throw away" (198). Similarly, Boldwood's "fearful sense of exposure," we are told, "is the usual experience of strong natures when they love" (127). The two characters are both equally conscious of a painful loss of dignity in this loss of strength: after her marriage to Troy Bathsheba mourns, "Now, anything short of cruelty will content me. Yes the independent and spirited Bathsheba is come to this!" (284), and when Boldwood pleads with Bathsheba he says in anguish, "I am come to that low, lowest stage—to ask a woman for pity" (212). There is a telling contrast, however, in Hardy's handling of Bathsheba's and Boldwood's respective "weaknesses," as I remarked in Chapter One. What amounts to a sort of "natural" feminine frailty in Bathsheba—her willingness to surrender her personal power as a result of love—displays itself as a genuine pathology in Boldwood, an indication of total personality disintegration and finally of insanity. Boldwood's shame and self-blame are more acute and more intolerable, we realize, because they are gendered: while Bathsheba bemoans the loss of her strength ("the independent and spirited Bathsheba is come to this"), Boldwood bemoans the loss of something far more crucial, namely his male identity. Thus for him the crowning indignity, the "lowest stage," is "to ask a *woman* for pity." Boldwood finds himself—incongruously, inappropriately, unnaturally—in the feminine position of submission, in which he has lost all his power to a woman. Madness and death, apparently, are the predictable outcomes of such a fall.

And it is romantic love that wreaks all this havoc. Even in this relatively early novel, we can see evidence of Hardy's deep-rooted cynicism about the possibility of successful love relationships between men and women. Apropos of Boldwood's infatuation with Bathsheba, the narrator sagely remarks, "The rarest offerings of the purest loves are but a self-indulgence, and no generosity at all. . . . It appears that ordinary men take wives because possession is not possible without marriage, and that ordinary women accept husbands because marriage is not possible without possession" (136). The characters, too, comment cynically on romance; Bathsheba declares, "Loving is misery for women always" (207), and Troy states flatly, "All romances end at marriage" (281). The only healthy love between the sexes, apparently, is the solution the book offers in the form of the ultimate alliance between Bathsheba and Gabriel: a connection based on affection rather than romance, described in detail in the narrator's well-known aside after the two agree to be married.

Theirs was that substantial affection which arises . . . when the two who are thrown together begin first by knowing the rougher sides of each other's character, and not the best till further on, the romance growing up in the interstices of a mass of hard prosaic reality. This good-fellowship—*camaraderie*—usually occurring through similarity of pursuits, is unfortunately seldom superadded to love between the sexes, because men and women associate not in their labours but in their pleasures merely. Where however happy circumstance permits its development the compounded feeling proves itself to be the only love which is strong as death—that love which many waters cannot quench, nor the floods drown, beside which the passion usually called by the name is evanescent as steam. (409)

A love based on *camaraderie*: this sounds progressive, a step beyond the usual domination/submission hierarchy of romantic love. It sounds, in fact, very similar to the love between Lucy Snowe and Paul Emanuel described by Charlotte Brontë in *Villette*. Brontë's description of this kind of bond, we will recall, runs as follows:

The love born of beauty was not mine; . . . another love, venturing diffidently into life after long acquaintance, furnace-tried by pain, stamped by constancy, consolidated by affection's pure and durable alloy, submitted by intellect to intellect's own tests, and finally wrought up, by his own process, to his own unflawed completeness, this Love that laughed at Passion, his fast frenzies and his hot and hurried extinction, in *this* Love I had a vested interest. (585)

Like Hardy, Brontë stresses "affection's durable alloy" and scorns the "hot and hurried extinction" of conventional "passion." There are other parallels as well between the two novels: Lucy, like Bathsheba, has known the pangs of unrequited romantic love before finding this "other," truer love. Why, then, do the outcomes of the novels seem so different? Why does Bathsheba's discovery of this new kind of love seem like a failure, or at best ambivalent, while Lucy's seems triumphant, a genuine progression in both the wisdom and the fortunes of the heroine?

Partly, I think, the answer lies in the visual dynamics of *Far from the Madding Crowd* that I discussed earlier, in which the female character's point of view is consistently elided in favor of the male's. We do not know how satisfying this new kind of love is for Bathsheba (as witnessed in the heated critical debate on this point) partly because we see her only from the outside. Before the wedding, we are told, there is a "mischievous smile in her bright eyes" and she "laughed with a flushed cheek" (412); after it, however, we are informed that "she never laughed readily now" (415). These are skimpy clues to her degree of satisfaction, especially in comparison with the detail in which Gabriel's impressions are recorded, including his impression of Bathsheba ("She seemed in his eyes remarkably like the girl of that fascinating dream," 413). As is so often the case in Hardy's novels, we cannot know the heroine's thoughts or feelings because we are simply not given them. The other stumbling-block to our belief in this new kind of love, at least from the heroine's point of view, is the "lesson" implicit in it within the context of the novel as a whole. As we have seen, Bathsheba learns the lesson that she must distinguish between a male desire that is worthy to respond to (which may not be very exciting) and one that isn't (which will in all likelihood appeal to her feminine vanity through some kind of flattery). Her failure to make this distinction results in the kind of comeuppance played out in the events of the novel, which teach her the error of her ways in a graphic and painful manner. The resulting alliance (this time with the "right" suitor) seems a reward not so much for Bathsheba as for Gabriel, who duly claims the prize he has so patiently won. Within the terms of my inquiry, therefore, it is difficult to posit Bathsheba as a female subject of desire, or even as having achieved an increased subjectivity over the course of the novel. She remains the beautiful object of male desire, to which she finally learns to respond in a fitting manner.

Lucy Snowe, on the other hand, comes to the realization that "the love, born of beauty was not mine" (585). She, too, learns a lesson about the vagaries of male desire, ultimately choosing to respond to a man whose feeling for her is affectionate and constant; but in no sense is this lesson a "punishment" in the way that Bathsheba's appears to be. Lucy, as much as Paul Emanuel, feels abundantly rewarded by the discovery of their love for each other, and we know this by means of direct access to her consciousness ("Penetrated with his influence, and living by his affection, having his worth by intellect, and his goodness by heart—I preferred him before all humanity," 613). In these two novels, in fact, we can see the difference between a male-centered and a female-centered account of a heroine's progress from romantic to affectionate love. Bathsheba merely learns to make better use of her status as a desirable object, while Lucy relinquishes this status and learns to love a man who admires and encourages her subjectivity. In conceptual terms, it is as if Hardy is still working within the classic subject/object paradigm, while Charlotte Brontë attempts, at least, to challenge its hegemony by working outside it. In spite of its narrative grammar, then, which places a female at the center of the story's action, *Far from the Madding Crowd* can hardly be termed a feminist novel in respect to either its ideological framework or the extent of its heroine's erotic subjectivity. It is a deceptively lighthearted love story, partaking of an underlying sexism that manifests itself in the "lesson" it finally teaches its recalcitrant heroine.

THE RETURN OF THE NATIVE

Hardy's next major work, *The Return of the Native*, was to continue the trends that came to mark his novel-writing career. As in *Far from the Madding Crowd*, the course of love does not run smoothly; desire tends to be triangular, the presence of a rival acting as a catalyst in the love plots; and the ending, while making a gesture toward peaceful reconciliation, is basically tragic. It is altogether a more somber novel than *Far from the Madding Crowd*, and one that is more interesting for the feminist critic. We can immediately notice, for instance, a marked decline in the number of sexist generalizations made by the narrator. The "Quiet Woman" with her head under her arm is a sexist symbol, of course, and we are informed of "the fact of the indirectness of a woman's movement towards her desire" (249) by the same authoritative voice that comments, "Once let a maiden admit the possibility of her being stricken with love for some one at some hour and place, and the thing is as good as done" (142). But such comments are rare, and there are anti-male generalizations as well: for instance, Mrs. Yeobright, a fairly reliable character, asks, "Why is it that a woman can see from a distance what a man cannot see close?" (214). The narrator in this novel is not nearly so sure of himself in the area of sexual psychology as the narrator was in *Far from the Madding Crowd*, and it would seem that this decrease in sexist asides corresponds to a decrease in Hardy's confidence that he could analyze and categorize women's behavior with perfect ease and accuracy. The issues in this novel are not so clear-cut, either, and the characters are not such bold "types": the swashbuckling Troy has dwindled to the vacillating Wildeve, Gabriel Oak the hero has become Venn the minor character, and the feisty Bathsheba has metamorphosed into the sultry Eustacia. As readers, we are generally less sure of what our responses to these more amorphous characters should be, and this is especially true of our responses to Eustacia, one of Hardy's most interesting heroines.

Our first glimpse of this unusual personage is appropriately enigmatic. Seen by Venn, Eustacia initially appears to be part of the heath, an "it" that rises from the barrow "like a spike from a helmet" (11). She continues to be described as an object, a "form," a "figure," until she moves, at which time Venn and the reader are able to discern "more clearly the characteristics of the figure: it was a woman's" (12). This is obviously not the standard introductory "portrait" of the Victorian novel-heroine. Our next information about her, too, downplays the visual; we simply overhear the heath-dwellers referring to her as a "lonesome dark eyed creature . . . that some say is a witch, . . . a fine young woman" (47–48). This obliquely received information is also ambiguous, telling us nothing definite about Eustacia's character: she is "lonesome," she may be evil, and she is young. Curiously, too, we hear her before we see her clearly. In Chapter Six, "The Figure Against the Sky," Eustacia is again approached from the point of view of an anonymous observer, who is introduced in Hardy's typically oblique fashion in such scenes ("Had the reddleman been watching he might have recognized her. . . . ," 50). This observer hears "the woman" (as she is called at this point) "break silence" in the following way: "What she uttered was a lengthened sighing, apparently at something in her mind which had led to her presence here. There was a spasmodic abandonment about it as if, in allowing herself to utter the sound, the woman's brain had authorized what it could not regulate" (52).

This spasmodic sigh precedes the first extended visual description of Eustacia, a description that is extremely interesting in terms of its scopic elements. In it, a female character is actually exercising the power of the gaze: Eustacia is watching Wildeve's inn through her telescope, an un-equivocally erotic situation. Somewhat surprisingly, however, she does not thereby function as an erotic subject. A close reading of this scene reveals that the viewing paradigm I discussed at the beginning of this chapter is firmly in place, so that instead of looking with Eustacia through her telescope and sharing her point of view, the reader is invited to share the perspective of the unspecified male observer and to "look at her looking":

Far away down the valley the faint shine from the window of the inn still lasted on; and a few additional moments proved that the window, or what was within it, had more to do with the woman's sigh than had either her own actions, or the scene immediately around. She lifted her left hand, and revealed that it held a closed telescope. This she rapidly extended. . . .

The handkerchief which had hooded her head was now a little thrown back, her face being somewhat elevated. A profile was visible against the dull monochrome of cloud around her; and it was as though side shadows from the features of Sappho and Mrs. Siddons had converged upwards from the tomb to form an image like neither but suggesting both. (52)

We are given here neither a description of the object of Eustacia's attention—the object, indeed, is "far away down the valley"—nor admit-tance to her perceptions; instead, the scene is recounted, like so many scenes in Hardy's novels, from the viewpoint of an amorphous, anonymous narratorial spectator. Eustacia herself, by a deft adjustment of narrative focus ("The handkerchief which had hooded her head was now a little thrown back. . . . A profile was visible") becomes the observed object, even though it is she who is doing the looking. In fact, the scene constitutes a perfect example of Mary Ann Doane's findings in her investigation of the female gaze in women's cinema. Such a scopic adjustment, according to Doane, is a standard device in such scenes: the female gaze on the cinema screen is typically "framed" in some way (by the use of mirrors, eyeglasses, etc.) in order to "to contain an aberrant and excessive female sexuality. For framing is the film's preferred strategy when it wishes to simultaneously state and negate. . . . The male gaze erases that of the woman" (100). Eustacia's telescope is just such a framing device, and it seems reasonable to conclude that Hardy's reasons for its use are similar to those of the filmmakers Doane describes.

In addition, we can see that what we have here is a voyeuristic scene similar to that which opens *Far from the Madding Crowd*. The observer-cum-reddleman watching Eustacia as she gazes through her telescope corresponds paradigmatically to Gabriel Oak watching Bathsheba as she gazes in the mirror (another framing device). In both instances the woman's gaze is powerless, negated by virtue of the narratorial perspective, and in both cases her gaze is eroticized and thus invested with (sexual) guilt. Just as Gabriel concludes that

Bathsheba is engaging in a display of vanity, the observing narrator refers to Eustacia's "spying attitude" (53), even though what he (and the reader) is doing is in fact spying on her. Also like Gabriel, this observer focuses on the action the female character performs (in this case the action of looking) rather than on her appearance ("The night revealed little of her whose form it was embracing, for the mobile parts of her countenance could not be seen"). In a moment, however, the observer's sexual curiosity is partially satisfied (as Gabriel's is when Bathsheba throws off her shawl in the cowshed) by Eustacia blowing on a live coal, which discloses "two match-less lips and a cheek only, her head being still enveloped."

The narrator tantalizes us yet further before revealing the details of his character's beauty: a few pages later, for example, Eustacia taunts Wildeve by "throwing back the shawl so that the firelight shone full upon her face and throat, [and saying] with a smile, 'Have you seen anything better than that in your travels?' " (60). This visual suspense finally culminates in the "Queen of Night" chapter, which encompasses an extended fetishistic close-up, a halt in the narrative for a moment of erotic contemplation, in which the heroine's bodily parts are atomized and described in a rhapsody of aesthetic perfection. "To see her hair," we read, "was to fancy that a whole winter did not contain darkness enough to form its shadow. It closed over her forehead like nightfall extinguishing the western glow" (63). Her eyes, we are told, were "pagan. . . , full of nocturnal mysteries. Their light, as it came, and went, and came again, was partially hampered by their oppres-sive lids and lashes; and of these the under lid was much fuller than it usually is with English women" (63). And her mouth, Hardy's aesthetic and erotic "weak spot," is dissected to the point of absurdity: it

seemed formed less to speak than to quiver, less to quiver than to kiss . . . less to kiss than to curl. Viewed sideways the closing-line of her lips formed, with almost geometric precision, the curve so well-known in the arts of design as the cima-recta, or ogee. . . . One had fancied that such lip-curves were mostly lurking underground in the South as fragments of forgotten marbles. So fine were the lines of her lips that, though full, each corner of her mouth was as clearly cut as the point of a spear. This keenness of corner was only blunted when she was given over to sudden fits of gloom. (64)

So far, then, Eustacia follows the predictable pattern of Hardy's custom-ary visual dynamic, functioning largely as the object rather than the subject of the look of desire, even when she is doing the looking. When she returns Clym's look after they are married, for instance (a potentially erotic mo-ment in the novel), the desire in the mutual gazing turns out once again to be male and unilateral: "In the quiet days since their marriage, when Yeobright had been poring over her lips, her eyes, and the lines of her face, she had mused and mused on [Paris], even while in the act of returning his gaze" (242). At the end of the book she is returned, appropriately, to the status of a lovely aesthetic/sexual object, a level she rarely transcends during the course of the novel. It is Clym who, in a final act of proprietorship, exhibits her corpse to Charley and Venn.

Eustacia, . . . as she lay there still in death eclipsed all her living phases. Pallor did not include all the quality of her complexion, which seemed more than whiteness; it was almost light. The expression of her finely carved mouth was pleasant, as if a sense of dignity had just compelled her to leave off speaking. . . . Her black hair . . . surrounded her brow like a forest. The stateliness of look which had been almost too marked for a dweller in a country domicile had at last found an artistically happy background. (380–81)

In this cameo, the narrator, the reader and the three male characters all step back and admire a final fetishistic portrait of Eustacia, which is doubly reassuring to the male psyche: she is safely distanced, fragmented and objectified against her "artistically happy background," each of her parts extravagantly eulogized; and she is dead, a condition of perfect submission holding no more threat of rebellious power, which somehow allows her to "eclipse all her living phases." She has clearly reached a state of aesthetic and feminine perfection.

The enigmatic Eustacia, more beautiful in death than in life, in fact represents a failed experiment by Hardy, and the reasons for this failure are significant in terms of her erotic subjectivity. Critics have noted the sketchy, perfunctory nature of Hardy's characterization of this potentially interesting main character, the lack of verisimilitude that mars her portrayal. His other heroines, by and large, seem much more "real." But their erotic passivity allows Hardy free rein in constructing lovingly detailed portraits of them, as I shall show, while his portrayal of Eustacia is fatally hampered by both external and internal constraints. What Hardy attempts in his creation of Eustacia—a sympathetic heroine who is also an experienced, worldly sensualist—simply cannot survive the Victorian prohibition against the portrayal of explicit sex in novels, on one hand, or the limitations of Hardy's own erotic vision on the other.

The constraints of Victorian Grundyism, first of all, render such an endeavor almost impossible. Hardy's characterization of Eustacia is marred—far more than his characterization of more conventionally "good" women such as Bathsheba, Tess or Sue, for example—by his forced inability to portray explicit sexuality, to the point where his "Queen of Night" seems unconvincing and ultimately uninteresting. Penny Boumelha sees Eustacia as "both an expression and a critical placing of Hardy's anxious relationship to Romanticism" (50); I think she just as accurately represents his anxious relationship to his "respectable" reading public.

The application of such censorious limitations to Eustacia, in particular, is instructive. Hardy's depiction of Tess, for example, was to display no such descriptive constraints—and it is not just the intervening thirteen years that make the difference. Just as relevant is the kind of woman portrayed in each instance. Tess is described in the context of a passive object of male desire, as I shall show, while Eustacia dangerously approaches the verge of sexual subjectivity. She takes independent action in regard to the men in her life, and, unlike Bathsheba, Tess or Sue, she suffers few moral agonies in regard to her irregular sexual conduct; even when she is *in extremis* and trying to decide whether to run away with Wildeve near the end of the book, her concerns are primarily personal rather than ethical: " 'I can't go,' she moaned. 'No money; I can't go! And if I could, what comfort to me?. . . How I have tried and tried to be a splendid woman, and how destiny has been against me! . . . I do not deserve my lot!' " (359). This lack of moral compunction effectively removes her from the category of the remorseful but inherently virtuous heroine who has "given in" to the desire of one or more of the male characters in the novel (like Tess, for example, or George Eliot's Maggie Tulliver) and places her instead in the equivocal position of a female character who has followed her own desire—and is sorry only that it has not worked out as she had planned.

A basic incongruity, however, arises from the fact that Hardy is prevented from depicting this desire as straightforwardly sexual. Like George Eliot's Gwendolen Harleth (only less convincingly, less interestingly, since Gwendolen's lack of sexual interest comes across as authentic neurotic complexity), Eustacia is made to long for status, prestige and luxury rather than for erotic fulfillment, in an attempt to make her palatable for Victorian consumption. As much as Eliot's heroine, Eustacia primarily desires power (over other people, and particularly over men) and secondarily desires wealth, excitement and social conquests (represented by Paris, in Eustacia's case). The difference between them, however, is crucial: Gwendolen's lust for power is readily understood as a form of compensation for her neurotic frigidity, while Eustacia is portrayed as anything but frigid. Her sensuality is extremely convincing, in fact, causing her lack of erotic fervor to seem doubly incongruous. Of her long dark hair, for example, we are told,

Her nerves extended into those tresses, and her temper could always be softened by stroking them down. When her hair was brushed she would instantly sink into stillness and look like the Sphinx. If, in passing under one of the Egdon banks, any of its thick skeins were caught . . . by a prickly tuft of the large *Ulex Europaeus*— which will act as a sort of hair-brush—she would go back a few steps, and pass against it a second time. (63)

Her languid shudders and spasmodic sighs, similarly, contribute to the construction of Eustacia as a physically sensuous and self-indulgent heroine, but one who is curiously lacking in erotic awareness. Somewhat incredibly, Hardy even manages to follow her into her bedroom and undress her in a seemingly innocent manner: although the narrator describes her sigh as "no fragile maiden sigh, but a sigh which shook her like a shiver," the latter reaction is attributed not to emotion but to a "flash of reason" which also "moved through her when, ten minutes later, she lay on her bed asleep" (62).

So, although Boumelha accurately places her in the "literary lineage of the destructive and self-destructive *femme fatale*, which takes much of its impetus from Falubert's Emma Bovary, and culminates in Ibsen's Hedda Gabler" (55), Eustacia appears as a pale, watered-down version of such powerful and dangerous females. Like that of Flaubert's Emma Bovary, Eustacia's "great desire" is "to be loved to madness," and "love was to her the one cordial which could drive away the eating loneliness of her days.... She seemed to long for the abstraction called passionate love more than for any particular lover" (66). Like Emma, too, she is an epicure in sensations, tending toward "actions of reckless unconventionality, framed to snatch a year's, a week's, even an hour's passion from anywhere while it could be won. Through want of it she had sung without being merry, possessed without enjoying, outshone without triumphing" (66). Unlike Emma, however, Eustacia—no doubt partly in order to circumvent the forbidden portrayal of explicit sex—is weary of love before she has really experienced it, progressing directly to the point of satiety without first indulging her appetites. "On his head she knew by prevision what most women learn only by experience: she had mentally walked round love, told the towers thereof, considered its palaces; and concluded that love was but a doleful joy. Yet she desired it, as one in a desert would be thankful for brackish water" (66–67). The result is a character who is curiously apathetic, rather than tragic, no matter how much Hardy stresses her queenly bearing, and one who signally fails to engage the reader's sympathies or imagination.

Nor is the novel's eroticism simply displaced into metaphor as it is in much of George Eliot's writing, for example, or as it will be to some extent in *Tess*. Eustacia never experiences anything remotely like Emma's rendezvous in the woods, either, so exquisitely rendered in terms of Rodolph's whip and cigar and the long drawn-out cry. Instead, there is an excess of hand-holding: she pays Charley by "pull[ing] off [her] glove, and [giving] him her bare hand" (127), and later we are told that "it was a favourite way with [Clym and Eustacia] to walk bare hand in bare hand" (207). The most explicit erotic reference in the novel is to a kiss as "something which lingered upon [Clym's] lips like a seal set there. The abiding presence of this impress was so real that . . . it seemed as if his mother might say, 'What red spot is that glowing upon your mouth so vividly?' " (192). As for Eustacia's liaison with Wildeve, the supposed passion between them seems even less believable, even though she admits, "I have loved you, and have shown you that I loved you, much to my regret" (79), and later, after she is married, says to him, "We have been hot lovers in our time, but it won't do now" (286). Hardy seems too hurried, too perfunctory, in his depiction of this heroine's erotic adventures and feelings, for some reason, and the overall result is strangely flat and forced.

This elision of the erotic in *The Return of the Native* is made even more pronounced by the presence, one might even say the omnipresence, of quarreling scenes, which of course are subject to none of Mrs. Grundy's literary constraints. The quarrels are obviously meant to illustrate Eustacia's passionate nature without direct reference to her sexuality—in one of them we read that "she interrupted with a suppressed fire of which either love or anger seemed an equally possible issue" (81)—but the number and detail of such scenes create an overall impression that the lovers meet mainly to bicker, and their stilted dialogue causes them to seem petty rather than passionate. In the middle of one of their disputes, for instance, when Wildeve says, "Your eyes seem heavy, Eustacia," she replies, "It is my general way of looking. I think it arises from my feeling sometimes an agonizing pity for myself that I ever was born" (197). Such pomposity, offset by none of the suppressed erotic intensity that could (possibly) justify it, hardly approximates the language of desire, and finally seems ludicrous. In this novel, particularly in contrast to its French counterparts, we can see very clearly the basis for Henry James' remark that "our English system is a good thing for virgins and boys, and a bad thing for the novel itself" (241) or Thackeray's complaint that "since the author of *Tom Jones* was buried, no writer of fiction among us has been permitted to depict to his utmost power a MAN [*sic*]. We must drape him, and give him a certain conventional simper. Society will not tolerate the Natural in our Art" (viii).

In Eustacia, then, Hardy takes on a real challenge, the portrayal of a seductive heroine without overt reference to her sexuality. Her sensuality in other respects, depicted in detail, causes the deficiency to be even more apparent than it would be in a more demure or ascetic heroine. Such pronounced sensuality, which marks one of the ways in which Eustacia's portrayal departs from that of the stereotypical Victorian heroine, initially appears to be a bold stroke by Hardy. In employing it, however, he creates a double dilemma for himself which the novel never overcomes: her sensual nature not only causes Eustacia's lack of overt sexuality to seem like a blatant omission, thus undermining her verisimilitude, but it also prevents the narrator (and by extension the reader) from sympathizing wholeheartedly with her, thus undermining her subjectivity. Hardy's narrator does not precisely disapprove of Eustacia's strong-willed hedonism, but he refuses to endorse it in such a way that his character becomes an object to be judged rather than a sympathetic female subject. She is not discounted as simply coarse, as Arabella is, for example, but unlike Bathsheba, Tess or Sue, she is not quite taken seriously, and never quite becomes a full-fledged heroine of the novel she inhabits. It is as though Hardy is somewhat scandalized by his own creation; he is able to admire the idea of such a heroine, but in the end he has no real affection for her. And this narratorial withholding of approval has a subtle but damning impact on Eustacia's overall impression on the reader, in that the latter's response to a sensuous female who pursues her own desires without hesitation is already culturally programmed to veer toward the conventional negative judgment accorded the "selfish" woman.

But Hardy's experiment is illuminating from a feminist point of view, for both what it attempts and the reasons for its failure. Paradoxically, the novel containing the most seductive heroine is the least erotic of the four novels I discuss in this chapter (it contains nothing to equal the exquisite sexual tension of the swordplay scene in *Far from the Madding Crowd*, for example); further, although this seductive heroine is the least believable of the four I discuss, she comes closest to embodying a female subject of desire. Quite simply, she represents a missed opportunity for Hardy, who is seemingly able to imagine but not to condone female desire. Ruth Milberg-Kaye contends that Hardy distrusts and dismisses *all* sexual desire ("For Hardy, both men and women are good or bad depending on the degree of conscious, aggressive sexuality driving each person," 33), but on close examination this is much more true of his female characters. Gabriel, Clym, Angel and Jude all act in the ways they do precisely because of sexual desire; the degree to which this is "conscious" or "aggressive" is variable and highly dependent on critical interpretation. Intellectually, Hardy clearly approves of female desire—Eustacia is portrayed as a "woman of . . . spirit" (59), especially in contrast to the conventional but slightly insipid Thomasin, whom Wildeve impatiently characterizes as a "confoundedly good little woman" (80)—but he is hindered by his own deeply rooted conventionality from creating a wholly sympathetic desiring woman as his main character. Emotionally, Hardy seems much more comfortable with traditional erotic patterns of domination and submission, as we can later see in his lovingly appreciative portrait of Tess, a woman-as-object par excellence.

Hardy's portrayal of Eustacia could in fact be seen as a classic case of ambivalent representation, an excellent instance of the simultaneous "stating and negating" described by feminist film critics (see Doane's point discussed earlier). Eustacia is indeed allowed to look, speak, feel and enact her desire; but in each instance her active subjectivity is undermined by the narrator's ruling consciousness. When she looks, as we have seen, the look is turned back on her so that she herself becomes the observed object, largely through the narrator's refusal to enter her consciousness. Similarly, although she is permitted to feel desire, her emotions are consistently undercut by the cynical, scoffing narrator, who does not appear to take them seriously. This narrator, himself adopting a world-weary stance toward "the abstraction called passionate love" (66), is given to making somewhat bitter generalizations about it: he refers wryly to "the sentiment which lurks more or less in all animate nature—that of not desiring the undesired of others" (99); "that peculiar state of misery which is not exactly grief, and which specially attends the dawnings of reason in the latter days of an ill-judged, transient love" (100); "the modulating point between indifference and love, . . . the stage called 'having a fancy for,' [which] occurs once in the history of the most gigantic passions, . . . [at] a period when they are in the hands of the weakest will" (118); "the sickening feeling which . . . accompanies the sudden sight of a once-loved one who is beloved no more" (151); "that quality of selfishness which is frequently the chief constituent of [love], and sometimes its only one" (152); and "those who love too hotly to love long and well" (209). The cumulative force of these generalizations, scattered randomly throughout the narrative, works to forge a bond of wry superiority between narrator and reader, who then tend to view the characters—and particularly Eustacia—from a slightly condescending vantage point.

Although at times she appears to share in this general ennui with regard to love (of her desire for Wildeve, for instance, she thinks, "Was it really possible that her interest in [him] had been so entirely the result of antagonism that the glory and the dream departed from the man with the first sound that he was no longer coveted by her rival? . . . . What was the man worth whom a woman inferior to herself did not value?" 98–99), for the most part Eustacia's romantic feelings are described by the narrator in overtly disparaging terms. His pronouncements about women in general ("Once let a maiden admit the possibility of her being stricken with love for some one at some hour and place, and the thing is as good as done," 142) and about women like Eustacia in particular ("To court their own discomfiture by love is a common instinct with certain perfervid women," 145) are notably sour, and even his most laudatory descriptions of his heroine are delivered in a slightly derogatory manner. In the "Queen of Night" chapter, for instance, we are told, "In Eustacia's brain were juxtaposed the strangest assortment of ideas . . . . There was no middle-distance in her perspective. . . . Every bizarre effect that could result from the random intertwining of watering-place glitter with the grand solemnity of a heath, was to be found in her" (65). Labels like "strange" and "bizarre" reflect both the narrator's judgmental distance from Eustacia and Hardy's own uneasiness about his creation; he appears both fascinated and repelled by her in a way that effectively negates her point of view even when we are allowed to share it. And, as I noted at the beginning of this chapter, this does not happen very often, as Hardy tends to eschew the use of free indirect speech in his portrayal of female characters.

This stylistic tendency becomes more obvious if we compare Hardy's handling of female consciousness to that of a more traditional Victorian novelist such as George Eliot. A passage of inner musing by Gwendolen Harleth, the Eliot heroine who most closely resembles the strong-willed Eustacia, for example, occurs when Herr Klesmer informs her of her lack

of musical talent. When Klesmer leaves, Eliot's narrator reports Gwendolen's state of mind in the following way:

The "indignities" that she might be visited with had no very definite form for her,
but the mere association of anything called "indignity" with herself, roused a
resentful alarm. And along with the vaguer images which were raised by those
biting words, came the more precise conception of disagreeables which her experience enabled her to imagine. How could she take her mamma and the four sisters
to London, if it were not possible for her to earn money at once? And as for
submitting to be a *protegée*, and asking her mamma to submit with her to the
humiliation of being supported by Miss Arrowpoint—that was as bad as being a
governess; nay, worse; for suppose the end of all her study to be as worthless as
Klesmer clearly expected it to be, the sense of favours received and never repaid,
would embitter the miseries of disappointment. Klesmer doubtless had magnificent
ideas about helping artists; but how could he know the feelings of ladies in such
matters? It was all over: she had entertained a mistaken hope; and there was an end
of it. (244–45)

This rather unremarkable passage is an utterly typical instance of how
Eliot (as well as most of her contemporaries) handles the thought processes,
the consciousness, of the important characters in her novels. In this reverie,
for example, Gwendolen's thoughts are reported in ordinary indirect
speech up to the sentence beginning "How could she take her mamma and
the four sisters to London," after which point they are couched in free
indirect speech, indicated by the questions ("how could he know the
feelings of ladies . . .?"), the vocabulary ("as bad as being a governess";
"Klesmer doubtless had magnificent ideas") and the overall sense of despair evinced by the abrupt phraseology ("nay, worse"; "It was all over . . .;
and there was an end of it"). In such passages we are made aware not only
of what the character is thinking and feeling, but also of the narrator's
opinion of such musings; in the preceding excerpt, for instance, Eliot's
narrator (as she so often does with Gwendolen) stands aside with a sort of
ironic pity. Overall, such passages yield freer and more intimate access to
a character's consciousness than either ordinary direct speech (" 'How can
I take my mamma and four sisters to London?' thought Gwendolen") or
ordinary indirect speech ("Gwendolen wondered how she could take her
mother and four sisters to London").

In Hardy's novel, Eustacia experiences a similar moment of disillusionment after Clym tells her that he intends to stay on Egdon Heath. Her
experience of this moment is expressed in the following passage:

When he was gone she rested her head upon her hands and said to herself, "Two
wasted lives—his and mine. And I am come to this! Will it drive me out of my
mind?"
    She cast about for any possible course which offered the least improvement on
the existing state of things, and could find none. She imagined how all those

Budmouth ones who should learn what had become of her would say, "Look at the girl for whom nobody was good enough!" To Eustacia the situation seemed such a mockery of her hopes that death appeared the only door of relief if the satire of Heaven should go much further.

Suddenly she aroused herself and exclaimed, "But I'll shake it off. Yes, I *will* shake it off! No one shall know my suffering. I'll be bitterly merry, and ironically gay, and I'll laugh in derision! And I'll begin by going to this dance on the green."

She ascended to her bedroom and dressed herself with scrupulous care. To an onlooker her beauty would have made her feelings almost seem reasonable. . . .

It was five in the afternoon when she came out from the house ready for her walk. There was material enough in the picture for twenty new conquests. (259–60)

The contrast in technique between this and Eliot's passage is telling. Eustacia's thoughts and feelings are conveyed either directly ("Two wasted lives—his and mine"; "But I'll shake it off") or indirectly ("She cast about . . ."; "She imagined . . ."; "To Eustacia the situation seemed . . ."). Within the latter mode, there are no indications of Eustacia's emotions or vocabulary: "mockery of her hopes," "door of relief" and "satire of Heaven" (the most emotive of these indirect utterances) sound unequivocally like the dispassionate, observing narrator. And "observe" is exactly what this narrator does, inviting the reader to do the same. The sentence "To an onlooker her beauty would have made her feelings almost seem reasonable" encompasses a characteristic Hardyesque shift of perspective, from Eustacia's point of view to that of an unspecified, unobtrusive onlooker. Such unobtrusive refocusing is a device that occurs with great regularity in Hardy's representations of women characters, reaching its culmination in *Tess of the d'Urbervilles*, in which, as Kaja Silverman points out, the unspecified onlooker is invoked again and again ("History," 10–11). From this anonymous vantage point the narrator is free to distance himself from Eustacia and also to objectify her (her feelings "almost seem reasonable" from this purely external viewpoint, for example). When she emerges from the house, this viewpoint is still operational and her objectification is complete: Eustacia has become a "picture" which can only be interpreted from the outside. The sentences that follow simply elaborate on the details of this picture ("The rebellious sadness that was rather too apparent when she sat indoors . . . was cloaked and softened by her out-door attire . . .; so that her face looked from its environment as from a cloud, with no noticeable lines of demarcation between flesh and clothes").

The shift is subtle, but what has happened in this passage is a typical alteration of narrative focus, from Eustacia's internal musing to her external appearance. The solid physical details of this appearance, so carefully and elaborately constructed and so freely interpreted by the observing narrator (the "rebellious sadness" is such an interpretation), produce the effect of "knowing" the character in some detail, obscuring the fact that the consciousness being explored in such passages is not that of the female character at all, but that of the male observer, whose objective distancing subtly undermines the reader's sympathy for the observed character.

Eustacia's speech and actions, like her thoughts and feelings, also evince a narratorial ambivalence that ultimately works to negate her erotic subjectivity. She herself is made to acknowledge the "unwomanly" nature of her statements of desire both for Wildeve ("Must I go on weakly confessing to you things a woman ought to conceal?" 60) and for Clym ("I love you. . . . There's my too candid confession," 200). Her bold enactment of desire, too, is portrayed as selfish and not quite properly feminine. Just as Henry James categorized Emma Bovary as masculine, Hardy's narrator remarks of Eustacia, "Her plans showed rather the comprehensive strategy of a general than the small arts called womanish" (68), and her grandfather complains, apropos of her mumming episode, "One would think you were one of the bucks I knew at one-and-twenty" (148). (The latter episode, by the way, innocuous in comparison with Emma's desperate transvestite search for an evening's pleasure, further emphasizes Hardy's swerving from the erotic in this novel.) And, like Flaubert's main character, Hardy's actively desiring heroine must be punished for her behavior by the end of the novel. Unlike Tess, for instance, who is punished as an innocent sacrificial victim of the misdemeanors of others, Eustacia in a sense "gets what she deserves" within the ethos of the novel she inhabits. "What she deserves" is death, obviously, and she deserves it because of her aberrant and independent—almost masculine—sexuality. She does not even feign feminine passivity (as George Eliot's Rosamond does, for example); after she has summoned Wildeve with her bonfire, she looks at him "as upon some wondrous thing she had created out of chaos" (58) and gloats, "Say what you will, try as you may, keep away from me all that you can, you will never forget me. You will love me all your life long. You would jump to marry me!" (81)

So, even though her "power" is necessarily limited to the power of attracting rather than actively pursuing the males in the novel, Eustacia operates far enough outside the conventional domination/submission hierarchy to make the narrator (and his reader) distinctly uncomfortable. Even though Hardy admires her boldness, he feels constrained to punish her for it, a not uncommon configuration in the Victorian novel. As Richard Barickman, Susan MacDonald and Myra Stark observe in their study of the Victorian "sexual system,"

In order for the woman of traditional Western literature to act on her own rather than as a reflex of men . . . she has to usurp a male position of power. This action, so contrary to the daily experience of the culture, is necessarily aberrant, atypical, and short-lived. However heroic, however much power it temporarily confers on the female character, it is purchased through a kind of self-annihilation: all pretense to an independent feminine nature is abandoned. . . . The divine and demonic roles assumed by female characters in much Western literature are extreme projections of the subservient and the usurping woman, and ultimately just as subject to masculine patterns of will and desire. Both are temporary transfers of a male commodity. (57)

Viewed in this light, Hardy's ambivalence toward his character is perhaps more easily understood, as is the failure of his experiment. To the extent that Eustacia is portrayed as demonic (an impression fostered by the witch rumors) and usurping, her female subjectivity is thereby discounted, and conventional erotic configurations are left undisturbed.

Hardy's stiffness in Eustacia's portrayal, we can conclude, is only partly due to the constraints of Victorian publishing. His ambivalence about his heroine's erotic independence would likely have prevented him from depicting her sexuality with any more clarity or enthusiasm, even if Mrs. Grundy had not been looking over his shoulder. He does not loathe her, as Flaubert loathes Emma Bovary, for example, but insofar as she feels and enacts her own desire she becomes an ambiguous and dangerous signifier for him, preventing him from endorsing the subjectivity he allows her. What he gives with one hand he takes away with the other, so to speak, so that his experiment is doomed from its inception. In this novel, more than in any other, we can see clearly the gender anxieties that feminist critics in particular have always sensed in Hardy's work.[5] However, this is not to say that The Return of the Native is a failed novel. Other aspects of the book—the heath-dwellers, Clym's wonderfully oedipal relationship to Mrs. Yeobright, the heath itself—are extremely convincing, creating a solid fictional reality in which the inconsistencies in Eustacia's characterization might easily go unnoticed. And, to give Hardy credit, he can at least imagine unabashed female desire, even if he cannot approve of it, a not inconsiderable achievement within the confines of the Victorian novel.

TESS OF THE D'URBERVILLES

> What can we possibly deduce from this fact that [woman] can be everything, but the knowledge that she is nothing? She seems everywhere present in art, but she is in fact absent. She is not the expression of female experience, she is a mediating sign for the male. (Tickner 264)

Tess of the d'Urbervilles, Hardy's most erotic novel by a considerable margin and surely one of the most erotic novels of the Victorian era, is of absorbing interest in terms of my present study. A particularly interesting— and revealing—inquiry is simply to ask what makes it such an erotic novel. As a novel which is undubitably "about" a female character, and one which is saturated with sexual desire, Tess would seem the ideal setting for an erotic subjectivity that is distinctively female. Astonishingly, however, this is not the case. Hardy's penultimate novel has at its center an absent subject, and the desire the book exudes is not Tess's but the (male) narrator's:

ultimately Hardy's, to put not too fine a point on it. As I shall show, what makes *Tess* so erotic is in fact its complex conformity to the domination/submission fantasy I outlined in Chapter One, a conformity that shares to an uncomfortable degree the pathological appeal of much male pornography. The look, the language and the enactment of desire in the tale of Hardy's milkmaid, despite its compelling heroine, ultimately do not belong to her.

The gaze in this novel, first of all, differs markedly in intensity from the gaze in Hardy's other works. Instead of Gabriel Oak observing Bathsheba as she gazes in her mirror or the reddleman spying on Eustacia as she looks through her telescope, we have in *Tess* a much more direct path of observation. No such framing devices are needed, because Tess herself does none of the looking. Nor is there a male spy as such; the gaze in *Tess* travels unmediated from male observer to female object, the voyeuristic spying of the early novels being succeeded, apparently, by Laura Mulvey's "fetishistic scopophilia" in which "the powerful look of the male protagonist . . . is broken in favor of the image in direct erotic rapport with the spectator. . . . The woman as object . . . is no longer the bearer of guilt but a perfect product, whose body, stylized and fragmented by close-ups, is the content of the film" (22). Tess as a "bearer of guilt" is a complex question, which I shall discuss presently; there is no doubt, however, that she functions physically as a "perfect product, whose body, stylized and fragmented by close-ups," in an important sense forms the content of Hardy's novel. These close-ups, occurring at regular intervals, have been well documented: Tess's "mobile peony mouth" (20) and "ever-varying pupils, with their radiating fibrils of blue, and black, and grey, and violet" (172) are repeatedly displayed in all their beauty, at once objectifying Tess and creating one of the most obvious erotic effects of the novel. Tess is delectable to look at, and it is the male narrator who focuses the zoom lens, so that the look of desire, unfiltered through the point of view of a male protagonist, falls on her with a peculiarly relentless scopophilic intensity.

According to Mulvey (who is referring in particular to Josef von Sternberg's films starring Marlene Dietrich), the look of desire in such films is unmediated for a specific reason: "The male hero misunderstands and, above all, does not see" (23). The function of seeing—and therefore accurately apprehending—the heroine is reserved for the filmmaker and his viewer, or in Hardy's case for the narrator and his reader. The perspective of the male characters, as Kaja Silverman points out in her excellent account of figuration and subjectivity in *Tess*, is sidestepped precisely because they "do not see." Quoting one of the well-known passages describing Tess's lips ("To a young man with the least fire in him that little upward lift in the middle of her red top lip was distracting, infatuating, maddening. He had never seen a woman's lips and teeth which forced upon his mind, with such insistent iteration, the old Elizabethan simile of roses filled with snow"),

Silverman points out that although it is ostensibly Angel's gaze that is turned upon Tess, the passage is less an account of Angel's perceptions than "an ironic admonition" to a young man who obviously does *not* have "the least fire in him." The admonition, of course, is given by the narrator himself, who *is* able to "see" Tess appropriately and who is revealed to be "the speaking subject, the one whose desires structure our view of Tess" ("History" 11). This is confirmed by the next few sentences of the "lips" quotation: "Perfect, he, as a lover, might have called [Tess's lips] off-hand. But no: they were not perfect. And it was the touch of the imperfect upon the would-be perfect that gave the sweetness" (152).[6]

This narrator who knows better (and who clearly has the requisite "fire" in him) is a constant hovering presence in the close-up scenes in *Tess*, correcting the perceptions of both Angel and Alec and subtly complicating the seemingly simple question of point of view in each instance. In another famous scene, Angel sees Tess "yawning, and he saw the red interior of her mouth as if it had been a snake's. She had stretched one arm so high above her coiled-up cable of hair that he could see its satin delicacy above the sunburn; her face was flushed with sleep, and her eyelids hung heavy over their pupils." So far, we see Tess's sensuous mouth and arm from Angel's somewhat voyeuristic point of view ("She had not heard him enter, and hardly realized his presence there"); but the next (transitional) sentence— "The brim-fulness of her nature breathed from her"—could belong either to Angel or to the overseeing, omnipresent narrator, who rounds off the description with a confident generalization: "It was a moment when a woman's soul is more incarnate than at any other time; when the most spiritual beauty bespeaks itself flesh; and sex takes the outside place in the presentation" (172). Other descriptions, too, are similarly glossed by the narrator's wise and watchful consciousness (the rape/seduction scene, initially rendered from Alec's point of view, is a good example), and, inevitably, "sex takes the outside place in the presentation." As Silverman rather wryly remarks, "What the narrator characterizes as [Tess's] 'soul' or 'consciousness' is often so fully exteriorized as to bear little resemblance to any classical definition of those terms" ("History" 22).

Thus we have one cause of the erotic immediacy in *Tess*: we are privileged to participate directly in the emotions and fantasy life of the doting, gloating narrator as he scrutinizes his nearly perfect heroine. Hardy's personal identification with this (unquestionably male) narrator is clear: "I have not been able to put on paper all she was or is to me," he admitted (Gittings 68). "All she was" to Hardy consisted simply of an ideal woman, gazed upon and longed for by the males in the novel, by the male reader, and by the narrator himself (whom together Silverman refers to as a "trio of exegetes" who produce an "alarmingly centered" reading of the text, "History" 20). This ideal vision is objectified not only through the cinematic sense of sight, but also—an effect made possible by the narrative medium—

through the other senses as well: we are made to feel "her arm, . . . cold and damp to [Angel's] mouth as a new-gathered mushroom" (178), to taste her (her arm "taste[s] of the whey," and Angel experiences her mouth and breath as tasting "of the butter and eggs and milk and honey on which she mainly lived," 238) and to hear the "stop'd-diapason note which her voice acquired when her heart was in her speech." In a physical sense, then, Tess is vividly and immediately present, to an extent that tends to obfuscate the fact that a key constituent of her subjectivity—what several critics have called her "interiority"—is missing. James Kincaid observes that "what disappears most emphatically in *Tess* is Tess. . . . Tess's being . . . disappears into form; put another way, her being is never more than the formulations of others and of herself. Others objectify her by separating her into parts, only to submit these parts to a curious blurring process and then to eroticise this blur as a wonderfully malleable or chameleon image. Tess takes on any shape for those she meets, but it is a conveniently empty shape, ready to be filled in and then longed for" (" 'You did not come' " 13).

At the heart of this novel so obviously "about" a woman, there is a blank space, an absent heroine. Its sense of felt life, so present and palpable, derives from the highly implicated narrator and his vividly realized erotic vision. Tess's "interiority"—her consciousness, in other words—is deftly elided in a series of unobtrusive omissions. Most obviously, we are never told what she is thinking or feeling, even at key points in the novel (the seduction, the moment she discovers she is pregnant, the baby's birth, her execution); as Penny Boumelha remarks, "Tess is asleep, or in reverie, at almost every crucial turn of the plot. . . . Tess is most herself—and that is, most woman—at points where she is dumb and semi-conscious" (121–22). Such instances of obliterated consciousness are multiple, and if we examine them carefully, we can see that usually what Tess is unconscious of is her own sexuality. Alec watches her "pretty and unconscious munching" (45) of the strawberry he feeds her and is "nettled" when she wipes his kiss away with her handkerchief, "for the act on her part had been unconsciously done" (58); later she lets him kiss her "as though she were nearly unconscious of what he did" (84); as she listens to Angel's flute in the garden she is "conscious of neither time nor space" (127); when Angel first embraces her she "yield[s] to his embrace with unreflecting inevitableness" (153); when he helps her with the skimming she is "in a dream wherein familiar objects appeared as having light and shade and position, but not particular outline" (172); before the wedding she is "whirled onward . . . by the mastering tide of her devotion to [Angel], which closed up further meditation" (210); at the wedding itself she "did not see anything; did not know the road they were taking to the church. . . . Angel was close to her; all the rest was a luminous mist" (211). This repeated elision of Tess's awareness results in a curious disjunction: everything is told from her point of view—and yet nothing is. The narrator retains absolute control of both his heroine and his narrative, without the necessity of exploring female consciousness (particularly sexual consciousness) in any depth or detail.

A less obvious erasure of Tess's interiority is effected by Hardy's general tendency, which I noted earlier, to avoid the use of free indirect speech in the musings of his female characters. On the whole this is a more insidious omission than Tess's obliviousness, as it can easily pass unnoticed. Occasions which would normally give rise to reverie on Tess's part, thus revealing her autonomous thoughts and feelings, her subjective impressions, are subtly overlaid with other impressions, usually the narrator's. Just after the wedding, for example, we are briefly given access to Tess's thoughts in the following way: "She was Mrs Angel Clare, indeed; but had she any moral right to the name? Was she not more truly Mrs Alexander d'Urberville? Could intensity of love justify what might be considered in upright souls as culpable reticence? She knew not what was expected of women in such cases; and she had no counsellor" (212). The first two sentences of this can readily be construed as Tess's free indirect speech: the questions indicate her anxiety, and the straightforward diction could easily be attributed to her consciousness. The second question, in particular, is convincingly naïve, true to her character as it is delineated in the novel. But the diction in the third question undergoes a slight but important shift, characteristic of many such passages: the "culpable reticence" adheres firmly to the sensibility not of Tess but of the narrator, whose voice unmistakably utters the final, more discursive sentence ("She knew not what was expected. . . .").

This narratorial shift is repeated again and again, effectively circumventing the thought processes of the construct that is Tess. Even the most obvious instances of Tess's free indirect speech are similarly re-aligned with the narrator's overriding consciousness. When Tess finally acknowledges Angel's harsh treatment of her, for instance, we read, "Her husband, Angel Clare himself, had, like others, dealt out hard measure to her—surely he had! She had never before admitted such a thought; but he had surely! Never in her life—she could swear it from the bottom of her soul—had she ever intended to do wrong; yet these hard judgments had come" (343). To this point, this musing is linguistically marked as Tess's, with the repeated exclamations, "surely he had!" and "he had surely!" and the avowal "she could swear it from the bottom of her soul." The next sentence, however ("Whatever her sins, they were not sins of intention, but of inadvertence, and why should she have been punished so persistently?"), performs the familiar sidestep into the narrator's diction and observation, so that we are never more than fleetingly in touch with thoughts, feelings or perceptions attributable to the novel's heroine.

A variant of this sidestep serves to emphasize the narrator's obsessive focus on Tess's corporeal being, her lovable exterior, a text in itself that the narrator is privileged to interpret. The fact that even he cannot always "read" Tess accurately fosters the impression of a mysterious reality called "Woman" at the same time that it obviates the need for the reconstruction of female consciousness. After her baby is born, for instance, the narrator engages in a philosophical aside of some length, beginning, "She [Tess] might have seen that what had bowed her head so profoundly . . . was founded on an illusion. She was not an existence, an experience, a passion, a structure of sensations, to anybody but herself." At the conclusion of these existential insights (which Tess "might have seen" had she been on the narrator's intellectual level), the narrator recommences his recital of the events of the story in the following way: "Whatever Tess's reasoning, some spirit had induced her to dress herself up neatly as she had formerly done" (96). The dismissive, even perfunctory tone of "Whatever Tess's reasoning" underlines the narrator's fundamental lack of interest in depicting his main character's inner workings in any detail. The narrator "guesses" at Tess's thoughts and motives at other key points in the novel as well; we are told that she looks at Angel when they are courting "*as though* her heart had said, 'Is coyness longer necessary?' " (178, my emphasis), and when she goes to seek help from her in-laws we are rather offhandedly informed, "*There is no doubt* that her dream at starting was to win the heart of her mother-in-law" (287, again my emphasis). Such conjectures by the narrator keep Tess at a slightly unknowable distance, in the manner of most erotic fantasies, and also help to explain why she remains such an elusive literary figure (as we can observe in the voluminous critical debate her character has occasioned).

This absence at the heart of Tess's portrayal is made more pronounced by the fact that we are given direct access, through free indirect speech, to Angel's consciousness. Occasionally, in fact, Angel, like the narrator, speculates about Tess's inner life. When he is first in love with her, for example, Angel (or perhaps the narrator—their idiom is similar), after noting Tess's individuality, asks, "How then should he look upon her as of less consequence than himself; as a pretty trifle to caress and grow weary of; and not deal in the greatest seriousness with the affection which he knew that he had awakened in her—so fervid and impressionable as she was under her reserve?" (158). Here we have, not Tess's feelings, but rather a report of her feelings ("the affection which he knew that he had awakened in her"), filtered through the consciousness of a male character. Thus the reader is invited to identify subjectively with Angel's "seriousness" rather than with Tess's "affection," and once again female experience is deftly elided in favor of male experience. Angel, like the narrator, expresses a distinctive (male) point of view; Tess's female consciousness, on the other hand, remains a somewhat amorphous matter of objective conjecture, for the reader as well as for the narrator and for the male characters in the novel.

Even when the narrator is most in sympathy with Tess—perhaps even especially at such times, in fact—he typically steps back and "places" her in his moral universe, at once objectifying her and interpreting her for the reader. In the midst of her struggle over whether to tell Angel of her past, for instance, he reminds us, "It was no mature woman with a long dark vista of intrigue behind her who was tormented thus; but a girl of simple life, not yet one-and-twenty, who had been caught during her days of immaturity like a bird in a springe" (196); similarly, on her journey to Flintcomb-Ash, he mourns, "Inside this exterior, over which the eye might have roved as over a thing scarcely percipient, almost inorganic, there was the record of a pulsing life which had learnt too well, for its years, of the dust and ashes of things, of the cruelty of lust and the fragility of love" (273). This pitying, protective narrator, in fact, so personally involved in his own creation, constitutes the voyeuristic consciousness in *Tess*. There is no male spy in the book for the same reason that the scopophilic gaze is unfiltered: the narrator participates directly in the psychic defenses of both voyeurism and fetishism in a way that renders the mediation of the male characters redundant. Tess's physical/aesthetic perfection, so lovingly dwelt on, ensures that she is "reassuring rather than dangerous" in Mulvey's terms (21). As I remarked earlier, however, she never appears to be "caught" in an act that points to her sexual guilt/castration, thus pleasurably invoking the observer's control and punishment/forgiveness (the basic mechanism of voyeurism, according to Mulvey). But the voyeurism in *Tess* is much more thoroughly pervasive than such a straightforward account can describe; there is no single instance of it in the book because the entire text consists, on a deep level, of an act of objectification and violence toward its heroine.

The "act" Tess is caught in the middle of is, quite simply, her life, as it is lived out in the course of the novel. Her "guilt" (her irresistible sexuality) is established at the outset, and her punishment (her suffering and death) is reluctantly but pleasurably overseen by the wise and yearning narrator. Several critics have noted the violence and ambivalence implicit in Hardy's presentation of the rape/seduction scene in particular, but I think a similarly voyeuristic pathology permeates the text as a whole.[7] Such an effect, of course, runs directly contrary to Hardy's conscious and professed intention in recounting Tess's story; but, as Joseph Allen Boone observes, "Hardy's language of sympathy virtually commits the violence his direct representation avoids. . . . The very concern with maligned female sexuality that leads Hardy to make Tess's consciousness the center of his narration ironically turns her into a recumbent object of the text's and thence the reader's fetishizing desire" (*Tradition* 109–10).

Tess is a text saturated with cruelty and suffering of a particularly detailed and gratuitous kind, if we use Constance Penley's criterion of "gratuitous" suffering as that which fails to lead to "women coming to realizations of self-knowledge through their struggles." If it does not lead to such self-knowledge, Penley maintains (she is referring in particular to

Bergman's *Cries and Whispers*), then such suffering "must serve some other function" (207).

On the surface, one obvious function Tess's suffering serves is purely aesthetic: she suffers beautifully, nobly, and in great detail as recounted by the observing, sorrowing narrator. The "beautiful feminine tissue, sensitive as gossamer, and practically blank as snow" (77) inevitably evokes a positive aesthetic/erotic response at the same time that it evokes the expected horror and repugnance—an effect only made possible, we may note, by the externalized point of view of the male observer. (The female victim's point of view in such cases, needless to say, would be unambiguously negative.) This feminine tissue is inscribed with suffering again and again in the course of the novel, thereby fulfilling the less obvious voyeuristic/sadistic function of pleasurably invoking the (male) observer's punishment and control of the guilty (female) object. If this reading of the novel seems disturbingly close to the motives and mechanisms of male pornography, it is simply because the objective depiction of a suffering and beautiful female object in our culture, no matter how sympathetically rendered, is inevitably eroticized. (This precept is forcibly underlined in the contrast between *Tess* and George Moore's *Esther Waters*, for instance, another tale of the trials of a working girl written at about the same time: Esther is plain, and her suffering—predictably—is far from erotic.) And, as in Hardy's other novels, the reader who is invited to observe and deplore/enjoy such suffering is male. As James Kincaid remarks, "If we find Tess's career both terrifying and attractive, tragic and titillating, then we are doing no more than dutifully playing the part of the implied reader" (" 'You did not come' " 14).[8]

Hardy's narrator, then, is implicated in a particularly inextricable and convoluted way in the domination/submission paradigm as it is manifested in the psychic structures inherent in *Tess*. Tess herself is so thoroughly objectified that it makes little sense to question the degree of her erotic subjectivity; quite simply, she has none. Both the surface features of the novel and its underlying structures conform rigidly, even brutally, to the very marginalizing discourse Hardy believed himself to be writing against. Tess fits to perfection the role of the submissive object in the erotic paradigm. She does not initiate or return the look of desire (when Angel is about to carry her across the flooded road, "her cheeks burned to the breeze, and she could not look into his eyes," 148), and she is likewise removed from the language of desire. She is often mute—Hardy even refers to the unlikely construct of the "mute obedience characteristic of impassioned natures at times" (188)—and when she does speak her desire for Angel, we significantly do not hear the words she uses. The latter are reported from the point of view of the dairy workers, who, when Tess walks outdoors with Angel during their courtship, hear "her impulsive speeches, ecstasized to fragments, though they were too far off to hear the words discoursed; noted the spasmodic catch in her remarks, broken into syllables by the leapings of her heart, . . . her contented pauses, the occasional little laugh, upon which her soul seemed to ride" (195). Obviously playing "nature" to Angel's "culture" in this passage, Tess is made to speak in a pre-symbolic, formless discourse, pure (womanly) emotion as opposed to male reason. Her speech is presented as a code requiring interpretation according to its sound values; her verbal expression is impulsive, fragmented, spasmodic, broken (the "stop'd diapason note" and the "syllable UR, probably as rich an utterance as any to be found in human speech" [21], are further instances of such fragmentation). And she is thereby rendered more lovable, at least to the dominant male narrator and his implied male reader, to whom these formless sounds are at once reassuringly child-like and comfortingly maternal. (Tess herself, of course, displays both of these quintessentially female attributes in the course of the novel, a particularly delectable combination.) Even her language is emphasized as a function of Tess's body, of her exterior as opposed to her interior being.[9]

Tess's behavior, too, enacts perfectly the pattern of submission required by the conventional erotic hierarchy. She displays the required reluctance in the face of Angel's advances, both when he first woos her—" 'She'll kick over the milk!' exclaimed Tess, gently striving to free herself. . . . As she saw and felt more clearly the position she was in she became agitated and tried to withdraw" (153)—and later when she is all but won: "Every time she held the skimmer under the pump to cool it . . . her hand trembled, the ardour of his affection being so palpable that she seemed to flinch under it like a plant in too burning a sun" (172–73). Angel, of course, interprets this reluctance in the conventional way, "his experience of women [being] great enough for him to be aware that the negative often meant nothing more than the preface to the affirmative" (176), and is appropriately titillated by it (as is the narrator and, vicariously, the reader).

In such predictable ways—blushing, demurring, not looking, not speaking—Tess simply plays out the role assigned to the heroine in much Victorian literature. But her enactment of the submissive position in the erotic paradigm goes far beyond such conventions, so that *Tess of the d'Urbervilles*, like Charlotte Brontë's *Jane Eyre*, becomes a sort of quintessential prototype of the domination/submission fantasy. The difference between these two very different novels, however, is telling: while *Jane Eyre* is a novel about female desire—the desire to submit, recounted by the central female character—*Tess* is only ostensibly about female desire. It is really a novel about the male desire to observe such female submission, recounted by the desiring male narrator. Nor is the difference simply a function of first-person as opposed to third-person narration; as I have shown, the absence of a female consciousness in *Tess* profoundly affects the overall ideological impression the novel makes. The erotic "thrill" in Jane's account is the thrill of merging with another, superior consciousness, in which the (female) reader vicariously participates, while the corresponding *frisson* in Tess's story lies in the fetishistic/voyeuristic observation of female beauty and beautiful suffering, in which the (male) reader vicariously participates. Female readers of *Tess* have a complex choice of identification, either with the narrator through an act of "transvestite" empathy, or with Tess herself through what Mary Ann Doane calls "a narcissistic identification with the female figure as spectacle" (19).

It is also no coincidence that Brontë's novel about female desire is a tale of triumph, while Hardy's is a tragedy. Jane's ultimately fulfilled desire, oedipal and regressive, is to be "mastered" by (but in her own way to master) the older, stronger, socially superior Rochester, and finally to merge her being with his as he becomes her permanent protector. In *Tess*, there is no suitable male protector (the latter seems to be a position jealously reserved for the narrator himself, who "knows better" than the deficient male characters), and hence the tragedy. In Hardy's novel, what is projected as female desire is simply the desire to submit to male desire in the name of love, no matter how destructive this might be. We are told of "the mastering tide of [Tess's] devotion to [Angel]. . . . Her one desire [was] . . . to make herself his, to call him her lord, her own—then, if necessary, to die" (210), and later, after her confession, she explains why she wants him to kill her: "To do it with my own hand is too good for me, after all. It is you . . . who ought to strike the blow. I think I should love you more, if that were possible, if you could bring yourself to do it. . . . I have no wish opposed to yours" (236).

Moreover, although it finally does kill her, this desire is seen by the narrator as laudable. One unmistakable message of the novel is that *a good woman loves like this*, in utter submission to her lord and master to the point of sacrifice. She is willing to die for him, and she is ultimately willing even to kill for him, in the violent manner demanded by the domination/submission fantasy in its extreme form. The relation between Tess and Angel is eroticized precisely in terms of the uneven power dynamics between them: Angel stoops to woo her "as no milkmaid was ever wooed before by such a man" (183) and finally becomes the man "for whom she lived and breathed" (199), to whom she prays ("She tried to pray to God, but it was her husband who really had her supplication," 212) and of whom she begs forgiveness on her knees, telling him, "I will obey you, like your wretched slave, even if [you order me] to lie down and die" (227). She endures her punishment at his hands with concomitant meekness, writing to him from Flintcomb-Ash, "I would be content, ay glad, to live with you as your servant, if I may not as your wife; so that I could only be near you, and get glimpses of you, and think of you as mine" (326). That the narrator unequivocally approves of this self-immolating desire of his heroine to merge her will entirely in that of another is made clear in the romanticized gloss on such behavior that we are given through the narrator's comment on

Angel's perceptions: "Clare knew that she loved him . . . but he did not know . . . the full depth of her devotion, its single-mindedness, its meekness; what long-suffering it guaranteed, what honesty, what endurance, what good faith" (211). Such a worthy submissive object clearly deserves protection by a strong male subject, and the love story in *Tess* goes awry because Angel (unlike Rochester, for example) fails to recognize this.

The yearning, tender, protective narrator, on the other hand, recognizes Tess's worth abundantly. Tess somehow seems more morally worthy than many of Hardy's heroines, in fact, and it is interesting to note the source of this impression. At least partly, it derives from her lack of erotic subjectivity, her lack of sexual awareness and desire. Hardy's other heroines are all culpable (and therefore punished) in some measure because of their sexuality, which in turn manages to wreak havoc in the lives of unsuspecting male characters. Bathsheba is punished for her vanity, Eustacia is punished for her wantonness, Sue is punished for her failure to follow through with her liberated ideas. All are punished for their sexual awareness, and for their failure to recognize and then submit to the most suitable male in the novel. Tess, on the other hand, displays no such erotic awareness; she maintains her child-like "innocence" to the end. Combined with her "luxuriance of aspect," this unawareness contributes to her existence as a perfect male fantasy, a sort of nineteenth-century Marilyn Monroe. She is totally sexual, yet totally non-threatening: beautiful, silent, submissive, accessible but reluctant, in need of male protection. And yet she is dealt the severest retribution of any of Hardy's female characters, as severe as that of the wanton Eustacia. Like them, in fact, she is punished for her womanhood, in Tess's case simply for being, for existence itself. The only glimmering of consciousness she herself experiences as to the origin of her suffering is indicative: when Alec asks her not to look at him, "there was revived in her the wretched sentiment which had often come to her before, that in inhabiting the fleshly tabernacle with which Nature had endowed her, she was somehow doing wrong" (301). The too-tantalizing female creates havoc in the male psyche by her very presence, and must be dealt with accordingly. She is beautiful, she suffers, and she finally dies, a sequence of events not inaccurately described by James Kincaid as "a titillating snuff movie we run in our own minds" (" 'You did not come' " 29).

We can see, then, that Hardy's most beautiful main character is a lovely fantasy, and the novel she inhabits is clearly one of the most erotic novels of the Victorian period. But in an important sense this lovely main character is missing, and the novel itself is pornographic. If this reading of the novel seems unduly hard on Hardy, it is because in *Tess* he has unwittingly created a flagrantly misogynistic ideal, a non-subject, a victim in need of rescue, whose suffering adds immeasurably to her erotic appeal. Far more than Sue Bridehead, Tess is "a fraction wanting its integer," a woman desperately in need of the right man. Nor is the novel's ideology redeemed by its "narrative grammar." Although a woman is center stage in *Tess*, and although she has two lovers, it is emphatically not a novel that explores the two-suitor plot that is evident in many of Hardy's other works, in which a heroine must decide between competing lovers and life-styles. Bathsheba finally chooses the "right" suitor, for example, while Sue ultimately chooses the wrong one, and Eustacia eludes both of her; but Tess, significantly, never gets to choose. Instead, she has choices forced upon her, none of which is satisfactory. Within the terms of my inquiry, in fact, she lacks the subjectivity necessary to make such choices; first to last, she is the perfect sexual object. That such a worthy object deserves protection, not castigation, forms a large part of Hardy's theme in *Tess*, leaving the terms of the domination/submission paradigm firmly intact. Tess is simply never dominated by the right male (who would implicitly resemble Hardy's narrator), and the result is the delectable tragedy that constitutes her story.

JUDE THE OBSCURE

A curious and bitter work, Hardy's last novel explores male-female relationships in a way that is significantly different from his approach in any of his other works. For one thing, it is unabashedly male-centered; for another, it is much more painful than erotic. In a sense, it is an elaborate answer to the question posed in the epigraph from Esdras:

Yea, many there be that have run out of their wits for women, and become servants for their sakes. Many also have perished, have erred, and sinned, for women. . . . O ye men, how can it be but women should be strong, seeing they do thus? (2)

The novel's reply, which forms one of the important strands of Hardy's theme, is that women are indeed strong, with the unfair, manipulative strength of "The Weaker" member of the sexual hierarchy. In that sense, *Jude* voices a protest against conventional gender relations, this time from the male subject's point of view; but as in *Tess*, the protest is muted and undercut by powerful and unstated ideological assumptions embedded in the text in fairly subtle ways. These ideological complexities are centered in the character of Sue, whom Katharine Rogers refers to as "at once Hardy's major contribution to feminism and the expression of his doubts about it" (254).

What, exactly, is Hardy trying to say about women, or about a certain kind of woman, in his portrait of Sue? Critics before and after D. H. Lawrence have noted the mass of contradictions of which she is composed—Kathleen Blake, for example, sees her as "rent between the poles of feminist erotic ambivalence, between ascetic and hedonistic tendencies . . . an emancipated woman but a repressive personality, advanced but infantile, passionate but sexless, independent but in need of men, unconventional but conventional, a feminist but a flirt" (148). But the most significant contradiction, I think, lies not so much in Hardy's portrait (which is quite believable) as in his own reaction to it, which is intensely problematic. The ideological confusion created by Sue's character is reflected in the narrator's ambivalence about various aspects of her personality. He (once again, Hardy's implied narrator is male) clearly approves of her intellect, and especially endorses her views on marriage. He equally clearly disapproves of her weakness of character, her inability to maintain the courage of her convictions in the face of adversity. What is not so clear is the narrator's opinion of Sue's sexuality; not surprisingly, the textual ambivalence has its origins in the erotic. To simplify the issue, we can see that on one hand, the narrator endorses Sue's "ethereal" nature, while on the other, he castigates her for the behavior arising from this attribute, her coyness, her "inability to love." Rosemarie Morgan resolves this conundrum by asserting that the approval of Sue's sexlessness has its origins not in the narrator's consciousness, but in Jude's ("It is not Hardy who idealises Sue, not he who perpetuates her mystification, her sexlessness. It is Jude and Jude alone," 143). This reading—which relies on Morgan's discernment of an independent point of view that attaches to Sue, in the statuette incident, for example—enables her to see *Jude the Obscure* as a feminist text that protests the resulting denial of Sue's sexual equality. I read the statuette incident very differently, as I shall show presently; and I think that Morgan's interpretation of Hardy's erotic ideology, while it is appealing, is mistaken. There are simply not enough narratorial clues that we are to read Jude's favorable response to Sue's "uncarnate," "phantasmal," "bodiless" nature (195, 272) as anything but appropriate. The narrator (and his reader) is just as charmed as Jude is by this "bodiless creature" (205), this "most ethereal, least sensual woman" (364), who is "a sort of fay, or sprite" (372). In fact, I think Sue's sexlessness is extremely revealing in terms of Hardy's own erotic imagination: it is as though he can conceive of a sensual woman, and also of an intellectual woman, but not of both at once (a threatening enough construct even in twentieth-century terms).[10]

Morgan's feminist approach to *Jude* is appealing because the novel is in one sense an exceedingly brave attempt to expose and examine the emotional hardships imposed on women as well as on men by the idealized Victorian institution of marriage. It is also an attempt to portray a New Woman, an emancipated, intellectually equal partner capable of teaching the most conventional of men (which Jude surely is at the beginning of the novel) a new way of thinking. Also, and not least importantly, it represents an entirely new departure in Hardy's method of portraying a female character, a seemingly conscious attempt to avoid the objectification of his heroine. In his portrayal of Sue, Hardy deliberately works outside the scopic structures that are so integral to his other works, in which the woman's beauty is held up for examination by the male gaze of the narrator, the reader and the male characters. Instead, Sue's physical appearance is left purposely vague, a somewhat blurred impression filtered through Jude's and Phillotson's perceptions. Even though Jude somewhat voyeuristically spies on Sue as she works in the bookshop before he gets to meet her, for instance, her appearance is not reported in any detail: we are merely told that "she was so pretty that he could not believe it possible that she should belong to him" (89). More surprisingly, when Jude considers the scene in retrospect, its scopic potential is entirely defused in precisely the same manner: "He had been so caught by her influence that he had taken no count of her general mould and build. He remembered now that she was not a large figure, that she was light and slight, of the type dubbed elegant. That was about all he had seen. There was nothing statuesque in her; all was nervous motion. She was mobile, living, yet a painter might not have called her handsome or beautiful" (90). This portrait—all the more significant since it is the first appearance of a female character—consists of a skillful and conscious re-working of the "normal" viewing paradigm. The usual scopic elements are present in the mention of Sue's "mould," "build" and "figure" as well as the imaginary painter, but these are conveyed in negatives: Jude takes "no count" of her mould and build, she is "not a large" figure, and the painter "might not have called her" beautiful. The result is a de-emphasis of Sue's presence as an aesthetic/sexual object in favor of an emphasis on her force as a personality (she is "nervous") and her general "mobility." Hardy does not take the step of creating in Sue a plain heroine, as Charlotte Brontë does in Jane Eyre and Lucy Snowe, for example, but his refusal to dwell on his character's physical beauty effects a similar deflection of the male gaze and a corresponding reduction in the fetishistic potential of such scenes.

In fact, *Jude the Obscure* is Hardy's least scopophilic novel. Although there is plenty of spying, for example, just as there is in Hardy's other work, none of it is particularly visual. Jude spies on Sue not only at her job but at church (where once again he notes not so much her appearance, her "pretty shoulders," as her movements, her "easy, curiously nonchalant, risings, and sittings, and her perfunctory genuflexions," 98). Phillotson spies on Sue as she goes to school; Jude spies on Phillotson and Sue walking together; Jude spies on Sue when she contemplates (possibly his) photograph; Phillotson admits to spying on Jude and Sue in the schoolhouse; and Arabella spies on Jude and Sue at the Agricultural Exhibition. Although Sue is always the spied-upon and never the spy in these instances, none of this secret looking participates to any significant extent in the voyeuristic dynamic so prevalent in the earlier novels. Just as the close-ups of Sue are blurred, thus reducing their fetishistic potential, the observations of Sue's actions, either alone or with other characters, are similarly lacking in visual detail and thus shorn of voyeuristic significance except insofar as they enhance the triangular rivalry in each case. We can see, then, that one aspect of the domination/submission configuration is thereby inactivated, namely the domination of the male subject over the female object via the gaze.[11]

Other aspects of this erotic configuration, however, are very much in place. Declining to make his heroine attractive by virtue of her physical appearance, Hardy substitutes another, equally invidious characteristic in place of her beauty: Sue is "cute." From her "little thumb stuck up by the stem of her white cotton sunshade" (306) to her "too excitable" nature (148), Sue is described again and again in terms of her child-like qualities; indeed, the word "little" is used to characterize her more than any other, and her very name is diminutive (only Phillotson calls her "Susanna"). The narrator tells us that Sue's manner is "that of a scared child" (178); that she sends Jude a "contrite little note . . . in which she said, with sweet humility, that she felt she had been horrid" (204); that she "silently sob[s] in little jerks" (253); that she is a "slim little wife,. . . [an] ethereal, fine-nerved, sensitive girl, quite unfitted by temperament and instinct to fulfil the conditions of the matrimonial relation . . . with scarce any man" (229); that she is "so sophisticated in many things [but] such a child in others" (254); that she speaks to Phillotson "with a child-like, repentant kindness" (263); that she "tremulously nestles up to [Jude] with damp lashes" (just after she asks him to "kiss [her], as a lover, incorporeally," 297); that "her mouth shap[es] itself like that of a child about to give way to grief" (298); that "her tender little mouth beg[ins] to quiver" (328); and that Jude "press[es] her little face against his breast as if she were an infant" (364). This sample by no means exhausts the instances of such cloying characterization in the novel, but I have quoted these at some length to indicate the cumulative effect of such repeated diminutives. Sue is in the end simply too precious, her child-like behavior finally becoming annoying, at least to the modern reader. And yet this diminutive quality is the very characteristic that is attractive to Jude, as his many fond endearments show: he constantly calls her by epithets such as "my dear girl" (109), "my poor little bird" (221), "my curious little comrade" (289), "jealous little Sue" (292), "you baby" (311), "dear little girl" (314), "poor little girl" (395) and "you darling little fool" (410). Even Mrs. Edlin calls Sue a "poor dear little thing," a "poor little quivering thing" (387–88).[12]

In making his New Woman into an emotional infant in this manner, Hardy irredeemably flaws her portrayal: she is thereby an unfit and unequal partner for Jude, lacking the strength and insight to stand by either her lover or her convictions in the face of opposition. Also, because Sue is so child-like herself, we never really believe in her motherhood (any more than we believe in Tess's aspirations to be a teacher—just as Hardy's intellectual woman is not convincingly sexual, neither is his most sexual woman convincingly intellectual), even though Sue's motherly feelings are ostensibly the reason for her breakdown. More importantly, however, Sue's infantilism renders her safely powerless, enabling Hardy to maintain his own conservative notions of gender politics. She is indubitably "The Weaker," needing and inspiring male protective instincts (the narrator's, Jude's), and—even more significantly—she almost entirely lacks erotic desire, conforming perfectly, in fact, to the most rigid Victorian notions of female sexuality. When she informs Jude that "an average woman . . . never instigates, only responds" to sexual advances (372), she not only voices the received wisdom of mid-nineteenth-century patriarchy, but she also reveals the limits of Hardy's ability to imagine a desiring adult female subjectivity. Like Tess's, Sue's unorthodox sexual conduct conceals a core of conventional feminine sexuality—passive, alluring and "innocent," that is, non-subjective and non-threatening. It is as though Hardy cannot imagine a lovable woman who lacks such innocence. In conformity with the traditional domination/submission scenario, the erotic feeling between Sue and Jude is generated by her reassuring reluctance (she "says no" even more often than Hardy's other, more conventional female characters), followed by her "capture" by the dominant male ("I do love you," she tells Jude. "I ought to have known that you would conquer in the long run. . . . the little bird is caught at last!" 281). Jude's response to this helpless innocence, tacitly shared by the sympathetic narrator, is psychologically accurate in its ambivalence: he is moved to love and protect her at all costs, at the same time that he feels angry at her power over him ("Jude felt that she was treating him cruelly, though he could not quite say in what way. Her very helplessness seemed to make her so much stronger than he," 120). The female who lacks desire herself continues to be threatening in her potential ability to control the male through the manipulation of his own desire. (Indeed, this is surely part of the novel's message: *all* women are dangerous, whether fleshly or spiritual, causing men to "run out of their wits . . . and become servants for their sakes.")

So far, then, we can see that Hardy has created in Sue a very different character from any of his previous heroines, a female who is present in the novel in a new way. Scopically, as we have seen, her character is de-cathected, insofar as Hardy declines to make her the focus of the look of desire (a maneuver which should theoretically work to enhance her subjectivity). Although we do not "see" Sue very clearly, she nevertheless seems physically present in the novel, an interesting effect achieved through another, less eroticized sense, that of hearing. Her appearance may be blurred, but her voice is described with minute accuracy, every tone and nuance of it examined again and again. Disappointingly, however, most of such descriptions serve to enhance Sue's child-like impression. The first time we hear it, "her voice, though positive and silvery, [is] tremulous" (101), and it continues to be rendered in similarly pathetic terms: she "breathed plaintively" (152); "a contralto note of tragedy [came] suddenly into her silvery voice" so that Jude "could hear that she was brimming with tears" (153–54); her voice takes on "an emotional throat-note" (155); she speaks "in the tone of a child" (157); "her voice seemed trying to nestle in [Jude's] breast" (158); she speaks "in quick, uneven accents not far from a sob" (194); there is a *"tremolo"* in her voice, a "tragic contralto note" (214); she speaks "in the tone of one brimful of feeling" (215); her voice "undulated, and [Jude] guessed things" (220); she speaks "in a vanquished tone, verging on tears" (223) and "in a tragic voice" (273); her voice "quavered as she spoke" (275) and "came in plaintive accents" (277); she speaks in a "little voice" (299), "a sweet and imploring voice" (370), in "trembling accents" (379) and in "hurt tones" (381). Once again, I have quoted at length to show the cumulative effect of such descriptions. We do not see Sue very clearly, but we certainly hear her—and she sounds like a rather spoiled child, an impression which insidiously undermines everything she says. Even though she voices many of the narrator's own opinions, therefore, particularly on the marriage question, she is vocally denied a fully adult subjectivity. As for the language of erotic desire, needless to say it could not be employed by such a voice; Sue has desires, as indicated by her plaintive tones, but they are significantly not sexual ones.

Sue's subjectivity is undermined in another, less obvious way as well. Because she is such a cerebral character, and because she articulates a good deal of the novel's polemic, it would seem that she must have in abundance what Tess, for instance, so signally lacks, namely an inner self, a sense of "interiority." Theoretically, Sue should be present and knowable to the reader in a sense that Tess is not, Tess being "exteriorized" to the point of total obliteration of her perceptions. Sue is certainly not objectified in the same way, but unfortunately, her perceptions are excluded just as completely. We are made aware of her thoughts and feelings only through direct speech and through the observations of the other characters, never through the more intimate device of free indirect speech, which once again Hardy omits in his presentation of a female character. This omission is all the more glaring by virtue of its contrast with the abundant use of the device in Jude's portrayal.

From the beginning of the novel, which recounts Jude's childhood perceptions in detail, we are made privy to his inner musings. Sue's inner life, however, is habitually only guessed at, either by the narrator or by the males in the novel. Before he meets her, for example, Sue's eyes *"seemed to [Jude]* to combine keenness with tenderness, and mystery with both" (90, my emphasis); when he tells her about Arabella, Sue speaks to him "with a gentle seriousness which did not reveal her mind" (174); before her wedding we are told that "what she felt he did not know" (178); at the wedding itself he speculates, apropos of "the frightened light in her eyes," "that Sue had acted with such unusual foolishness as to plunge into she knew not what for the sake of asserting her independence of him" (182); later, *"he knew that . . . Sue felt that* she had done what she ought not to have done" (198, my emphasis); at their aunt's funeral, Jude is moved by the pathos of the scene, but notes that "Sue either saw it not at all, or, seeing it more than he, would not allow herself to feel it" (220). Thus Sue herself functions as a text that Jude constantly interprets, with limited degrees of success. The cumbersome locutions, which I have emphasized in these examples, indicate the lengths to which Hardy goes to sidestep the direct rendition of her perceptions. In almost any given scene, in fact, the narrative sympathy is unobtrusively aligned with the male point of view. When Jude and Sue share an illicit kiss after she is married, for example, they part "with flushed cheeks on her side, and beating heart on his" (227), a seemingly innocuous construction that nevertheless privileges Jude's feelings, felt from within, over Sue's, observed from without.

Nor are her perceptions pre-empted exclusively in favor of those of Jude, the novel's main character; we are also admitted directly to the conscious-ness of Phillotson, a more minor character, who muses freely about the events of the novel and about Sue herself. We enter his point of view immediately after Sue asks him whether they might live apart, for instance ("Sue enter[ed] the class-room, where he could see the back of her head. . . . Phillotson bent a dazed regard upon her through the glazed partition; and he felt as lonely as when he had not known her," 235–36), and we are similarly made privy to his perceptions when Sue jumps from the window ("There on the gravel before him lay a white heap," 237) and when they eat their last meal together ("How permanently it was imprinted upon his vision; that look of her as she glided into the parlour to tea; a slim flexible figure; a face, strained from its roundness," 244). As to Sue's perceptions of any of these events, the reader, like the male characters, can only speculate.

Even when she is alone—as in the statuette episode—Sue's conscious-ness is withheld in favor of a direct narratorial report of her speech and actions. The closest this report comes to any mention of Sue's thoughts and feelings is the nebulous statement that the statuettes, "being almost in a line between herself and the church towers of the city, . . . awoke in her an oddly foreign and contrasting set of ideas by comparison" (94), as well as the observation (verging on free indirect speech) that "they seemed so very large now that they were in her possession, and so very naked" (95). The latter is immediately followed, however, by the narrator's own observa-tions that "being of a nervous temperament she trembled at her enterprise" and that she "seemed almost to wish she had not bought the figures" (77). Such conjectures on the part of the narrator as to Sue's thoughts and feelings are common throughout *Jude*, and together they constitute a subtle distanc-ing device; she is thereby constituted as an enigma, not only for the male characters but also for the narrator himself and for the implied reader, reinforcing the theme of woman as mysterious Other that informs the novel as a whole. The narrator often assumes the role of anonymous observer, whose guess as to Sue's feelings is no better informed than anyone else's:

just before her wedding, for instance, we are told that Sue *"could almost be seen to feel* that she was undeserving [Phillotson's] adoration" (181, my emphasis), and when she reads the marriage licence over Jude's shoulder we read that "her face seemed to grow painfully apprehensive" (295). This observer is also present at the open grave, where Sue's colored clothing "suggested to the eye a deeper grief than the conventional garb of bereavement could express" (359). This anonymous "eye" fulfills the same distancing function as the narratorial observers in Hardy's other novels, even if it does not observe its object in the same erotic detail.

Thus we can see that *Jude the Obscure*, even though it contains what Katharine Rogers calls "the single thinker among Hardy's women" (254), is an exclusively male-centered novel. Superficially, it seems to be about both Sue and Jude, but a careful examination of point of view reveals a constant privileging of Jude's consciousness over that of Sue. We are permitted to share her thoughts, usually through direct speech, but her feelings are rendered opaque in the ways I have indicated, so that her story is never really told. As Penny Boumelha puts it, Sue "is made the instrument of Jude's tragedy, rather than the subject of her own" (148). In spite of her intellectual acuity, therefore, and in spite of Hardy's avoidance of erotic objectification in her portrayal, Sue lacks any significant degree of subjectivity. Insofar as she is infantilized and in need of the protection and guidance of a male subject, she (disappointingly) occupies the object-position in the conventional erotic hierarchy. She neither gives nor receives the look of desire; the language of desire all belongs to Jude; and although she appears to enact her desire by running away to Jude, first from the training school and then from Phillotson, Sue's psychological configuration does not admit of erotic motives. Rosemarie Morgan reads Sue as having "dormant powers which . . . testify less to an insipid sexual drive than to deeply repressed sexual impulses" (124), but presumably all libidinal inadequacy could be similarly interpreted. The real puzzle is why Hardy chose to sabotage his portrait of an intellectual woman in this particular way. Eustacia's lack of erotic drive was partly enforced, in that Hardy could not have got her past the censors without it; but by the time he wrote *Jude*, publishing constraints had relaxed enough so that he could have permitted Sue much more erotic subjectivity, had he chosen to do so. Part of the explanation is undoubtedly what John Fowles sees as Hardy's "violent distaste for resolution, or consummation," in the interests of the deep pleasure he finds "in the period when consummation remains a distant threat" (36). I think Fowles is closer to the mark, however, when he characterizes the "luring-denying nature" of Hardy's heroines as "not too far removed from what our more vulgar age calls the cock-tease," insofar as the deep anger this epithet implies points to anxiety, rather than pleasure, as the driving force in Hardy's construction of such female characters. The "deadly war between flesh and spirit" is Hardy's as well as Jude's, and he deeply resents the power over him that the former grants to women, the "conjunctive orders from headquarters, unconsciously received by unfortunate men when the last intention of their lives is to be occupied with the feminine" (36), the "compelling arm of extraordinary muscular power . . . which . . . seemed to care little for [a man's] reason and his will, . . . and moved him along, as a violent schoolmaster a schoolboy he has seized by the collar" (40–41). This is indeed the helpless cry of the falsely differentiated male subject, terrified of his own dependence on the dependent female object.

Hardy's deeply ingrained Victorian ambivalence appears to have intensified over the course of his career, as we can see in his portrayal of women in particular and of male-female relationships in general. His inability to see women as both good and sexually desiring reaches its extreme in *Jude*, in which the alternative to the sexless Sue is Arabella, "a complete and substantial female animal—no more, no less" (36), a "woman of rank passions" (399) who is "thick in the flitch" (404)—in other words, a perfect illustration of the grossness of active female desire. Several critics see Arabella as a sort of liberated triumph for Hardy (Patricia Ingham, for instance, sees in her the picture of "a fallen woman who refuses to fall; . . . Unlike all her predecessors . . . she is guilt free," 74), but within the terms of my study she remains merely a discounted sexual subject, a sort of Mae West figure at best, whose boldness (apart from the tragedy it wreaks) borders on comedy. Women are agents of temptation and disruption in Hardy's work, and men are rewarded or punished because of the women they choose, or fail to choose: Gabriel Oak is ultimately rewarded for choosing Bathsheba (although Troy and Boldwood die for making the same choice); Clym and Wildeve are both punished for choosing Eustacia; Alec is punished for choosing Tess, while Angel is punished for not choosing her; and Jude seems to be punished for choosing any woman at all. "Strange that his first aspiration towards academical proficiency had been checked by a woman, and that his second aspiration—towards apostleship—had also been checked by a woman" (228), the narrator muses, and Jude's following speculation, as to whether it is "women [who] are to blame, or . . . the artificial system of things," does little to temper the bitterness of this musing, borne out as it is by the events of the novel.

So, although we must give him credit for his attempts to protest the inequalities of women's position in the gender hierarchy, and particularly for his attempt to create, in Sue, a heroine who is compelling by virtue of qualities other than her beauty, it must be acknowledged at the same time that Hardy's concept of desire remains unassailably traditional. It is the male, not the female, who is the active subject of desire in his novels, and desire itself tends to be triangular and competitive rather than reciprocal and nurturing. His view of gender relations seems to become progressively blacker as his career progresses, so that by the end of the century the tinge of hopefulness that marked the resolutions of his earlier plots has been replaced by a hopeless bitterness. Certainly the "artificial system of things" is partly to blame for his disaffection, but in examining his novels for traces of desiring female subjectivity, we can see that Hardy's own inability to break free of patriarchal psychic configurations constitutes his most restrictive limitation.

NOTES

1. See, for example, Elaine Showalter's well-known objection to Irving Howe's praise of the opening of *The Mayor of Casterbridge* ("Unmanning" 102).

2. T. R. Wright contends that the heroines of Hardy's "middle period" (from *Far from the Madding Crowd* to *Two on a Tower*) progress beyond the mere objecthood of the earlier novels to full-fledged erotic subjectivity. "From Bathsheba Everdene onwards," Wright remarks, "Hardy's heroines are not content simply to remain passive. They actively enjoy exploiting their charms, increasing the element of mystery which they recognise to be part of their fascination, exercising power and control over their male victims" (49). But within the terms of my study such an ability to manipulate male desire by the female object constitutes female subjectivity only in the most traditional view of gender relations; I think it would be more accurate to speak of a "progression" from voyeurism to fetishism in these novels, as I shall show.

3. For a detailed exploration of Hardy's use of free indirect speech, see Christine Brooke-Rose, who, although she does not discuss this device specifically in terms of gender, acknowledges the "rare examples" of it in connection with Sue's presentation, while Jude is "treated constantly" with it ("Ill Wit" 38–42).

4. Rosemarie Morgan labels Bathsheba's blushing look in the mirror "autoeroticism" (35). It may well be, but as we only have Gabriel's perceptions of Bathsheba's thoughts and feelings and not her own, the overall erotic impression of the scene remains voyeuristic.

5. For example, Rosalind Miles refers to "the perennial tension of Hardy's ambivalence about women" (36); Marjorie Garson suggests that "Hardy's fiction expresses certain anxieties about wholeness, about maleness, and particularly about woman" (3).

6. Janet Freeman, too, stresses that the ability to "see" Tess correctly functions "as if it were a test, a measure of value. . . . None of [the male characters] sees her as she is. That distinction is reserved for Hardy himself" (314–15).

7. Kaja Silverman comments of the seduction scene that "the action taken by Alec . . . has assumed the status of a seduction in some analyses of the novel not so much because Tess's 'own' sexuality seems at any point engaged, as because the narrator entertains a complexly ambivalent relation to that action projected onto her as acquiescence" ("History" 9); more generally, Penny Boumelha notes that "all the passionate commitment to exhibiting Tess as the subject of her own experience evokes . . . in the narrative voice . . . erotic fantasies of penetration and engulfment [that] enact a pursuit, violation and persecution of Tess in parallel with those she suffers at the hands of her two lovers" (120). Jean Lecercle, too, argues that "the violence of style is Hardy's main object in *Tess*" (2).

8. Dianne Sadoff, in her excellent account of female representation in fiction and film, discerns a similar pathology in Roman Polanski's film version of *Tess*: "Polanski represents female sexuality as tragic: the male hates to hurt her but nevertheless to see her in pain pleases and arouses him" ("Looking" 154).

9. For a positive analysis of the non-verbal qualities of Tess's speech, see Adrian Poole (337) and Margaret Higonnet, whose detailed and sensitive account of the novel as a "metanarrative about voice" ("A Woman's Story" 26) raises extremely interesting questions about authorial voice and female discourse.

10. For an illuminating explanation of Sue's contradictory portrayal in particular and Hardy's typically ambivalent narrator in general, see Kristin Brady, who accurately locates Hardy in the nineteenth-century's "hysterical discourse about the female body" (89). "Like Sue Bridehead, his most hysterical symptom," says Brady, "[Hardy] ultimately submits to the oppressive codes he has set out to challenge" (90).

11. For a reading of the novel as voyeuristic, see James Kincaid's fascinating "Girl-watching" article, especially 44 ff. I find Kincaid's analysis of the erotic sadism in *Jude* compelling, even though my reading of Hardy's scopic structures is so obviously different.

12. For an interesting analysis of Sue's "infantile posturing" as a manifestation of her cultural conditioning, see Rosemarie Morgan 116–20.

5

✧   ✧   ✧

CONCLUSION

The application of twentieth-century gender-relations theory to the nineteenth-century novel is a fascinating exercise, producing genuinely new feminist readings of canonical texts as well as some extremely interesting bases for conjecture about their authors' psychic wounds and defenses. Like classical Hollywood cinema and realist painting, the realist novel is particularly amenable to such an inquiry because its overt gender ideology is so rigidly defined, making its covert agendas all the more powerful and compelling. The refusal of the feminist reader to read these texts on their own terms exposes their ideological underpinnings, throwing into sharp relief each novelist's relation to the reigning patriarchal norm.

The vexed question of female desire is especially revealing of such relationships, running counter to the prevailing ethos in a particularly subversive way. Nineteenth-century females, fictional and otherwise, were culturally constructed as aesthetic and sexual objects, existing to be looked at, spoken to (and of) and actively desired by male subjects inside and outside novels. The extent to which novelists contravened this cultural imperative provides a useful index to their dissatisfaction with women's traditional position in the gender hierarchy, and with the hierarchy itself. Such an investigation goes beyond a traditional "representation of women" approach to an analysis of representational structures, and an assessment of each novelist's attempt to work within or around them. A novelist's attempt to create room for a desiring female subjectivity, either within or in spite of these structures, constitutes, I believe, a strong measure of that novelist's feminism. A full-fledged female subject of desire, so difficult to envisage even in twentieth-century terms, is unlikely to be found in the nineteenth-century novel; but the tendency of each novelist to push toward such a possibility signals a significant disruption of traditional erotic paradigms. The female characters in the novels of Charlotte Brontë, George Eliot and Thomas Hardy are not always permitted to look, speak or enact their desire (and they are not always permitted to feel any). But sometimes they are, and such instances of active female involvement create enlarged possibilities for a new mode of interaction between the genders, the replacement of the traditional unhealthy subject/object relation with a fulfilling mutual subjectivity.

All three writers are significantly feminist in terms of the surface polemic of their novels, with Hardy being the most vociferously so. There is no "progress" as such over the course of the century in terms of the disruption of traditional erotic paradigms, however, as Brontë is the most disruptive of such paradigms while Hardy is the most supportive of them. Brontë also makes the most individual progress over the course of her career, from an uncanny understanding of the domination/submission paradigm from the point of view of both the male subject (in *The Professor*) and the female object (in *Jane Eyre* and *Shirley*) to an explicit rejection of it in favor of a more mutually subjective interaction (in *Villette*). Brontë's total indulgence in the female's "submission" fantasy in *Jane Eyre*, especially, allows her to re-write this fantasy in female terms: she avoids the objectification of her heroine by making her plain, and she allows her heroine to employ both the look and the language of her desire for the male hero, who eventually becomes the heroine's equal instead of her superior. Magically, Jane gets all of the pleasure, but none of the pain, of the traditional domination/submission arrangement. The "fairy-tale" aspect of this idyllic scenario is implicitly acknowledged in *Shirley*, however, whose heroine endures the pain inherent in such a relationship for the passive female object, the pain of waiting, of rejection, of helplessness—of the forced inability to express desire. Finally, in *Villette*, Brontë has her heroine grow beyond her longing for the domination/submission form of interaction (the "love born of beauty") to attain a more mutual and nurturing relationship in which she functions as a friend and an equal. Most importantly, desire in all of Brontë's novels (apart from *The Professor*, a deliberate and notable exception) is related from the female's point of view. The erotic is of central concern in Brontë's work, which can be said to consist of a thorough and courageous exploration of what she perceptively recognizes as the reigning (and unsatisfactory) gender hierarchy of her day.

George Eliot's work represents a more muted, less straightforward protest against the conventional erotic paradigm. Because she never acknowledges the power or potential of the domination/submission relation, Eliot never moves beyond it. The patriarchal ideal of transcendence, so compelling for most Victorian intellectuals, was no less compelling for Eliot, so that the erotic itself is repressed and de-valued in her work to an unparalleled extent, at least on the surface. Predictably, however, it re-emerges in complicated ways. Female beauty, for instance, a generally reliable erotic catalyst, is de-eroticized and invested with "higher" values in Eliot's work—but these include submissive devotion to a worthy male subject, thus reinscribing the erotic paradigm as a function of spiritual "duty." Eliot's relation to patriarchal norms is thus complex and ambivalent. The erotic gaps, silences and refusals function to create a powerful unstated erotic energy in her novels, and although she creates conventional good/bad oppositions among her female characters (such as Dinah and Hetty, Dorothea and Rosamond), she also creates strong female subjects such as Maggie and Gwendolen. Maggie, in particular, represents a missed opportunity for Eliot in terms of her erotic potential—which clearly cannot be expressed or fulfilled within the patriarchal system, a constraint which Eliot adheres to with some ambivalence.

Of the three novelists in my study, Thomas Hardy struggles the most openly with issues of gender politics, yet fails the most completely to disrupt patriarchal ideology. There is a failure at the heart of Hardy's attempt to portray sympathetic female characters, resulting in the first instance from his seemingly unconscious reinforcement of patriarchal modes of perception and the resulting elision of his female characters' points of view. Hardy approaches his heroines externally (through the vision of his male characters or the male narrator) rather than internally (through the reconstruction of female consciousness), and his novels tend to be highly scopophilic as a result. This scopophilic reader-narrator-character dynamic, which can be read as an indicator of Hardy's underlying anxiety and ambivalence in regard to female desire, prevents him from ever escaping the confines of the domination/submission hierarchy, even though he ponders openly about the restrictions such a hierarchy imposes on women. Most of Hardy's female characters, therefore, function ideologically as objects of male desire, even though the surface polemic of the novels they inhabit indicates a need for a new basis of interaction between the genders. Bathsheba and Tess, for instance (and the latter in particular, whose objectification is so complete that her portrayal verges on the pornographic), fall into this category. But even Hardy, implicated as he is in patriarchal paradigms, explores to some extent the concept of female subjectivity: Eustacia, although she is not a fully sympathetic subject, is permitted some measure of desire, and Sue, while she is not permitted an adult sexuality, is at least not constructed as an erotic object.

The feminist goal of a mutually desiring subjectivity, still beckoning on the horizon of gender politics in the twentieth century, was barely conceivable, much less attainable, for Brontë, Eliot or Hardy, simply because of the sexual ethos of the time. But the tentative gestures of these novelists, their subliminal disruptions, their barely concealed anger with the passive feminine role, constitute subtle feminist adjustments to the reigning gender hierarchy. Some of their works explore notions of female subjectivity, others query the objectification of women, and a few probe the notion of active eroticism in relation to female consciousness, actually endowing their female characters with the power to speak, look and enact their desire—all significant steps in the evolution of a new paradigm for erotic relations in the nineteenth-century novel and in our culture as a whole.

WORKS CITED

Armstrong, Nancy, and Leonard Tennenhouse. "The Literature of Conduct, The Conduct of Literature, and the Politics of Desire: An Introduction." In *The Ideology of Conduct: Essays on Literature and the History of Sexuality*. Ed. Nancy Armstrong and Leonard Tennenhouse. New York: Methuen, 1987, 1–24.

Auerbach, Nina. "The Power of Hunger: Demonism and Maggie Tulliver." *Nineteenth-Century Fiction* 30 (1975): 150–71.

———. *Woman and the Demon*. Cambridge, Mass.: Harvard University Press, 1982.

Bailin, Miriam. " 'Varieties of Pain': The Victorian Sickroom and Brontë's *Shirley*." *Modern Language Studies* 48 (1987): 254–78.

Barickman, Richard, Susan MacDonald, and Myra Stark. *Corrupt Relations: Dickens, Thackeray, Trollope, Collins, and the Victorian Sexual System*. New York: Columbia University Press, 1982.

Barrett, Dorothea. *Vocation and Desire: George Eliot's Heroines*. London: Routledge, 1989.

Beer, Gillian. *George Eliot*. Brighton: Harvester, 1986.

Bellis, Peter. "In the Window-Seat: Vision and Power in *Jane Eyre*." *English Literary History* 54 (1987): 639–52.

Benjamin, Jessica. "The Bonds of Love: Rational Violence and Erotic Domination." Eisenstein and Jardine 41–70.

———. "A Desire of One's Own: Psychoanalytic Feminism and Intersubjective Space." In *Feminist Studies/Critical Studies*. Ed. Teresa de Lauretis. Bloomington: Indiana University Press, 1986, 78–101.

Benveniste, Emile. *Problems in General Linguistics*. Coral Gables, Fla.: University of Miami Press, 1971.

Berger, John. *Ways of Seeing*. Harmondsworth: Penguin, 1972.

Bernheimer, Charles. "Huysmans: Writing Against (Female) Nature." Suleiman 373–86.

Blake, Kathleen. *Love and the Woman Question in Victorian Literature: The Art of Self-Postponement*. Brighton: Harvester, 1983.

Blom, Margaret Howard. *Charlotte Brontë*. Boston: Twayne Publishers, 1977.

Boone, Joseph Allen. *Tradition Counter Tradition: Love and the Form of Fiction*. Chicago: University of Chicago Press, 1987.

———. "Depolicing *Villette*: Surveillance, Invisibility, and the Female Erotics of 'Heretic Narrative.' " *Novel* 25 (Fall 1992): 20–42.

Boumelha, Penny. *Thomas Hardy and Women: Sexual Ideology and Narrative Form*. 1982. Madison: University of Wisconsin Press, 1985.

Brady, Kristin. "Textual Hysteria: Hardy's Narrator on Women." Higonnet 87–106.

Brontë, Charlotte. *Jane Eyre*. 1847. Ed. Margaret Smith. Oxford: Oxford University Press World's Classics, 1991.

———. *The Professor*. 1857. Ed. Margaret Smith and Herbert Rosengarten. Oxford: Clarendon Press, 1987.

———. *Shirley*. 1849. Ed. Herbert Rosengarten and Margaret Smith. Oxford: Oxford University Press World's Classics, 1981.

———. *Villette*. 1853. Ed. Margaret Smith and Herbert Rosengarten. Oxford: Oxford University Press World's Classics, 1990.

Brooke-Rose, Christine. "Ill Wit and Sick Tragedy: *Jude the Obscure*" In *Alternative Hardy*. Ed. Lance St. John Butler. Basingstoke: Macmillan, 1989, 26–48.

———. "Woman as a Semiotic Object." Suleiman 305–16.

Brooks, Peter. *Reading for the Plot: Design and Intention in Narrative*. New York: Alfred A. Knopf, 1984.

Buchanan, Robert. "The Fleshly School of Poetry: Mr. D.-G. Rossetti." *Contemporary Review* 18 (1871):334–50.

Carroll, David. *George Eliot: The Critical Heritage*. London: Routledge and Kegan Paul, 1971.

Chatman, Seymour. *Coming to Terms: The Rhetoric of Narrative in Fiction and Film*. Ithaca: Cornell University Press, 1990.

Chodorow, Nancy. "Gender, Relation, and Difference in Psychoanalytic Perspective." Eisenstein and Jardine 3–19.

Clark, Kenneth. *Feminine Beauty*. London: Weidenfeld and Nicolson, 1980.

Coward, Rosalind. *Female Desires: How They Are Sought, Bought and Packaged*. 1984. New York: Grove Weidenfeld, 1985.

Culler, Jonathan. *On Deconstruction: Theory and Criticism After Structuralism*. Ithaca, N.Y.: Cornell University Press, 1982.

Davis, Lennard J. *Resisting Novels: Ideology and Fiction*. New York: Methuen, 1987.

de Lauretis, Teresa. *Alice Doesn't: Feminism, Semiotics, Cinema*. Bloomington: Indiana University Press, 1984.

de Rougement, Denis. *Love in the Western World*. 1956. Trans. Montgomery Belgion. Princeton, N.J.: Princeton University Press, 1983.

Dinnerstein, Dorothy. *The Mermaid and the Minotaur: Sexual Arrangements and Human Malaise*. New York: Harper and Row, 1976.

Doane, Mary Ann. *The Desire to Desire: The Woman's Film of the 1940's*. Bloomington: Indiana University Press, 1987.

Doane, Mary Ann, Patricia Mellencamp, and Linda Williams, eds. *Re-Vision: Essays in Feminist Film Criticism*. Frederick, Md.: University Publications of America, 1984.

Donovan, Josephine. "Beyond the Net: Feminist Criticism as a Moral Criticism." *Denver Quarterly* 17, 4 (Winter 1983): 40–57.

Dworkin, Andrea. "Pornography and Grief." In *Take Back the Night: Women on Pornography*. Ed. Laura Lederer. New York: William Morrow, 1980, 286–92.

Eisenstein, Hester, and Alice Jardine. *The Future of Difference*. Boston: G. K. Hall, 1980.

Eliot, George. *Adam Bede*. 1859. Ed. Stephen Gill. London: Penguin Classics, 1985.

_____. *Daniel Deronda*. 1876. Ed. Graham Handley. Oxford: Clarendon Press, 1984.

_____. *Middlemarch*. 1872. Ed. David Carroll. Oxford: Clarendon Press, 1986.

_____. *The Mill on the Floss*. 1860. Ed. Gordon S. Haight. Oxford: Clarendon Press, 1980.

Ermarth, Elizabeth. "Fictional Consensus and Female Casualties." In *The Representation of Women in Fiction*. Ed. Carolyn C. Heilbrun and Margaret R. Higonnet. Baltimore: John Hopkins University Press, 1983, 1–18.

_____. *George Eliot*. Boston: Twayne Publishers, 1985.

_____. "Maggie Tulliver's Long Suicide." *Studies in English Literature* 14 (1974): 587–601.

Federico, Annette. " 'A Cool Observer of Her Own Sex Like Me': Girl-Watching in *Jane Eyre*." *Victorian Newsletter* 80 (Fall 1991): 29–34.

Fetterley, Judith. *The Resisting Reader: A Feminist Approach to American Fiction*. Bloomington: Indiana University Press, 1978.

Foucault, Michel. *The History of Sexuality*. Vols. 1–3. Trans. Robert Hurley. New York: Pantheon Books, 1978–86.

Fowles, John. "Hardy and the Hag." In *Thomas Hardy After Fifty Years*. Ed. Lance St. John Butler. London: Macmillan, 1977, 28–42.

Freeman, Janet. "Ways of Looking at Tess." *Studies in Philology* 79 (1982): 311–23.

French, Marilyn. *Beyond Power: On Women, Men and Morals*. London: Jonathan Cape, 1985.

Froula, Christine. "When Eve Reads Milton." *Critical Inquiry* 10 (Dec. 1983): 321–47.

Garson, Marjorie. *Hardy's Fables of Integrity: Woman, Body, Text*. Oxford: Clarendon Press, 1991.

Gaskell, Elizabeth. *The Life of Charlotte Brontë*. Ed. Winifred Gerin. London: The Folio Society, 1971.

Gentile, Mary C. *Film Feminisms: Theory and Practice*. Westport, Conn.: Greenwood Press, 1985.

Gilbert, Sandra, and Susan Gubar. *The Madwoman in the Attic*. New Haven: Yale University Press, 1979.

_____. "Sexual Linguistics: Gender, Language, Sexuality." *New Literary History* 16, 3 (Spring 1985): 515–43.

Girard, René. *Deceit, Desire, and the Novel: Self and Other in Literary Structure*. Trans. Yvonne Freccero. Baltimore: Johns Hopkins University Press, 1961.

Gittings, Robert. *The Older Hardy*. London: Heinemann, 1978.

Gledhill, Christine. "Developments in Feminist Film Criticism." Doane et al. 18–48.

Glen, Heather. Introduction. *The Professor*. By Charlotte Brontë. London: Penguin Books, 1989, 7–31.

Griffin, Susan. *Pornography and Silence: Culture's Revenge Against Nature*. New York: Harper and Row, 1981.

Gubar, Susan. " 'The Blank Page' and the Issues of Female Creativity." *Critical Inquiry* 8 (Winter 1981): 243–63.

Haight, Gordon S. *George Eliot and John Chapman; With Chapman's Diaries*. New Haven, Conn.: Yale University Press, 1940.

Hardy, Thomas. *Far From the Madding Crowd*. 1874. Ed. Suzanne B. Falck-Yi. Oxford: Oxford University Press World's Classics, 1993.

———. *Jude the Obscure*. 1895. Ed. Patricia Ingham. Oxford: Oxford University Press World's Classics, 1985.

———. *The Return of the Native*. 1878. Ed. Simon Gatrell. Oxford: Oxford University Press World's Classics, 1991.

———. *Tess of the d'Urbervilles*. 1891. Ed. Juliet Grindle and Simon Gatrell. Oxford: Oxford University Press World's Classics, 1988.

Heath, Stephen, and Patricia Mellencamp. *Cinema and Language*. Frederick, Md.: University Publications of America, 1983.

Higonnet, Margaret R. "A Woman's Story: Tess and the Problem of Voice." Higonnet 14–31.

———. "Speaking Silences." Suleiman 68–83.

Higonnet, Margaret R., ed. *The Sense of Sex: Feminist Perspectives on Hardy*. Urbana: University of Illinois Press, 1993.

Hochman, Baruch. *The Test of Character: From the Victorian Novel to the Modern*. London: Associated University Presses, 1983.

Homans, Margaret. *Bearing the Word: Language and Female Experience in Nineteenth-Century Women's Writing*. Chicago: University of Chicago Press, 1986.

———. " 'Syllables of Velvet': Dickinson, Rossetti, and the Rhetorics of Sexuality." *Feminist Studies* 11, 3 (Fall 1985): 569–93.

Huysmans, Joris-Karl. *A Rebours*. 1884. Trans. Robert Baldick. Baltimore: Penguin, 1959, as *Against Nature*.

Ingham, Patricia. *Thomas Hardy*. London: Harvester, 1989.

Irigaray, Luce. "This Sex Which Is Not One." In *This Sex Which Is Not One*. Trans. Catherine Porter with Carolyn Burke. Ithaca, N.Y.: Cornell University Press, 1985, 23–33.

Jacobus, Mary. "Men of Maxims and *The Mill on the Floss*." In *Reading Woman: Essays in Feminist Criticism*. New York: Columbia University Press, 1986, 62–79.

Jalland, Pat, and John Hooper, eds. *Women from Birth to Death: The Female Life Cycle in Britain 1830–1914*. London: Harvester, 1986.

James, Henry. "Nana." *Documents of Modern Literary Realism*. Ed. George J. Becker. Princeton, N.J.: Princeton University Press, 1963, 236–43.

Janeway, Elizabeth. "Who is Sylvia? On the Loss of Sexual Paradigms." Stimpson and Person 4–20.

Jardine, Alice A. *Gynesis: Configurations of Women and Modernity*. Ithaca, N.Y.: Cornell University Press, 1985.

Jehlen, Myra. "Archimedes and the Paradox of Feminist Criticism." In *The Signs Reader: Women, Gender, and Scholarship*. Ed. Elizabeth Abel and Emily Abel. Chicago: University of Chicago Press, 1983, 69–95.

Johnson, Patricia E. " 'This Heretic Narrative': The Strategy of the Split Narrative in Charlotte Bronte's *Villette*." *Studies in English Literature* 30 (1990): 617–31.

Johnston, Ruth D. "*The Professor*: Charlotte Brontë's Hysterical Text, or Realistic Narrative and the Ideology of the Subject from a Feminist Perspective." *Dickens Studies Annual* 18 (1989): 353–80.

Jones, Ann Rosalind. "Writing the Body: Toward an Understanding of *l'écriture féminine*." Newton and Rosenfelt 86–101.

Kaplan, E. Ann. *Women and Film: Both Sides of the Camera*. New York: Routledge, 1983.

Kappeler, Susanne. *The Pornography of Representation*. Minneapolis: University of Minnesota Press, 1986.

Keefe, Robert. *Charlotte Brontë's World of Death*. Austin: University of Texas Press, 1979.

Kennard, Jean. *Victims of Convention*. Hamden: Archon Books, 1978.

Kent, Sarah. "The Erotic Male Nude." In *Women's Images of Men*. Ed. Sarah Kent and Jacqueline Morreau. London: Writers and Readers, 1985, 75–104.

———. "Looking Back." Kent and Morreau 55–74.

Kincaid, James. "Girl-Watching, Child-beating, and Other Exercises for Readers of *Jude the Obscure*." Higonnet 132–48.

———. "'You did not come': Absence, Death and Eroticism in *Tess*." *Sex and Death in Victorian Literature*. Ed. Regina Barreca. Bloomington: Indiana University Press, 1990, 9–31.

Kristeva, Julia. "Woman Can Never Be Defined." From "La femme, ce n'est jamais ça," an interview in *Tel Quel* 59 (Fall 1974). Trans. Marilyn A. August. In *New French Feminisms: An Anthology*. Ed. Elaine Marks and Isabelle de Courtivron. Amherst: University of Massachusetts Press, 1980, 137–41.

Kucich, John. *Repression in Victorian Fiction: Charlotte Brontë, George Eliot, and Charles Dickens*. Berkeley: University of California Press, 1987.

Kuhn, Annette. "Real Women." Newton and Rosenfelt 268–86.

Lacan, Jacques. *Feminine Sexuality: Jacques Lacan and the école freudienne*. Ed. Juliet Mitchell and Jacqueline Rose. Trans. Jacqueline Rose. London: Macmillan, 1982.

———. *The Four Fundamental Concepts of Psycho-Analysis*. Ed. Jacques-Alain Miller. Trans. Alan Sheridan. New York: Norton, 1978.

Lawrence, D. H. "Study of Thomas Hardy." In *Phoenix: The Posthumous Papers*. Ed. Edward D. McDonald. 1936. New York: Viking, 1972.

Lecercle, Jean Jacques. "The Violence of Style in *Tess of the d'Urbervilles*." In *Alternative Hardy*. Ed. Lance St. John Butler. Basingstoke: Macmillan, 1989, 1–25.

Lefkovitz, Lori Hope. *The Character of Beauty in the Victorian Novel*. Ann Arbor: UMI Research Press, 1987.

Lerner, Laurence, and Holmstrom, John, eds. *Thomas Hardy and His Readers*. London: The Bodley Head, 1968.

London, Bette. "The Pleasures of Submission: *Jane Eyre* and the Production of the Text." *English Literary History* 58 (1991): 195–213.

Lorde, Audre. *Uses of the Erotic: The Erotic as Power*. Paper, 1978. Trumansburg: Out & Out Books, The Crossing Press, 1984.

MacPherson, Pat. *Reflecting on Jane Eyre*. London: Routledge, 1989.

Maynard, John. *Charlotte Brontë and Sexuality*. Cambridge: Cambridge University Press, 1984.

McMaster, Juliet. "George Eliot's Language of the Sense." In *George Eliot: A Centenary Tribute*. Ed. Gordon S. Haight and Rosemary T. VanArsdel. Totowa, N.J.: Barnes and Noble, 1982, 11–27.

Michie, Helena. *The Flesh Made Word: Female Figures and Women's Bodies*. New York: Oxford University Press, 1987.

Milberg-Kaye, Ruth. *Thomas Hardy: Myths of Sexuality*. New York: The John Jay Press, 1983.

Miles, Rosalind. "The Women of Wessex." In *The Novels of Thomas Hardy*. Ed. Anne Smith. London: Vision, 1979, 23–44.

Miller, Nancy K. "Emphasis Added: Plots and Plausibilities in Women's Fiction." *Publications of the Modern Language Association* 96 (1981): 36–48.

Millett, Kate. *Sexual Politics*. New York: Ballantine Books, 1969.

Mitchell, Juliet. *Women: The Longest Revolution*. New York: Pantheon, 1966.

Morgan, Robin. *The Anatomy of Freedom: Feminism, Physics, and Global Politics*. Oxford: Martin Robertson, 1982.

Morgan, Rosemarie. *Women and Sexuality in the Novels of Thomas Hardy*. London: Routledge, 1988.

Mullins, Edwin. *The Painted Witch: Female Body: Male Art: How Western Artists Have Viewed the Sexuality of Women*. London: Secker and Warburg, 1985.

Mulvey, Laura. *Visual and Other Pleasures*. Bloomington: Indiana University Press, 1989.

Murray, Janet Horowitz. *Strong-Minded Women and Other Lost Voices from Nineteenth-Century England*. New York: Pantheon, 1982.

Myers, William. *The Teaching of George Eliot*. Leicester: Leicester University Press, 1984.

Nestor, Pauline. *Charlotte Brontë*. London: Macmillan, 1987.

Newman, Beth. " 'The Situation of the Looker-on': Gender, Narration, and Gaze in *Wuthering Heights*." *Publications of the Modern Language Association* 105 (1990), 1029–41.

Newton, Judith, and Deborah Rosenfelt, eds. *Feminist Criticism and Social Change: Sex, Class, and Race in Literature and Culture*. New York: Methuen, 1985.

Nin, Anaïs. *The Diary of Anaïs Nin*. Vol. III (1939–44). New York: Harcourt Brace Jovanovich, 1969.

Nye, Andrea. *Feminist Theory and the Philosophies of Man*. London: Croom Helm, 1988.

Oates, Joyce Carol. *Black Water*. New York: Dutton, 1992.

Orel, Harold, ed. *Thomas Hardy's Personal Writings: Prefaces, Literary Opinions, Reminiscences*. Lawrence: University Press of Kansas, 1966.

Penley, Constance. "Cries and Whispers." In *Movies and Methods: An Anthology*, Vol. I. Ed. Bill Nichols. Berkeley: University of California Press, 1976, 204–7.

Person, Ethel Spector. "Sexuality as the Mainstay of Identity: Psychoanalytic Perspectives." Stimpson and Person, 36–61.

Poole, Adrian. " 'Men's Words' and Hardy's Women." *Essays in Criticism*, 31 (1981): 328–45.

Rabinowitz, Nancy Sorkin. "'Faithful Narrator' or 'Partial Eulogist': First-Person Narration in Brontë's *Villette*." *Journal of Narrative Technique* 15 (1985): 244–55.

Radway, Janice A. *Reading the Romance: Women, Patriarchy, and Popular Literature.* Chapel Hill: University of North Carolina Press, 1984.

Réage, Pauline. *Story of O.* Trans. Sabine d'Estrée. New York: Grove, 1965. Trans. of *Histoire d'O.*

Rich, Adrienne. "Compulsory Heterosexuality and Lesbian Existence." In *Powers of Desire: The Politics of Sexuality.* Ed. Ann Snitow, Christine Stansell and Sharon Thompson. New York: Monthly Review Press, 1983, 177–205.

Rich, Ruby. "Feminism and Sexuality in the 1980's". *Feminist Studies* 12, 3 (Fall 1986): 525–61.

Rogers, Katharine. "Women in Thomas Hardy." *Centennial Review* 19, 4 (1975): 249–58.

Rooney, Ellen. "Criticism and the Subject of Sexual Violence." *Modern Language Notes,* 98 (1983): 1269–78.

Sadoff, Dianne F. "Looking at Tess: The Female Figure in Two Narrative Media." Higonnet 149–71.

——— . *Monsters of Affection: Dickens, Eliot, and Brontë on Fatherhood.* Baltimore: Johns Hopkins University Press, 1982.

Schweickart, Patrocinio. "Reading Ourselves: Toward a Feminist Theory of Reading." In *Gender and Reading: Essays on Readers, Texts, and Contexts.* Ed. Elizabeth A. Flynn and Patrocinio P. Schweickart. Baltimore: Johns Hopkins University Press, 1986, 31–62.

Scruton, Roger. *Sexual Desire: A Philosophical Exploration.* London: Weidenfeld and Nicolson, 1986.

Sedgwick, Eve Kosofsky. *Between Men: English Literature and Male Homosocial Desire.* New York: Columbia University Press, 1985.

Showalter, Elaine. *The Female Malady: Women, Madness and English Culture 1830–1980.* New York: Pantheon, 1985.

——— . "The Unmanning of the Mayor of Casterbridge." In *Critical Approaches to the Fiction of Thomas Hardy.* Ed. Dale Kramer. London: Macmillan, 1979, 99–115.

Showalter, Elaine, ed. Introduction. *The New Feminist Criticism: Essays on Women, Literature, and Theory.* New York: Pantheon Books, 1985.

Sichtermann, Barbara. *Femininity: The Politics of the Personal.* Oxford: Polity, 1983.

Silverman, Kaja. *The Acoustic Mirror: The Female Voice in Psychoanalysis and Cinema.* Bloomington: Indiana University Press, 1988.

——— . "Dis-Embodying the Female Voice." Doane et al. 131–49.

——— . "*Histoire d'O*: The Construction of a Female Subject." In *Pleasure and Danger: Exploring Female Sexuality.* Ed. Carole S. Vance. Boston: Routledge and Kegan Paul, 1984, 320–49.

——— . "History, Figuration and Female Subjectivity in *Tess of the d'Urbervilles*" *Novel* 18 (Fall 1984): 5–28.

Snitow, Ann Barr. "The Front Line: Notes on Sex in Novels by Women, 1969–1979." Stimpson and Person, 158–74.

Steiner, George. *On Difficulty and Other Essays.* Oxford: Oxford University Press, 1978.

Stimpson, Catherine R., and Ethel Spector Person, eds. *Women: Sex and Sexuality,* Chicago: University of Chicago Press, 1980.

Suleiman, Susan, ed. *The Female Body in Western Culture: Contemporary Perspectives.*
    Cambridge: Harvard University Press, 1986.
Sutphin, Christine. "Feminine Passivity and Rebellion in Four Novels by George
    Eliot." *Texas Studies in Literature and Language* 29, 3 (Fall 1987): 342–63.
Thackeray, William Makepeace. Preface. *The History of Pendennis.* 1850. New York:
    A. L. Burt, 1901.
Thomas, D. M. *The White Hotel.* Toronto: Clarke, Irwin, 1981.
Thurston, Carol. *The Romance Revolution: Erotic Novels for Women and the Quest for a
    New Sexual Identity.* Urbana: University of Illinois Press, 1987.
Tickner, Lisa. "The Body Politic: Female Sexuality and Women Artists Since 1970."
    In *Framing Feminism: Art and the Women's Movement, 1970–1985.* Ed. Rosz-
    ika Parker and Griselda Pollock. London: Pandora, 1987, 263–76.
Williams, Linda. "When the Woman Looks." Doane et al. 83–99.
Wittenberg, Judith Bryant. "Early Hardy Novels and the Fictional Eye." *Novel* 16
    (Winter 1983): 151–64.
Wright, T. R. *Hardy and the Erotic.* New York: St. Martin's Press, 1989.
Wyatt, Jean. "A Patriarch of One's Own: *Jane Eyre* and Romantic Love." *Tulsa
    Studies in Women's Literature* 4, 2 (Fall 1985): 199–215.

INDEX

Acton, William, 23, 28 n.14
Animal metaphors: in Brontë's novels, 34, 38, 73; in Eliot's novels, 117, 124, 128, 140; in Hardy's novels, 206
Anorexia, as symbol of emotional starvation in Brontë's novels, 67, 73. *See also* Food/drink metaphors; Hunger/thirst metaphors
Auerbach, Nina, 8, 154 n.2
Autoeroticism, 27 n.5, 83 n.10

Bailin, Miriam, 83 n.7
Barrett, Dorothea, 85, 88, 89, 93, 100, 107, 111, 113, 125, 135–36, 154 n.3
Bede, Adam: as exonerated by Eliot's narrator, 91, 93–95, 129; as dominant subject, 102; as gazing subject, 101–2
Beer, Gillian, 112, 139, 148
Benjamin, Jessica, 4, 7–8, 119, 149
Blake, Kathleen, 24, 25, 198–99
Blom, Margaret, 58
Boone, Joseph Allen, 83 nn.8, 10, 193
Boumelha, Penny, 178, 180, 190, 205, 207
Bovary, Emma: as absent voice, 19; comparison with Rosamond Vincy, 126–27; comparison with Eustacia Vye, 180, 186, 187

Brady, Kristin, 208 n.10
Bretton, Graham (Dr. John): as less interesting character than Paul Emanuel, 70; as object of the gaze, 78–79; as object of Lucy's unrequited love, 69–74, 80, 81–82; relationship with Paulina, 71, 73, 74–75, 77–78, 80, 81
Bridehead, Sue: as effaced subject, 203–5; as erotic subject, 199; as feminist character, 198–99, 208 n.10; as frigid, 199, 205; as infantilized character, 201–3; as object of the gaze, 199–202; as speaking subject, 203; as submissive object, 202
Brontë, Emily, as model for Shirley Keeldar, 60
Brooke, Dorothea: comparison with Dinah Morris, 122–23, 130; as desiring subject, 88, 133; as embodying Eliot's feminist contempt for feminine stereotype, 130; as non-erotic subject, 132; as selfless character, 89, 109; as spiritual character, 87, 108, 123; as submissive ideal, 126, 130–34, 135; as unconscious of her own beauty, 100, 105. *See also* Friendship, male-female
Brooke-Rose, Christine, 19, 207 n.3

About the Author

JUDITH MITCHELL is Associate Professor of English at the University of Victoria in Canada. A frequent commentator on feminist issues and the nineteenth-century novel, she has published in *Modern Fiction Studies*, *The Victorian Newsletter*, *English Literature in Transition*, *Modern Language Studies*, and several other journals.

ISBN 0-313-29043-1

EAN

9 780313 290435

90000>

HARDCOVER BAR CODE